Celebrations . . .
Food, Family, and Fun!

A collection of recipes from
The Fayetteville Academy Family

Published by
The Fayetteville Academy
Fayetteville, North Carolina

Celebrations ... Food, Family, and Fun! is a collection of recipes from alumni, students, families, and friends of The Fayetteville Academy. We are grateful to them for their overwhelming response and support. Proceeds from the sale of this cookbook will be used to continue the tradition of academic and athletic excellence at The Fayetteville Academy.

Additional copies may be obtained by using the order forms in the back of this book or by writing to:

The Fayetteville Academy
Attn: Cookbook Request
3200 Cliffdale Road
Fayetteville, NC 28303
910-868-5131
(Fax) 910-868-7351

Library of Congress Catalog Card Number: 99-72906
ISBN 0-9674254-0-9

Printed in the USA by

WIMMER
The Wimmer Companies
Memphis
1-800-548-2537

People celebrate birthdays and anniversaries. We throw parties for graduations and weddings, and we gather to support the home team. Every fun event calls for an appropriate menu. The Fayetteville Academy has your solution in Celebrations ... Food, Family, and Fun!

Our school family enjoys celebrating together and invites you to join in the fun. From the First Day of School to the Fourth of July, we have a recipe for your festivity. Whether you are wearing school colors or silk and sequins, your table will be spread in the best of taste. Plan a Teen Fiesta or Thanksgiving Feast using one of the scrumptious menus outlined in these pages.

Above all, have fun with our collection. The Cookbook Family celebrates each other and all of the cooks who will find this book to be an invaluable addition to their kitchen libraries.

Since 1969, The Fayetteville Academy has grown from the vision of a dedicated group into an excellent institution. Students in grades Pre-Kindergarten through 12 come from surrounding neighborhoods, communities, and military bases to learn in a nurturing, college-preparatory environment. We are proud of our programs and the families and faculty that make them possible. Please visit us when you can!

Cookbook Committee

Co-Chairs
Kim Howell and Chris Kastner

Jane Buryk	Kelley Ebel	Sharon McDaniel
Linda Blair	Ann Erteschik	Cathy Monaghan
Gloria Bownas	Mary Frederick	B.G. Moore
Jennifer Britt	Maggie Franzeen	Jean Moore
Elizabeth Carter	Sandra Jameson	Linda Myers
Libbie Crabtree	Marymelda Kizer	Celine Shoup
Catherine Earle	Susanne Long	Susan Spell

Cover design
Kelley Ebel and Cathy Monaghan

Photography by
Wally Yoshimoto
with technical assistance by Bobby Williford

Cover models
Briggen Bownas, Ann Monaghan, and Philip Taylor

With special thanks to
Maggie Franzeen
For many hours of work, insight, and encouragement.

Benjamin M. Crabtree
Headmaster

F. Ted Ray, Jr.	Montague G. Ball	Frank R. Till
Lower School Director	Middle School Director	Upper School Director

Contents

Celebrations...
Menu Ideas

August: Home from the Beach

Crab Cakes p. 97
Tomato Pie p. 198
Pasta Salad p. 89
Classic Cheesecake with Fresh Fruit p. 211

September: Back to School

Broccoli Salad p. 82
Chicken Lasagna p. 122
Spaghetti Bread p. 48
Pretzel Salad p. 257

October: Tailgate Party

Caramel Corn p. 23
Marinated Cheese p. 18
Texas Caviar with Corn Chips p. 32
Baked Wing Drumettes with Tangy Sauce p. 20
Hanky Panky p. 25
Amaretto Fruit Dip with Sliced Fresh Fruit p. 33
Grilled Margarita Chicken (sliced) p. 118
Grandma Anderson's Chocolate Chip Cookies p. 227
Linda's Spiced Tea p. 38

November: Feast on Tradition

Baked Potato Soup p. 70
Pumpkin Seed Muffins p. 52
Cranberry "Red Stuff" p. 92
Broccoli with Balsamic Butter p. 183
Sweet Potato Casserole p. 197
Cornelia's Corn Pudding p. 185
Garlic and Rosemary Roasted Pork p. 156
Pumpkin Roll p. 223
Sour Cream Apple Pie p. 245

December: Primary Party Pizzazz

Puppy Kibbles p. 241
Caramel Apple Dip with Apple Slices p. 33
Self-filled Cupcakes p. 216
Cheese and Ham Muffins p. 52
Noel Cookie Gems p. 226
Lemon Crisp Cookies p. 231
Wood Pile Candy p. 240
Lime Punch p. 34

January: Teen Fiesta

Black Bean Salsa with Tortilla Chips p. 26
Fiesta Cheesecake p. 27
South of the Border Dip p. 28
Taco Soup p. 67
Chicken Fajitas p. 129
Bean and Cheese Enchiladas p. 177
Cookie Dough Brownies p. 236

February: Homecoming Gathering for a Crowd

Chicken Tortilla Soup p. 72
Roasted Vegetables with Dip p. 201
Cashew and Pea Salad p. 83
Golden Potato Casserole p. 191
Sloppy Joes for a Crowd p. 150
Chicken and Sausage Casserole p. 115
Love Cake p. 212
Wedding Ring Cookies p. 231

March: Too Busy to Cook

Rick's Chili p. 73
Ganny's Cornbread p. 47
Easy and Good Salad p. 93
Seven Layer Bars p. 235

April: Fantastic Faculty Luncheon

Strawberry Spinach Salad p. 84
Swiss Ham Ring Around p. 162
Fruited Chicken Salad p. 80
Ginger Glazed Carrots p. 184
Patsy's Asparagus p. 182
Yeast Biscuits p. 50
Dead Teacher's Cake p. 217
Auntie Em's Crème de Menthe Bars p. 234
Lemonade Iced Tea p. 34

May: After the Prom Breakfast

Monkey Cake p. 54
Sausage Breakfast Casserole p. 60
Ice Cream Sweet Rolls p. 51
Macadamia Nut French Toast p. 64
"Special K" Cookies p. 229
Frozen Banana Punch p. 35
Instant Hot Chocolate p. 40

June: Pomp and Circumstance Celebration

Southern-Style Bruschetta p. 9
Glazed Bacon p. 15
Spiced Pecans p. 23
Crab Mold Carson with Crackers p. 30
Strawberry Cheese Mold p. 13
Antipasto Pizza p. 16
Prize Nut Cookies p. 233
Board of Trustees Bribe Chocolate Cream Cheese Pound Cake p. 222
Punch for a Bunch p. 34

July: Red, White, and Blue Picnic

Herb Cheese Spread with Crackers p. 10
Blueberry Salad p. 92
Barbequed Butter Beans p. 183
Summertime Cukes p. 186
Southern Fried Chicken p. 120
Red Velvet Cake p. 216

Appetizers
and
Beverages

Appetizers/Beverages

Appetizers
Mary Etta's Salmon Log

1 (14-ounce) can salmon, drained and flaked after removing skin and bones	2 teaspoons grated onion
	1 teaspoon horseradish
	¼ teaspoon salt
1 (8-ounce) package cream cheese, softened	¼ teaspoon liquid smoke
	½ cup chopped pecans
1 tablespoon lemon juice	5 tablespoons chopped parsley

Mix all ingredients except pecans and parsley. Chill. Shape into a log or round ball. Stir together pecans and parsley until well blended. Roll salmon log in pecan mixture. Serve with crackers.

Susan Spell, Parent of Laura Caroline

Southern-Style Bruschetta

1 French baguette	¼ cup finely chopped Spanish olives
¼ cup olive oil	
1 cup cooked grits, cooled	3 tablespoons minced onion
1½ cups shredded sharp cheddar cheese	2 tablespoons butter, softened
	1 egg, lightly beaten
2 tablespoons grated Parmesan cheese	1 teaspoon garlic salt
	1 teaspoon minced jalapeño pepper

Cut bread into ½-inch slices. Brush one side with olive oil. Bake in preheated 300° oven for 15 to 20 minutes or until light brown. Combine grits, cheeses, olives, onion, butter, egg, garlic salt, and jalapeño peppers. Mix until smooth. Spread this mixture on each toast slice. Broil until bubbly, watching carefully to avoid burning. Makes 30 pieces.

DeLafayette Restaurant

Fancy Fruit Spread

2 (8-ounce) packages cream
  cheese, softened
4 tablespoons margarine,
  softened
1 cup powdered sugar, sifted

2 tablespoons orange juice
1 tablespoon grated orange
  rind
½ teaspoon vanilla
1 cup chopped nuts

Beat all ingredients except nuts until smooth. Chill 2 hours or more. Garnish with chopped nuts. Use ginger snaps, fresh apple and/or pear slices for dipping.

Ruth Bowman, Grandparent of CoCo Smith

Herb Cheese Spread

This is a great spread for crackers. It goes well at parties.

2 cloves garlic, minced
1 cup butter, softened
2 (8-ounce) packages cream
  cheese, softened
½ teaspoon salt

½ teaspoon basil
½ teaspoon marjoram
¼ teaspoon thyme
¼ teaspoon pepper
1 teaspoon dill

Mix all ingredients. Refrigerate. Serve on crackers.

Mary Lyn Maulden Morgan '81

Chutney Cheese Mold

2 (8-ounce) packages cream
  cheese, softened
4 cups shredded sharp
  cheddar cheese, divided
1 teaspoon curry powder

2 to 4 drops hot sauce
1 (10-ounce) jar mango chutney
6 strips bacon, cooked and
  crumbled
6 green onions, chopped

Mix cream cheese, 3 cups cheddar cheese, curry powder, and hot sauce. Mold into disc approximately 1 to 1½-inches thick. Refrigerate. Before serving, spread with chutney. Sprinkle with bacon, then onion, then remaining cup of cheese. Serve with crackers.

Martha DeGaetano, Parent of Robert

Gouda Loaf

1 small wheel Gouda cheese with wax covering removed	1 (8-ounce) can refrigerated crescent rolls

Split Gouda horizontally. Unroll crescent roll dough and divide into two squares. Wrap each section of Gouda cheese in square of dough. Seal edges so cheese is covered completely. Bake in preheated 350° oven for 15 to 20 minutes. Slice and serve alone or with crackers.

Lois Hockstatter, Grandparent of Brooke, Garrett, Megan, and Seth Ebel

Mary's Cheese

1 (8-ounce) package sharp cheddar cheese, grated	5 green onions with tops, chopped
5 slices bacon, cooked and crumbled	½ cup sliced almonds, toasted
	Mayonnaise

Mix cheese, bacon, onions, and almonds with enough mayonnaise to hold them together. Serve with wheat crackers.

Jean Schaefer Moore '80, F.A. Faculty, Parent of Hampton and Kirkland

Edie's Cheese Ball

1 (8-ounce) package cream cheese, softened	Dash hot sauce to taste
2 tablespoons steak sauce	Dash garlic salt to taste
	1 cup chopped pecans, divided

Mix cream cheese, steak sauce, hot sauce, and garlic salt with ½ cup pecans. Form into ball. Roll cheese ball in remaining ½ cup chopped pecans. Refrigerate. Best when made a few days ahead.

Wanda Siewers, F.A. Staff

Pineapple Cheese Ball

2 (8-ounce) packages cream
  cheese, softened
1 (8-ounce) can crushed
  pineapple, drained
2 tablespoons chopped onion

¼ cup chopped green pepper
1 tablespoon seasoning salt
2 cups chopped pecans,
  divided

Mix cream cheese, pineapple, onion, green pepper, and salt. Stir in 1 cup chopped pecans. Shape into 1 large or 2 small balls and roll in nuts to cover outside of ball. Refrigerate.

Note: For a sweeter cheese ball, substitute 6 tablespoons sugar for onion, pepper, and salt.

Christine Holden, Grandparent of Candace
Dot Ray, Parent of Beth Ray (F.A. Faculty)

Shrimp Spread

12 ounces cooked shrimp,
  peeled and deveined, finely
  chopped
2 (8-ounce) packages cream
  cheese, softened
½ cup mayonnaise
½ cup ketchup
2 teaspoons grated onion

1 teaspoon salt
1 teaspoon mustard
1 teaspoon sugar
1 teaspoon Worcestershire
  sauce
½ teaspoon hot sauce
1 envelope unflavored gelatin
¼ cup water

Cream together cream cheese and mayonnaise. Heat, but do not boil, ketchup, onion, salt, mustard, sugar, Worcestershire, and hot sauce. Dissolve gelatin in water and stir into hot ketchup mixture. Blend with cream cheese mixture and shrimp. Pour into 4-cup mold. Refrigerate to congeal. Unmold and serve with crackers. Serves 25.

Libba Pate, Former F.A. Faculty

Cheese Ball

1 (8-ounce) package cream
  cheese, softened
3 green onions, diced

1 (2¼-ounce) jar dried beef,
  diced

Mix all ingredients together. Shape into ball. Wrap in plastic wrap and chill overnight. Serve at room temperature with crackers.

Laurie Duncan, Aunt of Kimberly Sansverie

Italian Cheese Ball

1 (8-ounce) package cream
  cheese, softened

1 envelope Italian dressing mix
1 cup chopped pecans

In food processor, blend cream cheese and dressing mix. Turn out on sheet of waxed paper; shape into ball. Chill 1 hour. Roll in chopped nuts and return to refrigerator for 24 hours. Serve with crackers.

Frances Bowyer, Former Trustee, Parent of Wendell '88 and Robert '90

Strawberry Cheese Mold

4 cups shredded cheddar
  cheese
1 small onion, grated
2 tablespoons milk
Cayenne pepper to taste

½ cup mayonnaise
1½ cups coarsely chopped
  pecans
1 (12-ounce) jar strawberry
  preserves

Combine cheese, onion, milk, pepper, and mayonnaise. Stir in pecans. Form cheese ring. Chill. Fill center of ring with strawberry preserves.

Bettye Grady, F.A. Faculty

Crab Bites

2 tablespoons butter, softened
1 jar Old English cheese
   spread, room temperature
1 tablespoon mayonnaise
½ teaspoon garlic salt
½ teaspoon seasoned salt
1 (7-ounce) can crabmeat,
   drained, rinsed, and shells
   removed
12 English muffins, split

Mix all ingredients except muffins. Spread on muffins. Cut muffins into quarters. Place on cookie sheet and freeze. When frozen, remove from cookie sheet. Store in plastic bag. No need to thaw when ready to serve. Place frozen muffins on cookie sheets and broil until bubbly.

Sharon McDaniel, Wife of Greg '76, Parent of Jack

Mushroom Palmiers

¾ pound mushrooms (2 cups,
   finely chopped)
1 medium onion, finely
   chopped
2 tablespoons butter
½ tablespoon lemon juice
1 teaspoon Worcestershire
   sauce
½ teaspoon salt
¼ teaspoon pepper
2 tablespoons mayonnaise
2 frozen puff pastry sheets,
   thawed
1 egg, lightly beaten
1 tablespoon water

Chop mushrooms and onion in food processor until fine. Add butter, lemon juice, Worcestershire sauce, salt, and pepper; microwave uncovered on high 12 to 15 minutes, stirring occasionally. Cook until <u>all</u> liquid is evaporated. Cool completely. Stir in mayonnaise.

Place 1 pastry sheet on work surface. Spread with ½ of mushroom mixture. Roll jellyroll fashion, starting at short side and ending at middle of pastry. Roll up from other side until both rolls meet. Repeat with other sheet of pastry. Wrap in plastic wrap and chill 1 hour or until firm.

Cut into ¼-inch slices. Place slices, cut side down, 1-inch apart on ungreased baking sheet. Combine egg and water; brush on slices. Bake in preheated 400° oven for 20 minutes or until golden. Serve warm.

Ann Erteschik, Parent of Elaine

Cocktail Reubens

1 (36 slices) loaf party-size rye bread
½ cup creamy Russian dressing
6 slices Swiss cheese

¼ pound thinly sliced corned beef
1 (8-ounce) can sauerkraut, drained well

Spread bread with dressing. Cut each slice of cheese into 6 pieces. Top bread with beef, sauerkraut, and cheese. Arrange on paper plate or serving platter; heat in microwave 2 to 3 minutes or until cheese melts.

Pom Fine, Parent of Jamie '98 and Justin

Parmesan Treats

½ to 1 cup grated Parmesan cheese
1 small red onion, chopped

½ to 1 cup mayonnaise
1 (36 slices) loaf party-size rye bread

Mix cheese, onion, and mayonnaise into thick paste. Spread generous amount on each slice of bread. Place on cookie sheet and either bake in preheated 350° oven until light brown or broil for 4 to 5 minutes until bubbly and light brown. Serve immediately. Serves 8 to 12.

Earnie Iuliucci, Grandparent of Natalie Royal
Mary Werner, Grandparent of Gordon McCambridge

Glazed Bacon

1 pound bacon, sliced
1 cup firmly packed light brown sugar

2 tablespoons Dijon mustard
4 tablespoons white wine

Fry bacon until almost crisp. Drain on paper towels. Mix brown sugar, Dijon mustard, and white wine. Place bacon in baking pan. Pour ½ of glaze over bacon; bake in preheated 350° oven for 5 minutes. Turn bacon and cover with remaining glaze. Bake for 5 more minutes. Remove and place on waxed paper. Serve warm or cold. Serves 6 to 8.

Ginny Lee Starke '73
Sharon McDaniel, Wife of Greg '76, Parent of Jack

Antipasto Pizza

1 (8-ounce) can refrigerated
  crescent rolls
2 (6-ounce) jars marinated
  artichoke hearts, drained
  and coarsely chopped
1 cup sliced mushrooms
6 ounces sliced pepperoni,
  finely chopped

1 cup shredded mozzarella
  cheese
2 tablespoons chopped onion
2 tablespoons chopped fresh
  parsley
¼ cup grated Parmesan
  cheese
12 pitted black olives, sliced
¼ cup chopped red bell pepper

Unroll crescent dough and place on pizza stone or baking sheet; press perforations to seal. Bake in preheated 375° oven for 8 minutes or until lightly browned. Remove from oven. Toss with sliced mushrooms. Sprinkle pepperoni over crust; sprinkle mozzarella cheese. Arrange mushrooms and artichoke hearts over cheese. Top with onions, parsley, and Parmesan cheese. Return to oven; bake additional 10 to 15 minutes or until crust is deep golden brown. Remove from oven and garnish with olive slices and chopped red pepper.

Sarah-Ann Howell, Student

Curried Deviled Eggs

8 hard-boiled eggs, peeled and
  sliced in half lengthwise
2 cloves garlic, minced
1 tablespoon curry powder
1 tablespoon butter

2 tablespoons chutney
2 tablespoons sour cream or
  mayonnaise
Chopped peanuts

Separate egg yolks from whites. Sauté garlic and curry in butter for 3 minutes. Combine with yolks and chutney. Blend in sour cream or mayonnaise. Fill egg white halves with mixture and garnish with chopped peanuts.

Ursula LeFevre, Grandparent of Jordan Ethington

Spanakopeta (Greek spinach roll-ups)

3 (10-ounce) packages frozen
  chopped spinach, thawed
1 (8-ounce) package cream
  cheese, softened
1 (8-ounce) carton cottage
  cheese
1 (8-ounce) carton ricotta
  cheese
1 (8-ounce) container feta
  cheese
¼ cup Parmesan cheese

2 tablespoons olive oil
½ small onion, grated
4 eggs
Pepper
Oregano
1 teaspoon salt
1 box phyllo sheets, thawed
  according to package
  directions
1 cup butter, melted

Squeeze spinach dry. Mix together all ingredients except phyllo and butter. Cut phyllo sheets in quarters. Keep moist between sheets of waxed paper with damp towel laid over top. Place 1 tablespoon spinach mixture on ¼ sheet of phyllo; brush lightly with melted butter. Tuck ends in and roll like an eggroll. (You may freeze at this point.) Place on cookie sheet and bake in preheated 350° oven for 45 minutes. Makes 65 roll-ups.

Teri Mascia Williams '80, Wife of Stuart '80,
Parent of Jared and Justin

Fried Zucchini

2 large zucchini
4 tablespoons salt
4 ounces ground round, finely
  minced
2 eggs, lightly beaten

8 ounces tofu, mashed
2 green onions, minced
2 cloves garlic, minced
½ cup all-purpose flour
1 red pepper for garnish

Cut the zucchini into ¼-inch thick slices and sprinkle with salt. Mix together beef, tofu, ½ beaten eggs, onion, and garlic. Dry zucchini slices; dip into flour. Spoon tofu mixture on center of zucchini slices. Dip into remaining beaten egg; redip into flour. Fry until golden brown. Decorate with red pepper and serve with oriental sauce of your choice. Serves 2.

Aeran Lee DelaCerna, Parent of Joonho '99 and Taeree Lee

Marinated Cheese

½ cup olive oil
½ cup white wine vinegar
3 tablespoons chopped fresh
  parsley
3 tablespoons minced green
  onions
1 teaspoon sugar
¾ teaspoon dried basil
½ teaspoon ground pepper

3 cloves garlic, minced
½ teaspoon salt
1 (2-ounce) jar diced pimento,
  drained
1 (8-ounce) block sharp
  cheddar cheese, chilled
1 (8-ounce) package cream
  cheese, chilled
Fresh parsley sprigs

Combine olive oil, vinegar, parsley, onions, sugar, basil, salt, pepper, garlic, and pimento in jar; cover tightly and shake vigorously. Set aside. Cut block of cheddar cheese in ½ lengthwise. Cut crosswise into ¼-inch thick slices; set aside. Repeat cutting procedure with cream cheese. Arrange cheese slices alternately in shallow baking dish, standing slices on edges. Pour marinade over cheese; cover and let marinate in refrigerator at least 8 hours. Transfer cheese slices to serving platter in same alternating fashion, reserving marinade. Spoon marinade over cheese slices. Garnish with fresh parsley sprigs. Serve with assorted crackers. Serves 16 to 20.

Kim Howell, Parent of Hunter and Sarah-Ann

Saucy Cocktail Meatballs

1 pound lean ground beef
2 tablespoons bread crumbs
1 egg, lightly beaten
½ teaspoon salt
⅓ cup finely chopped green
  pepper
⅓ cup finely chopped onion

2 tablespoons butter
1 can tomato soup
2 tablespoons brown sugar
4 teaspoons Worcestershire
  sauce
1 tablespoon dry mustard
1 tablespoon vinegar

Mix beef, bread crumbs, egg, and salt. Shape into 50 meatballs. Place in shallow baking pan. Broil until browned, turning once. Drain and place in large ovenproof casserole. In saucepan, sauté pepper and onion in butter until tender. Stir in remaining ingredients. Pour over meatballs. Cover. Bake in preheated 350° oven for 20 minutes.

Pom Fine, Parent of Jamie '98 and Justin

Crabmeat Stuffed Mushrooms

1 (8-ounce) can crabmeat,
   drained, rinsed, shells
   removed
1 cup shredded Swiss cheese
1 teaspoon lemon juice
⅛ teaspoon pepper

½ teaspoon curry powder
1 tablespoon chopped green
   onions
¼ cup mayonnaise
1 pound fresh mushrooms

Mix together all ingredients except mushrooms. Wash mushrooms and remove stems. Fill mushroom caps with crabmeat mixture. Place in 9x13x2-inch glass baking dish. Bake in preheated 400° oven for 10 minutes.

Note: For a variation, substitute English muffins or bread slices for mushroom caps.

Janet Robinson, Parent of Courtney and Hillary

Margarita Shrimp

5 tablespoons olive oil
1½ pounds large fresh shrimp,
   peeled and deveined
3 to 4 green onions, finely
   chopped

2 cloves garlic, minced
¼ cup tequila
2 tablespoons fresh lime juice
1 teaspoon margarita salt
Lime wedges

Heat oil in large skillet over medium-high heat. Add shrimp, onion, and garlic. Cook 1 to 2 minutes. Remove from heat and add tequila. Return to heat and bring to boil. Scrape up any browned bits in pan. Transfer to bowl. Toss with lime juice and salt. Cool. Dip rims of 6 margarita glasses in lime juice then in salt. Place cooled shrimp in glasses and garnish with lime wedges. Serves 6.

Kitty Proctor, Parent of Jamie

Vegetable Pizza

2 (8-ounce) cans refrigerated
   crescent rolls
2 (8-ounce) packages cream
   cheese, softened
1 cup mayonnaise
1 package ranch dressing mix
¾ cup chopped carrots
¾ cup chopped green pepper
¾ cup chopped broccoli
¾ cup chopped mushrooms
¾ cup chopped green onions
¾ cup chopped tomatoes
¾ cup chopped green or black
   olives

Unroll dough and press into 15x10x1-inch jellyroll pan. Bake in preheated 325° oven for 10 minutes until lightly brown. Let cool. Blend cream cheese, mayonnaise, and salad dressing mix. Spread over crust. Sprinkle vegetables on top. Chill for 1 hour before serving. Serves 10.

Sue Hockman, Aunt of Cassandra

Baked Wing Drumettes with Tangy Sauce

15 chicken wings (about 3
   pounds)
⅓ cup soy sauce
3 tablespoons sugar
3 tablespoons firmly packed
   light brown sugar
3 tablespoons cider vinegar
1 teaspoon ginger
1 small onion, minced
1 garlic clove, minced
Pepper to taste

Cut wing tips from chicken wings; place tips in large saucepan; add water to cover. Bring to a simmer; cover and cook 30 minutes. Drain; reserve liquid; discard tips. In large baking dish, combine ½ cup of reserved liquid and remaining ingredients; stir well. Add chicken wings. Cover with plastic wrap and marinate 2 hours, turning frequently. Place baking dish in preheated 325° oven. Bake uncovered until most of the marinade is gone, about 1½ hours. Serve in hot chafing dish.

Marge Koenig, Parent of John '79 and Patricia '79,
Grandparent of Stephen Nuttall

Bacon Swirls

6 slices bacon, cooked and crumbled
1 (4-ounce) can mushroom pieces, drained and chopped
¼ cup mayonnaise
½ teaspoon garlic powder
1 (8-ounce) can refrigerated crescent rolls
2 (3-ounce) packages cream cheese, softened
1 egg white, lightly beaten
Poppy seeds

Combine bacon, mushrooms, mayonnaise, and garlic powder; stir well and set aside. Separate crescent roll dough into 4 rectangles; press perforations to seal. Spread ¼ of cream cheese over each dough rectangle, leaving ¼-inch margin on one long side. Spread ¼ of bacon mixture evenly over cream cheese. Roll jellyroll fashion, starting at long sides. Pinch seams to seal. Cut rolls into ¼-inch slices; place cut side down on a lightly greased baking sheet. Brush each slice with egg white; sprinkle with poppy seeds. Bake in preheated 375° oven for 9 minutes or until lightly browned. Serve warm.

Susanne Hux Long '77, Parent of Caroline and Claire

Cheese Biscuits

2 cups shredded sharp cheddar cheese
1 cup margarine, softened
2 cups all-purpose flour
2 cups crisp rice cereal
Cayenne pepper to taste (⅛ - ¼ teaspoon)

Cream cheese and margarine until well blended. Slowly blend in flour. Stir in cereal and cayenne pepper. Form into 1-inch balls; place on ungreased cookie sheets and flatten in crisscross pattern with back of fork. Bake in preheated 375° oven for 10 minutes.

Beth Bradford Davis '84, Parent of Brawley and Dottie

Sausage Balls

1 pound good-quality bulk pork sausage
1 cup shredded sharp cheddar cheese

3 cups biscuit/baking mix

Mix sausage and cheese together. Add flour 1 cup at a time. Mix well and form into 1-inch balls. Bake in preheated 350° oven for 10 to 12 minutes. Makes approximately 90 balls. (Using maple flavored sausage adds wonderful flavor to this recipe.)

Charlotte Ingram '81
Elvina Spell, Grandparent of Laura Caroline
Florence Alvarez, Parent of Sean '79,
Grandparent of Jamie '94 and Ryan '98 Johnson, and Kristin Wellons

Ranch Oyster Crackers

¾ cup salad oil
1 envelope ranch dressing mix
½ teaspoon dill weed
¼ teaspoon lemon pepper

¼ teaspoon garlic powder
1 (12 to 16-ounce) package plain oyster crackers

Whisk together all ingredients except crackers. Pour over crackers; stir to coat. Bake in preheated 275° oven for 15 to 20 minutes.

Catharine Brown, Parent of Bobby and Bucky

Garlic Pretzels

1 (12-ounce) bottle butter-flavored popping corn oil
1 envelope ranch dressing mix
1 tablespoon dill

1 tablespoon garlic powder
2 (10-ounce) bags pretzels, broken into pieces

Blend together oil, dressing mix, dill, and garlic powder. Pour over broken pretzels in large baking pan. Bake in preheated 200° oven for 1 hour, turning pretzels every 10 minutes. Let cool.

Edith Bigler, Parent of Haley and Hunter

Caramel Corn

5 to 6 quarts unbuttered
  popped popcorn
1 cup butter or margarine
2 cups firmly packed brown
  sugar

½ cup light corn syrup
1 teaspoon salt
½ teaspoon baking soda

Spread freshly popped corn in large roasting pan with high sides (not a cookie sheet). Set oven at 250° and put popcorn in to keep warm. Combine butter, sugar, corn syrup, and salt in heavy saucepan. Stir over medium heat until sugar is dissolved. Bring to boil; boil 5 minutes. Stir continuously to prevent mixture from boiling over. Remove from heat and stir in baking soda. Pour over warm popcorn; stir to coat thoroughly. Return pan to oven and bake for 45 minutes to 1 hour, stirring every 15 minutes. Cool and serve.

Joyce Rhoads, Grandparent of Brian and Laura Kastner

Spiced Pecans

3 tablespoons butter
3 tablespoons Worcestershire
  sauce
1 teaspoon salt
½ teaspoon cinnamon

¼ teaspoon garlic powder
¼ teaspoon cayenne pepper
Dash hot pepper sauce
1 pound pecan halves

Melt butter in heavy skillet. Stir in all ingredients except pecans. Add pecans; toss until well coated. Place on baking sheet in single layer. Bake in preheated 300° oven for 20 to 30 minutes, stirring often, until pecans are brown and crisp. Makes approximately 4 cups.

Linda Lewis, Parent of Richard '81, Hardy '83, David, and Frank

Vegetable Sandwich Spread

1 (8-ounce) package cream
  cheese, softened
⅔ cup finely grated carrots
¼ cup minced onion
¼ cup finely chopped celery
¼ cup chopped cucumber

¼ cup finely chopped green
  pepper
2 teaspoons lemon juice
1 teaspoon mayonnaise
¼ teaspoon salt
⅛ teaspoon white pepper

Beat cream cheese until light and fluffy. Stir in remaining ingredients. Spread on cocktail bread or spoon into phyllo shells.

Susanne Hux Long '77, Parent of Caroline and Claire

Tootsy's Veggie Spread

1 green pepper
2 medium carrots
8 radishes
1 zucchini

1 (24-ounce) package cream
  cheese, softened
1 package ranch dressing mix
½ cup mayonnaise

Chop vegetables in food processor until fine but not puréed. Drain liquid by letting stand in colander. Cream together cream cheese and mayonnaise; add dressing mix and blend well. Add drained vegetables and mix until well blended. Serve with assorted crackers or as sandwich filling.

Barbara B. Lambert, F.A. Faculty, Parent of Barbara '76

Josephines

1 pound Monterey Jack
  cheese, grated
½ cup butter, softened
⅛ teaspoon garlic powder
1 cup mayonnaise
1 (4-ounce) can green chiles,
  chopped and drained

1 (7-ounce) can crabmeat,
  drained, rinsed, and shells
  removed (optional)
Toasted sourdough bread or
  baguette

Blend together cheese and butter. Add garlic powder, mayonnaise and chiles; stir until well mixed. Refrigerate until ready to serve. Spread mixture over one side of bread. If desired, sprinkle with crabmeat. Broil for 3 to 4 minutes until bubbly. Keeps in refrigerator for at least a week so it's great for busy families.

Mary Joan Fredette, Parent of Chris '94 and Jon

Hanky Panky

1 pound ground beef
1 pound hot Italian sausage,
  casings removed
½ teaspoon hot pepper flakes
1 teaspoon oregano

½ teaspoon Worcestershire
  sauce
1 pound processed cheese
  loaf, cubed
Party rye bread

In large saucepan, lightly brown ground beef. Add sausage and continue to brown, breaking up meat. Drain excess fat; add pepper flakes, oregano, and Worcestershire sauce. Stir in cheese cubes. Continue stirring until cheese melts. Serve hot on party rye bread.

Earnie Iuliucci, Grandparent of Natalie Royal

Bruschetta

8 Roma tomatoes, seeded and
  finely chopped
3 cloves garlic, finely chopped
5 tablespoons extra virgin
  olive oil
2 tablespoons balsamic vinegar
3 tablespoons finely chopped
  fresh basil

¾ teaspoon salt
½ teaspoon pepper
1 baguette, 2½ to 3-inches in
  diameter, cut in ¼-inch slices
3 whole garlic cloves, peeled

Stir tomatoes, chopped garlic, olive oil, vinegar, basil, salt, and pepper until well mixed; let rest at room temperature for 30 minutes. Toast both sides of bread slices under broiler until well browned. When cool enough to handle, rub slices on both sides with whole garlic cloves. Top each slice with heaping teaspoon of tomato mixture.

Blair Broadfoot Knowlton '84

Dips
Salsa

1 medium onion, finely
  chopped
1 large cucumber, finely
  chopped
2 green peppers, finely
  chopped
4 large ripe tomatoes,
  chopped
¼ cup olive oil

2 tablespoons vinegar
1 clove garlic, minced
3 to 4 dashes hot sauce
½ teaspoon salt
⅛ teaspoon pepper
2 chili peppers, seeded and
  chopped
¼ cup chopped cilantro

Mix all ingredients and chill 3 to 4 hours.

Liza Latella '94

Fresh Salsa

3 large tomatoes
2 large green peppers
2 large onions
1 bunch celery

4 jalapeño peppers, seeded
1 package taco seasoning mix
1 (8-ounce) bottle Italian
  dressing

Chop vegetables. Mix all ingredients and chill 3 to 4 hours. Serve with tortilla or corn chips.

Becky Frank, Parent of Rebecca '96

Black Bean Salsa

1 large avocado, peeled and
  chopped
2 (15-ounce) cans black
  beans, rinsed and drained
1 (17-ounce) can whole kernel
  corn, drained
1 purple onion, chopped

2 large tomatoes, seeded and
  chopped
⅛ to ¼ cup chopped cilantro
3 to 4 tablespoons lime juice
2 tablespoons olive oil
1 teaspoon salt
½ teaspoon pepper

Combine ingredients in large bowl. If desired, garnish with additional avocado slices and fresh cilantro. Cover and chill. Serve with tortilla chips.

Sharon Young, Parent of Allison and Stephanie

Cheese Dip

1 (16-ounce) jar processed
  cheese sauce
1 (16-ounce) jar processed
  jalapeño cheese sauce

1 can cream of mushroom
  soup, undiluted
1 pound lean ground beef,
  browned and drained

Heat cheese sauces and soup on medium heat until melted. Reduce heat to medium-low. Add beef to cheese mixture, stirring constantly. Serve hot with tortilla chips.

Happy Bleecker '96

Fiesta Cheesecake

This is a very attractive appetizer. During the holidays, the vegetables look very nice shaped into a tree. Use ripe olives for the trunk, green pepper for main tree branches, and colored vegetables scattered as ornaments/lights.

Crust:
1½ cups crushed tortilla chips
¼ cup butter, melted

Filling:
2 (8-ounce) packages cream
  cheese, softened
1 (3-ounce) package cream
  cheese, softened
2 eggs
2½ cups grated Monterey Jack
  cheese with jalapeños

1 (4-ounce) can green chiles,
  drained
¼ teaspoon ground red pepper
Fresh cilantro

Topping:
8 ounces sour cream
Red, green and yellow
  peppers, diced
Tomatoes, diced
Ripe olives, sliced
Green onion, chopped

Combine crushed tortilla chips and butter. Press into 9-inch springform pan. Bake in preheated 325° oven for 15 minutes. Cool on wire rack.

Beat cream cheese until fluffy. Add eggs one at a time. Stir in Monterey Jack cheese, chiles and ground red pepper. Pour onto shell. Return to 325° oven for 30 minutes. Cool 10 minutes on wire rack. Remove cheesecake from springform pan and place on bed of cilantro. Spread sour cream on top, then scatter chopped vegetables over it.

Toi McGary, Sister of Lulie Harry (F.A. Faculty)

Tex-Mex Dip

3 medium avocados, peeled, pitted, and mashed
2 tablespoons lemon juice
½ teaspoon salt
¼ teaspoon pepper
1 cup sour cream
½ cup mayonnaise
1 package taco seasoning mix
2 (10-ounce) cans jalapeño or mild bean dip
1 bunch green onions, chopped
3 medium tomatoes, chopped
1 (6-ounce) can black olives, chopped
8 ounces cheddar cheese, shredded

Stir together avocados, juice, salt, and pepper. In separate bowl, combine sour cream, mayonnaise, and taco seasoning. On large shallow serving platter, spread layer of bean dip; top with layer of avocado mixture; then spread layer of sour cream mixture. Sprinkle with onions, tomatoes, and olives. Cover with cheese. Serve chilled or at room temperature with tortilla chips. May be made ahead. Serves 10.

Kappy Prosch, F.A. Faculty, Parent of Bo
Mary Martinez, Parent of Mario

South of the Border Dip

2 (16-ounce) cans refried beans
1 package taco seasoning mix
1 (16-ounce) container sour cream
2 cups grated cheddar cheese

Mix beans with taco seasoning; spread into shallow 2-quart container. Spread sour cream over beans and sprinkle cheese on top. Bake in preheated 350° oven for 20 to 30 minutes. Serve with corn chips.

Mrs. Martin Davis, Grandparent of Brawley and Dottie

Layered Cheese Bean Dip

2 (16-ounce) cans refried
beans
1 (4-ounce) can chopped
green chiles
1 package taco seasoning mix
2 medium avocados, mashed
2 cups thick salsa, divided
1½ cups sour cream
3 cups shredded lettuce

½ cup shredded Monterey
Jack cheese
½ cup shredded Cheddar
cheese
3 tablespoons sliced ripe
olives
Chopped tomatoes
Chopped green onions

Mix together beans, chiles, and taco seasoning mix. Spread on 12-inch round platter. Mix together avocados and ½ cup salsa. Spread on top of bean mixture. Spread sour cream on top of avocado mixture. Top with shredded lettuce. Alternate cheese over top in sections resembling pie wedges. Sprinkle with sliced olives, chopped tomatoes, and green onions. Top with remaining salsa. Serve with taco chips or corn chips.

Prima Yoshimoto, Parent of Brendan

Shrimp Dip

3 pounds shrimp, cooked,
peeled, deveined, and
coarsely chopped
2 (8-ounce) packages cream
cheese, softened
1 cup mayonnaise
1 tablespoon finely chopped
green pepper
2 tablespoons finely chopped
celery

2 tablespoons grated onion
1 (8-ounce) container sour
cream
2 lemons, juiced and rind
grated
Salt
Paprika
Worcestershire sauce
Hot sauce

Mix shrimp, cream cheese, mayonnaise, pepper, celery, onion, sour cream, and lemon. Season to taste with salt, paprika, Worcestershire sauce, and hot sauce. Serve with crackers.

Sarah Moorman, Wife of Frank '79

Crab Mold Carson

2 (8-ounce) packages cream cheese, softened
1 tablespoon lemon juice
1 tablespoon grated onion (optional)
1 teaspoon hot sauce

1 teaspoon Worcestershire sauce
1 (12-ounce) jar chili sauce
1 (6½-ounce) can crabmeat or fresh crabmeat, drained, rinsed, and shells removed

Thoroughly mix cream cheese, lemon juice, onion, hot sauce, and Worcestershire sauce. Shape cheese mixture on serving tray. Cover with chili sauce. Top with crabmeat. Serve with crackers.

Sandra Jameson, Parent of Matt '97 and Cal

Tuna Party Dip

2 (6-ounce) cans tuna, drained and flaked
2 (8-ounce) packages cream cheese, softened
¼ cup sherry
2 teaspoons mustard

½ cup mayonnaise
⅛ teaspoon garlic salt
⅛ teaspoon onion salt
¼ teaspoon Worcestershire sauce

Mix all ingredients; heat in double boiler until thoroughly blended. Serve hot or cold with crackers, potato chips, corn chips, or in cocktail party shells. Recipe freezes well.

Ginny Lee Starke '73

Mary Helen's Crab Dip

2 (8-ounce) packages cream cheese, softened
3 tablespoons milk
1 pound crabmeat, drained, rinsed, and shells removed
4 tablespoons chopped onion

1½ teaspoons cream-style horseradish
1 teaspoon salt
½ teaspoon pepper
½ to ¾ cup toasted almonds

Blend all ingredients except almonds by hand in large bowl. Spoon into greased ovenproof dish. Sprinkle with toasted almonds. Bake in preheated 375° oven for 20 to 30 minutes until bubbly. Serve with crackers.

Pam Little, F.A. Staff

Spinach Beef Dip

1 (10-ounce) package frozen chopped spinach, thawed and drained
1 (8-ounce) package cream cheese, softened

1 cup mayonnaise
½ cup chopped green onion
1 tablespoon dill
1 (2½-ounce) jar dried beef, rinsed and chopped

Combine spinach, cream cheese, mayonnaise, onions, and dill in blender or food processor; process on high speed 1 to 2 minutes or until smooth and creamy. Fold in dried beef. Chill. Serve with crackers. Makes 3 cups.

Wanda Siewers, F.A. Staff

Hot Crab Dip

1 (8-ounce) package cream cheese, softened
1 (7-ounce) can crabmeat, drained, rinsed, shells removed

¼ cup mayonnaise
3 to 4 dashes hot sauce
1 teaspoon garlic salt
1 tablespoon Worcestershire sauce

Mix all ingredients, blending well. Place in small baking dish. Bake in preheated 350° oven for 20 to 25 minutes. Serve with crackers.

Elizabeth Nunalee Hood '77

Artichoke Dip

1 (8-ounce) can artichoke hearts, drained

1 cup grated Parmesan cheese
1 cup mayonnaise

Coarsely chop artichoke hearts. Mix in cheese and mayonnaise. Bake in preheated 350° oven for 20 minutes or until lightly browned. Serve as a dip with crackers or tortilla chips.

Variations: Add one of these ingredients—1 tablespoon garlic powder; ¼ teaspoon cayenne pepper; ½ package cheese Italian dressing mix.

Judye Bleecker, Parent of Happy '96
Kim Green, Parent of Mandy '99
Kim Howell, Parent of Hunter and Sarah-Ann
Irma Smith, Parent of Coco

Texas Caviar

2 (14-ounce) cans black-eyed
  peas
1 (15-ounce) can hominy or an
  additional can of peas
2 medium tomatoes, chopped
4 green onions, chopped
2 cloves garlic, chopped

1 medium green pepper,
  chopped
1 jalapeño pepper, chopped or
  1 small can green chiles
½ to ¾ cup chopped onion
½ cup chopped fresh parsley
1 (8-ounce) bottle Italian salad
  dressing

    Combine all ingredients except salad dressing. Mix well.
Pour dressing over mixture. Stir and cover tightly. Store in
refrigerator. Marinate overnight or at least 2 hours before
serving. Flavor is best if left overnight. Serve with corn chips or
as a side dish. Serves 6 to 8.

Carolyn Campbell, F.A. Faculty,
Parent of Kathryn '89, Kristen '93, and John '95

Beau Monde Dip

2 cups mayonnaise
2 cups sour cream
3 tablespoons dried minced
  onion

3 tablespoons dill weed
3 teaspoons beau monde
  seasoning
Rye bread round

    Mix dip ingredients thoroughly. Refrigerate overnight
before serving. Hollow rye loaf; cut into cubes. Pour dip into
hollowed loaf. Serve with cubed bread, crackers, or vegetables.

Diane Discavage, Parent of Beth '97 and Sara
Kelley Ebel, F.A. Staff, Parent of Brooke, Garrett, Megan, and Seth

Caramel Apple Dip

1 (8-ounce) package fat-free
  cream cheese, softened
¼ cup sugar

¾ cup firmly packed brown
  sugar
1 teaspoon vanilla

Mix all ingredients well. Chill for at least 2 hours. Serve with apple slices — it tastes just like caramel!

Maggie Franzeen, F.A. Staff, Parent of Matthew

Dip for Fruit

1 (8-ounce) package fat-free
  cream cheese, softened
1 (7-ounce) jar marshmallow
  creme

4 tablespoons orange juice
  (optional)
1 teaspoon grated orange rind
  (optional)

Mix well with electric mixer or food processor. Serve with fresh strawberries, melon, pear slices, etc.

Susan Williams, Parent of Catherine and Sam

Amaretto Fruit Dip

1 (3½-ounce) package instant
  vanilla pudding
1 cup milk

1 (12-ounce) container
  nondairy whipped topping
3 to 4 tablespoons amaretto

Mix vanilla pudding with milk. Add whipped topping and amaretto. Serve with sliced fruit—apples, banana, kiwi, strawberries, etc.

Chris Kastner, Parent of Brian and Laura

Quick Fruit Dip

1 (14-ounce) can sweetened
  condensed milk
1 (8-ounce) container sour
  cream

¼ cup lemon juice
1 teaspoon almond extract

Mix together and refrigerate. Great for fruit dip or as dressing for fruit salads.

Barbara B. Lambert, F.A. Faculty, Parent of Barbara '76

Cold Beverages
Punch for a Bunch

8 cups water, divided
1½ cups sugar
1 (7½-ounce) bottle frozen
   lemon juice, thawed
1 (6-ounce) can frozen orange
   juice, thawed and undiluted

2 (6-ounce) cans unsweetened
   pineapple juice (1½ cups)
1 (2-liter) bottle ginger ale,
   chilled

Combine 2 cups water and sugar in saucepan. Bring to boil; reduce heat and simmer 20 minutes. Cool. Stir in remaining 6 cups water and fruit juices. Cover and freeze at least 8 hours, stirring juice twice during freezing process. Remove from freezer 1 hour before serving. Break into chunks; add ginger ale and stir until slushy. Makes 5 quarts.

Chris Kastner, Parent of Brian and Laura

Lime Punch

2 (3-ounce) packages lime
   gelatin mix
2 cups sugar
1 quart boiling water
Juice of 6 lemons

1 (46-ounce) can pineapple
   juice
1 quart cold water
1 (2-liter) bottle ginger ale,
   chilled

Dissolve gelatin and sugar in boiling water. Add remaining ingredients except ginger ale and freeze. To serve, chop frozen mixture and add ginger ale to make slush. Serves 25.

Christine Holden, Grandparent of Candace

Lemonade Iced Tea

3 quarts sweet tea
1 (12-ounce) can frozen
   lemonade concentrate

1 liter ginger ale

Combine tea and lemonade. Just before serving, add ginger ale and serve over crushed ice.

Frozen Banana Punch

4 cups sugar
6 cups water
24 ounces frozen orange juice, undiluted
1 (12-ounce) can frozen lemonade, undiluted
1 (46-ounce) can pineapple juice
6 ripe bananas, mashed
3 quarts lemon-lime soda

Bring sugar and water to boil and cook for 3 minutes. Cool. Add remaining ingredients except soda. Freeze. Take from freezer 2 hours before serving and "slush down" with potato masher. Add soda before serving. Serves about 60 people at ½ cup each.

Sandra Jameson, Parent of Matt '97 and Cal

Vickymama's Chocolate Drink Mix

This is great for a lunchbox. Add milk at school.

1 (25.6-ounce) box powdered milk
1 (30-ounce) box chocolate powdered drink mix
1 (16-ounce) box powdered sugar
3 tablespoons cinnamon
2 tablespoons nutmeg

Mix all ingredients in large storage container. When ready to use, mix 3 to 4 tablespoons (or to taste) in milk or water. Can be served hot or cold.

Suzanne Coates Bullard '82

Lemonade

6 lemons
1 cup sugar
4 cups water

Squeeze lemons for juice. Add sugar and stir. Pour in water and stir until sugar dissolves. Chill. Serve over ice.

Wanda Siewers, F.A. Staff

Holiday Berry Punch

1 (10-ounce) package frozen
   strawberries with syrup,
   thawed
1 (12-ounce) can frozen cran-
   raspberry juice concentrate

1 (12-ounce) can frozen
   lemonade concentrate
1 liter ginger ale
2 liters seltzer water

Purée strawberries in blender. Combine with juices and
ginger ale. Stir in seltzer. Serves 25.

Chris Kastner, Parent of Brian and Laura

Lime Tea

5 regular size tea bags
5 cups boiling water
1 (6-ounce) can frozen
   limeade concentrate

1 cup sugar
Fresh lime
Fresh mint

Steep tea in boiling water for 5 minutes. Remove tea
bags. Add limeade and sugar; stir well. Serve cold. Garnish
with fresh lime slices and mint. Serves 8 to 10.

Cathy Monaghan, F.A. Faculty, Parent of Ann and Katie

Orange Slush

1 (6-ounce) can frozen orange
   juice concentrate
1 cup water
½ cup sugar

½ cup milk
1 teaspoon vanilla
18 ice cubes

Mix all ingredients in blender until ice cubes make slush.
Pour into glasses; drink immediately. Store any leftover slush
in the freezer.

Fruit Parfait Punch

4 ripe bananas
½ cup lemon juice
1 (16-ounce) can peeled
   apricots
3 cups sugar
1½ cups water
1 (16-ounce) can crushed
   pineapple

1 (6-ounce) can frozen orange
   juice concentrate
1 (8-ounce) jar maraschino
   cherries, drained and
   chopped
1 liter ginger ale

Mash bananas; add lemon juice. Mash apricots; add to bananas. In small saucepan, boil sugar and water. To banana mixture, add pineapple, orange juice, sugar water, and cherries. Mix well. Pour into plastic container with lid and freeze for at least 8 hours. Spoon into parfait glasses and pour ginger ale on top.

Kim Howell, Parent of Hunter and Sarah-Ann

Fruity Slush

1 (6-ounce) can orange juice
   concentrate
¾ cup water
½ cup sugar
1 (2-liter) bottle lemon-lime
   soda

1 (46-ounce) can pineapple
   juice
½ (6-ounce) jar maraschino
   cherries, chopped

Heat orange juice, water, and sugar in saucepan to make syrup. Cool. Add other ingredients. Put mixture in plastic container. Freeze for 24 hours. Stir 3 times while freezing. Let slush sit out before serving.

Linda Rosen, Parent of Ashley and Justin

Hot Beverages
Percolator Punch

3 cups unsweetened
   pineapple juice
3 cups cranberry juice cocktail
1½ cups water

⅓ cup firmly packed brown
   sugar
2 lemon slices
1 or 2 sticks cinnamon, broken
1½ teaspoons whole cloves

Pour pineapple juice, cranberry juice, and water into percolator. Place remaining ingredients in percolator basket. Perk. Enjoy!

Wanda Siewers, F.A. Staff

Jean's Spiced Tea

2 cups orange flavored instant
   drink mix
¾ cup instant tea
1 (¼-ounce) package
   unsweetened lemonade mix

1½ cups sugar
1 teaspoon cinnamon
½ teaspoon ground cloves
Cinnamon sticks

Mix all ingredients except cinnamon sticks. Use 2 level teaspoons mix per cup of hot water. (Use 3 teaspoons for mugs.) Garnish with cinnamon stick.

Julia Tingler, Parent of Lauren

Linda's Spiced Tea

4 cups boiling water, divided
2 tablespoons tea leaves or 4
   regular size tea bags
¼ teaspoon allspice
¼ teaspoon cinnamon

¼ teaspoon nutmeg
¾ cup sugar
2 cups cranberry juice cocktail
½ cup orange juice
⅓ cup lemon juice

Bring 2½ cups water to a boil; pour over tea leaves or bags. Add spices. Cover and steep for 5 minutes. Strain. Add sugar and stir until dissolved. Add juices and remaining 1½ cups water. Heat to serve. May be stored in refrigerator and heated as needed. Recipe can be doubled easily. Serves 8.

Linda Tillman, Parent of Scott '98

Party Perk Mulled Cider

1 gallon apple cider
2 teaspoons rum extract
2 (1-inch) cinnamon sticks
5 whole allspice

16 whole cloves
1 whole nutmeg
1 cup firmly packed light
   brown sugar

Pour cider and extract into large percolator. Place spices and brown sugar in percolator basket. Perk as you would coffee.

Susan Spell, Parent of Laura Caroline

Fireside Coffee

2 cups instant cocoa mix
2 cups powdered nondairy
   creamer
1 cup instant coffee granules

1½ cups powdered sugar
½ teaspoon nutmeg
½ teaspoon cinnamon

In large bowl, mix all ingredients well. Store in airtight container. When ready to use, mix 4 teaspoons into cup of boiling water. Stir well and enjoy.

Maggie Franzeen, F.A. Staff, Parent of Matthew

Spicy Wassail

2 cups water
2 (32-ounce) bottles
   low-calorie cranberry juice
1 (6-ounce) can frozen
   pineapple-orange or orange
   juice concentrate, thawed

3 to 4 whole cinnamon sticks
3 whole cloves
Orange slices and cinnamon
   sticks for garnish

In large kettle, combine water, juices, cinnamon sticks, and cloves. Bring to boil and reduce heat. Cover; simmer for 10 minutes. Remove cinnamon and cloves. Ladle juice mixture into cups and garnish with orange slices and stick cinnamon. Serves 20.

Karen Bullard, Parent of John

Instant Hot Chocolate

1 (8-quart) box powdered milk
1 (6-ounce) jar nondairy
  creamer
1 (16-ounce) box instant
  cocoa mix

1 (16-ounce) jar chocolate
  malted milk mix
½ cup powdered sugar

Combine small amount of each ingredient at a time in large container until all are mixed. Store in airtight container. To serve, use ⅓ cup mixture in boiling water for each serving. Serves about 55.

Doris Johnson, Grandparent of Matthew Franzeen

Hot Sassafras Tea

4 (3-inch) sassafras roots
1 cup boiling water

Place clean, washed roots in cup. Add boiling water. Steep 5 minutes. Strain and discard roots. Sweeten to taste.

Cal Jameson, Student

Breads
and
Brunch

Breads and Brunch

Quick Breads
Pineapple Macadamia Nut Loaf

½ cup shortening
1 cup sugar
2 eggs
1 teaspoon vanilla
1½ cups all-purpose flour
4 teaspoons baking powder

½ teaspoon salt
½ cup milk
1 cup chopped macadamia
nuts
1 cup chopped candied
pineapple

Cream shortening and sugar. Add eggs and vanilla; beat well. Sift together flour, baking powder, and salt. Add dry ingredients and milk alternately, beating well. Add nuts and pineapple. Pour into greased loaf pan. Bake in preheated 350° oven for 60 minutes.

Ululani Packett, Former Parent

Lemon Blueberry Poppy Seed Bread

1 blueberry muffin mix
(with crumb topping)
2 tablespoons poppy seeds
1 egg
¾ cup water

1 tablespoon grated lemon
peel
½ cup powdered sugar
1 tablespoon lemon juice

Rinse blueberries with cold water and drain. Empty mix into medium bowl. Add poppy seeds, egg, and water; stir until moistened, about 50 strokes. Fold in blueberries and lemon peel. Pour into greased and floured loaf pan. Sprinkle topping from packet over batter. Bake in preheated 350° oven for 55 to 65 minutes, or until toothpick tests clean. Cool in pan 10 minutes. Loosen loaf from pan. Lay foil over top when removing from pan to keep topping intact. Invert onto cooling rack. Turn right side up. Cool completely. Combine sugar and lemon juice; stir until smooth. Drizzle over loaf.

Sonya Jenkins, Parent of Sarah

Blueberry Orange Bread

2 tablespoons butter or
    margarine
¼ cup boiling water
½ cup orange juice
3 tablespoons grated orange
    rind
1 egg

1 cup sugar
2 cups all-purpose flour
1 teaspoon baking powder
¼ teaspoon baking soda
½ teaspoon salt
1 cup blueberries
2 tablespoons honey

In small bowl, melt butter in boiling water. Add orange juice and rind; set aside. Beat egg with sugar until light and fluffy. Sift together flour, baking powder, baking soda, and salt. Add dry ingredients to egg mixture alternately with orange liquid, beating well after each addition. Fold in berries. Grease 9x5x3-inch pan. Bake in preheated 325° oven for 70 minutes. Turn out on rack. Spread honey on warm loaf.

Betty Southard, Grandparent of Peter '99 and Anna Buryk

Banana Nut Bread

1½ cups all-purpose flour
1 teaspoon baking soda
½ teaspoon salt
½ cup vegetable oil
1½ cups sugar

2 eggs
3 to 4 ripe bananas, mashed
4 tablespoons buttermilk
1 cup chopped pecans

Sift together flour, baking soda, and salt in small bowl; set aside. Cream oil and sugar in large bowl. Add eggs and beat well. Add mashed bananas to sugar mixture. Add buttermilk, dry ingredients, and pecans. Pour in greased and floured loaf pan. Bake in preheated 375° oven for 45 minutes. Let stand 15 minutes before removing from pan.

Susan Williams, Parent of Catherine and Sam

Strawberry Banana Bread

3 cups all-purpose flour
2 cups sugar
1 teaspoon baking soda
1½ teaspoons cinnamon
1 (3-ounce) package
  strawberry gelatin

3 eggs
1 (16-ounce) package frozen
  strawberries, thawed
1 banana, mashed
¾ cup vegetable oil

Combine flour, sugar, soda, and cinnamon in large bowl. Make well in center. In separate bowl, mix gelatin, eggs, strawberries, banana, and oil. Pour fruit mixture into well; stir gently by hand. Pour mixture into 2 greased loaf pans. Bake in preheated 400° oven for 60 minutes or until toothpick tests clean. Let cool before slicing.

Lisabeth Wasson Peterson '86

Strawberry Bread

1¼ cups vegetable oil
3 eggs
2 cups sugar
3 cups all-purpose flour
1 tablespoon cinnamon

1 teaspoon baking soda
1 teaspoon salt
3 cups sliced strawberries
1 cup chopped pecans

Combine oil, eggs, and sugar. Add flour, cinnamon, and soda, stirring just until moistened. Stir in strawberries and nuts. Spoon into 2 greased and floured loaf pans. Bake at 350° for 1 hour or until toothpick tests clean.

Nan Williams, Grandparent of Jenna and Megan Bishop

My Grandfather's Cornbread

2 cups cornmeal, white or
yellow (no mixes or
leavening)
1 tablespoon salt

¼ cup cooking oil, shortening,
bacon fat, or lard
¾ cup buttermilk, divided
(water or milk may be
substituted)

Combine cornmeal and salt in mixing bowl; add oil. Mix until mixture looks like large crumbs. Add ½ cup buttermilk. Mix well and allow to set for 5 minutes. Meal will absorb liquid, and mixture will become very stiff. Add remaining ¼ cup of liquid; mix again.

Grease ovenproof skillet or glass baking dish. Place mixture in pan or dish; spread no thicker than ⅜ inch. Bake in preheated 450° oven until top of bread begins to brown. Remove and brush top with melted butter.

Robert Downing, Grandfather of Bobby and Ryan Brady

Corn Sticks

1½ cups self-rising corn meal
½ cup all-purpose flour
2 teaspoons baking powder
½ teaspoon baking soda
1 teaspoon salt

1 teaspoon sugar
2 eggs, lightly beaten
1½ cups buttermilk
¼ cup vegetable oil

Combine corn meal, flour, baking powder, baking soda, salt, and sugar in bowl; set aside. Combine eggs, buttermilk, and oil in separate bowl. Add liquid mixture to dry ingredients, stirring just until moistened. Place well-greased cast iron corn stick pan in preheated 450° oven for 3 minutes or until hot. Remove from oven and spoon batter into pan, filling ¾ full. Return to oven and bake 15 minutes or until lightly browned. Serves 12.

Mary Warren, Parent of Patrick

Broccoli-Cheese Cornbread

2 (7-ounce) cornbread muffin
   mixes
¼ cup margarine, melted

1 (10-ounce) box frozen
   chopped broccoli, thawed
3 cups shredded cheddar
   cheese, divided

Mix cornbread according to directions on box. Add margarine, broccoli and 1½ cups cheese. Pour into greased loaf pan. Bake in preheated 350° oven for 25 minutes. Sprinkle with remaining cheese; bake until cheese melts.

Martha DeGaetano, Parent of Robert

Broccoli Cornbread

1 (7-ounce) box cornbread mix
4 eggs
1 (8-ounce) container cottage
   cheese

½ teaspoon salt
½ cup butter, melted
1 (10-ounce) box frozen
   chopped broccoli, thawed

Mix all ingredients. Pour into greased 8x12-inch pan. Bake in preheated 350° oven for 30 minutes or until brown.

Julia Carter, Grandparent of Richard

Ganny's Cornbread

1 cup all-purpose flour
1 cup corn meal
½ cup sugar
3 teaspoons baking powder
1 teaspoon salt

1 cup milk
1 large or 2 small eggs
2 tablespoons softened bacon
   drippings or vegetable oil

Mix flour, corn meal, sugar, baking powder, and salt. Add milk, eggs, and grease. Pour into hot, greased 10-inch or 12-inch cast iron skillet. Bake in preheated 425° oven for 25 to 30 minutes or until brown on top. Serves 8 to 10.

Note: Be sure baking powder is fresh.

Nancy Goodrum, F.A. Faculty

Yeast Breads
Bread Machine
Quick Sourdough French Bread

2½ tablespoons white vinegar	1½ teaspoons salt
1 cup sour cream	½ teaspoon ginger
½ cup water	3½ cups all-purpose flour
2 tablespoons wheat germ	3½ teaspoons yeast
1 tablespoon sugar	

Place ingredients in bread machine in order recommended by manufacturer. Process on basic bread cycle according to manufacturer's directions.

B. G. Moore, Parent of Gray and Landis

Spaghetti Bread

1 package yeast	1 teaspoon dried Italian
3 cups bread flour	seasoning
1 tablespoon sugar	1 tablespoon olive oil
1 teaspoon garlic salt	1½ cups warm water
¼ cup grated Parmesan cheese	

In bread maker, add all ingredients in order recommended by manufacturer. Process on the white bread cycle according to manufacturer's directions. Bread takes approximately 4 hours to complete.

Florence Alvarez, Parent of Sean '79,
Grandparent of Jamie '94 and Ryan '98 Johnson, and Kristin Wellons

Quick Sourdough French Bread

4 to 5 cups bread flour,
  divided
2 tablespoons wheat germ
1 tablespoon sugar
2 teaspoons salt
½ teaspoon ginger
2 packages fast-acting dry
  yeast

1 cup warm water (120 - 130°)
1 cup sour cream, at room
  temperature
2 tablespoons white vinegar
1 egg white
1 tablespoon water
2 teaspoons poppy seed

In large bowl, combine 1½ cups flour, wheat germ, sugar, salt, ginger, and yeast. Add water, sour cream, and vinegar. Blend at low speed until moistened; beat 3 minutes at medium speed. Stir in an additional 2 to 2½ cups flour until dough pulls cleanly away from sides of bowl.

On floured surface, knead in remaining ½ to 1 cup flour until dough is smooth and elastic, about 5 minutes. Place dough in greased bowl; cover loosely with plastic wrap and cloth towel. Let rise in warm place (80 - 85°) until light and doubled in size, 25 to 35 minutes.

Grease large cookie sheet. Punch down dough several times to remove all air bubbles. Allow to rest on counter covered with inverted bowl for 15 minutes. Divide in half; roll each half to 14x8-inch rectangle. Starting with longest side, roll up; pinch edges firmly to seal. Place seam side down on greased cookie sheet; taper ends to a point. With sharp knife, make five ¼-inch deep diagonal slashes on top of each loaf. Cover; let rise in warm place until light and doubled in size, about 15 minutes.

Bake in preheated 375° oven for 25 minutes. In small bowl, beat egg white and 1 tablespoon water. Remove bread from oven; brush with egg white mixture. Sprinkle with poppy seeds. Return to oven. Bake an additional 5 to 10 minutes or until loaves sound hollow when lightly tapped. Immediately remove from cookie sheet; cool on wire racks. Makes 2 (17-ounce) loaves.

B. G. Moore, Parent of Gray and Landis

Yeast Biscuits

2 tablespoons dry yeast
2 cups lukewarm water
¼ cup sugar
½ cup powdered milk

3½ cups all-purpose flour
1½ teaspoons baking powder
1½ teaspoons salt
½ cup shortening

Mix yeast, water, and sugar. Let stand for 10 minutes. Sift milk, flour, baking powder, and salt. Cut shortening into flour mixture. Add yeast mixture. Mix well.

Roll to ½-inch thick; cut. Place on baking sheet brushed with melted butter. Let rise 30 minutes in warm place (80 - 85°). Bake in preheated 450° oven for 15 minutes. Makes 4 dozen.

Lucille West, Grandparent of Jason Schmidt

French Bread

5 cups bread flour, divided
2 packages rapid rise yeast
1 tablespoon salt
1 tablespoon sugar

2 cups very warm water
  (115 - 120°)
2 tablespoons vegetable oil
1 egg, beaten

Combine 3 cups flour, yeast, sugar, and salt; stir. Add warm water and oil; stir until glossy. Add 2 cups flour. Mix and turn out of bowl onto lightly floured surface. Knead 5 minutes. Add flour so dough does not stick to hands. Place dough in greased bowl; let rise one hour. Punch down. Cut in half. Cut each half into 3 portions. Braid each group of 3 portions , and brush with beaten egg. Let rise 30 minutes. Brush with egg again. Bake in preheated 375° oven for 15 to 20 minutes.

Liz Latella, Parent of Liza '94 and Leah

Pastries
Apricot Muffins

1 cup chopped dried apricots	2 cups all-purpose flour
1 cup boiling water	1 teaspoon baking soda
1 cup sugar	1 tablespoon grated orange
½ cup butter, softened	peel
1 cup sour cream	½ cup chopped nuts

Soak apricots in water for 5 minutes; drain, discarding liquid. Cream sugar and butter until fluffy. Add sour cream. Combine dry ingredients, and stir into creamed mixture. Fold apricots, orange peel, and nuts into mixture. Spoon batter into greased muffin cups. Bake in preheated 400° oven for 18 to 20 minutes. Serves 12.

Diane Glanville, F.A. Faculty, Parent of Lee '91

Blueberry Muffins

2 cups flour	1 egg
3 teaspoons baking powder	1 cup milk
½ teaspoon salt	1 pint blueberries, rinsed and
½ cup sugar	drained
3 tablespoons shortening	

Mix flour, baking powder, salt and sugar. Cut shortening into dry ingredients and mix like pie dough. In separate bowl, beat egg and milk together; add to dough mixture. Add berries. Spoon into muffin pans and bake at 400° for 25 minutes.

Mary Ksanznak, Grandparent of Karen Pittman

Ice Cream Sweet Rolls

2 cups self-rising flour	2 cups softened ice cream, any flavor

Mix flour and ice cream. Spoon into greased muffin tins about ⅔ full. Bake in preheated 400° oven for 10 to 15 minutes. Makes 12.

Note: Chocolate chip ice cream is our favorite!

Thora Davidson-White, Parent of Christopher '98

Pumpkin Seed Muffins

1¾ cups all-purpose flour
½ cup sugar
3 teaspoons baking powder
1½ teaspoons cinnamon
½ teaspoon salt

¼ cup toasted pumpkin seeds,
  shelled and chopped
¾ cup milk
½ cup canned pumpkin
⅓ cup oil
1 egg, beaten

Combine flour, sugar, baking powder, cinnamon, salt, and pumpkin seeds; set aside. Combine remaining ingredients. Stir into dry ingredients just until moistened; batter will be lumpy. Spoon batter evenly into greased muffin cups. Bake in preheated 400° oven for 20 to 25 minutes. Serve warm.

Diane Discavage, Parent of Beth '97 and Sara

Cheese and Ham Muffins

2 cups all-purpose flour, sifted
4 tablespoons sugar
3 teaspoons baking powder
½ teaspoon salt
1 cup grated cheddar cheese

1 cup diced boiled ham or
  bacon, cooked and
  crumbled
1 egg, slightly beaten
1 cup milk
2 tablespoons vegetable oil

Sift flour, sugar, baking powder and salt. Stir in cheese and ham. Mix egg, milk, oil and add to flour mixture. Stir lightly with fork until moistened. Fill greased muffin pan cups about ⅔ full. Bake in preheated 400° oven for 25 minutes. Serves 12 large or 24 miniature muffins.

Jennifer Britt, Parent of Daniel and Tyler

Night Owl Sticky Buns

1 cup pecan pieces
⅔ cup firmly packed brown
   sugar
⅓ cup butter

1 (3½-ounce) package cook
   and serve butterscotch
   pudding (not instant)
1 (25-ounce) package frozen
   white rolls

Lightly grease 9x13x2-inch pan. Layer pecans, rolls, sugar and pudding. Dot top with butter. Set on counter overnight to rise. Bake in preheated 350° oven for 15 to 20 minutes. Serves 6 to 8.

Sharon Young, Parent of Allison and Stephanie

Apple Walnut Coffeecake

2 eggs
1 cup oil
1 cup sugar
½ cup firmly packed brown
   sugar
1 teaspoon vanilla

2 cups all-purpose flour
1 teaspoon salt
1 teaspoon baking soda
1 teaspoon cinnamon
½ cup chopped walnuts
2 Granny Smith apples,
   unpeeled and diced

In large bowl, mix eggs, oil, sugars, and vanilla by hand. In separate bowl, combine flour, salt, baking soda, and cinnamon. Add to egg mixture, mixing well. Stir in walnuts and apples. Pour into greased Bundt pan or greased 9x13x2-inch baking pan. Bake in preheated 350° oven for 1 hour. Serve warm or cold.

Donna McCormick, Former Faculty, Former Trustee, Parent of Keith '87

Monkey Cake

4 (10-ounce) cans refrigerated biscuits
1½ cups sugar, divided

1 cup chopped pecans
1½ cups margarine
2 teaspoons cinnamon

Cut biscuits into fourths. Mix 1 cup sugar and cinnamon in large zippered plastic bag. Drop ¼ of biscuits into bag; shake well. Place sugar-coated biscuits into greased Bundt or 10-inch tube cake pan and sprinkle with nuts. Repeat until all biscuits are used (4 layers). In saucepan, melt margarine; add ½ cup sugar, and cinnamon. Cook and stir until heated thoroughly. Pour over biscuits and bake in preheated 325° oven 30 to 35 minutes. Serves 10 to 12.

Note: Maureen's tip is to use scissors to cut biscuits!
Maureen McNeill, Trustee, Parent of Dan
Doris Beaman, Grandparent of Grayson Chavonne

Sour Cream Coffeecake

Cake:
1 cup butter or margarine
1 cup sugar
2 eggs
1 teaspoon vanilla
2 cups all-purpose flour
1 teaspoon baking soda
½ teaspoon salt
1 cup sour cream (regular or nonfat)

Filling:
¾ cup sugar
⅓ cup brown sugar
½ cup ground nuts
1 teaspoon cinnamon

Cream butter and sugar; add eggs and vanilla and beat well. In separate bowl, combine dry ingredients. To egg mixture, add dry ingredients alternately with sour cream. In small bowl, combine filling ingredients. Spread half of batter in Bundt or 10-inch tube pan. Top with filling. Cover with remaining batter. Bake in preheated 350° oven for 45 minutes.
Ann Watts, Grandparent of Ashley Tinney

Cranberry Swirl Coffeecake

½ cup butter
1 cup sugar
2 eggs
1 teaspoon baking powder
1 teaspoon soda
2 cups all-purpose flour
½ teaspoon salt
12 ounces sour cream
1 teaspoon almond flavoring

1 (8-ounce) can whole berry
   cranberry sauce, divided
½ cup chopped pecans

Glaze:
¾ cup powdered sugar
½ teaspoon almond flavoring
1 tablespoon warm water

Cream butter; add sugar gradually. Add eggs one at a time, beating at medium speed. Sift together dry ingredients and add to butter mixture, alternating with sour cream. Add flavoring. Pour layer of batter in greased 8-inch tube pan. Swirl with half of cranberry sauce. Add another layer of batter, then remaining cranberry sauce. Sprinkle top with chopped pecans. Bake at 350° for 55 minutes. Cool for 5 minutes. Remove from pan. Mix glaze ingredients together. Drizzle over top and sides of cake.

Susanne Hux Long '77, Parent of Caroline and Claire

Low-Fat Scones

2½ cups all-purpose flour
¼ cup sugar
½ teaspoon salt
4 teaspoons baking powder
¼ teaspoon baking soda
1 egg

1 cup low-fat buttermilk
3 tablespoons vegetable oil
½ cup raisins, or frozen
   currants, cherries, blueberries (no need to defrost)

Whisk together flour, sugar, salt, baking powder, and baking soda in large bowl. In separate bowl, whisk together egg, buttermilk, vegetable oil and fruit. Add wet mixture to dry. With wooden spoon or rubber spatula, mix together only until all dry ingredients are moistened. Drop batter in 2½-inch mounds onto baking sheet or muffin pan. Sprinkle tops with cinnamon and sugar. Bake until tops are golden brown. Eat warm with hot tea or with frozen yogurt as a dessert.

Elizabeth Musselman, Sister of Mary Green '93

Brunch

Quick Quiche

½ pound bacon, fried and
crumbled
1 cup grated Swiss cheese
¾ cup onion, sautéed

1 cup biscuit/baking mix
4 eggs
2 cups milk
Salt and pepper to taste

Sprinkle bacon, cheese, and onion on bottom of 9-inch pie plate. Blend remaining ingredients and pour into dish. Bake at 400° for 30 minutes or until toothpick tests clean. Serves 4.

Mary Anne Ethington, Parent of Jordan

Zucchini Frittata

1 cup sliced onion
¼ cup oil, divided
2 tablespoons butter, divided
8 eggs

¼ cup grated cheese
1 teaspoon salt
¼ teaspoon pepper
2 cups thinly sliced zucchini

Heat 2 tablespoons oil and 1 tablespoon butter in large skillet. Add onion and sauté until soft. Remove and place in a sieve to drain. Beat eggs, cheese, salt, and pepper in large bowl. Add drained onion and zucchini; mix thoroughly. Heat remaining butter and oil in 9-inch skillet. When very hot, pour in egg mixture. Cook 5 minutes or until bottom and sides are set. Loosen edge with spatula. Place a plate over skillet – flip frittata onto plate and slide back into skillet, uncooked side down. Cook until completely set. Serves 6.

Marie Gagliano, Grandparent of Amanda and Lauren

Hamburger Quiche

½ cup mayonnaise
½ cup milk
1 teaspoon corn starch
2 eggs, beaten
Salt and pepper to taste

1 pound ground beef,
   browned and drained
8 ounces cheese, grated (your
   preference on flavor)
⅓ cup chopped green onion
1 (9-inch) pie shell, unbaked

Mix together mayonnaise, milk, corn starch, eggs, salt, and pepper. Fold in ground beef, cheese and green onion. Pour into pie shell. Bake in preheated 350° oven for 45 minutes.

Emily Schaefer, Wife of Dickson '84

Zucchini Sausage Quiche

1 (9-inch) deep dish pie crust,
   baked according to package
   directions
2 cups shredded zucchini
4 tablespoons butter, divided
½ pound sweet Italian
   sausage

1 cup grated Swiss cheese
3 eggs
½ cup half and half
¼ cup milk
½ teaspoon salt
½ teaspoon pepper
¼ cup Parmesan cheese

Sauté zucchini in 2 tablespoons butter for 5 minutes. Put in pie shell. Remove casings from sausage; brown in remaining butter. Crumble. Sprinkle sausage on top of zucchini. Top with Swiss cheese. Beat eggs; add milk, cream, salt, and pepper. Blend well. Pour over cheese; sprinkle with Parmesan. Bake in preheated 450° oven for 15 minutes. Lower oven temperature to 350° and bake an additional 15 minutes or until set.

D. Hanna, F.A. Faculty

Margaret's Ham/Cheese Souffle

16 slices day old bread, cubed
  without crust
1½ pounds cooked ham,
  cubed
1 pound sharp cheddar
  cheese, grated
1½ cups grated Swiss cheese

1 teaspoon minced onion
6 eggs
3 cups milk
½ teaspoon dry mustard
Salt and pepper to taste
3 cups crushed soda crackers
½ cup butter, melted

Grease 9x13x2-inch glass baking dish. Spread ½ bread cubes evenly over bottom. Top with cubed ham and cheeses; cover with remaining bread cubes. In large bowl, combine onion, eggs, milk, mustard, salt, and pepper. Blend well and pour slowly over the casserole until all milk and egg mixture is absorbed. Cover with plastic wrap and refrigerate overnight. When ready to bake, preheat oven to 375° and combine crushed crackers and butter in bowl. Spread cracker mixture over top and bake casserole until golden, about 40 minutes. Serves 10 to 12.

Marge Koenig, Parent of John '79 and Patricia '79,
Grandparent of Stephen Nuttall

Breakfast/Brunch Casserole

6 slices day old bread, cubed
1½ pounds sausage, cooked
  and drained
½ pound cheddar cheese,
  grated

4 eggs, beaten
¼ teaspoon salt
2 cups milk
¼ teaspoon dry mustard

Using 9x13x2-inch greased baking dish, layer bread crumbs, sausage, and cheese in that order. Mix eggs, mustard, salt, and milk; pour over sausage mixture. Cover and bake in preheated 325° oven 1 hour. Serves 6 to 8.

Sharon Bullard, Parent of Christopher

Susie's Brunch Casserole

2 eggs
2 cups milk
½ cup flour
Salt to taste

½ pound cheddar cheese,
grated
12 ounces cooked bacon or
1 jar real bacon bits

Mix eggs, milk, flour, salt, and pepper together well. Line 9x9-inch baking dish with cheese. Top with bacon. Pour mixture over bacon; bake in preheated 350° oven 45 to 50 minutes. Serves 4.

Susie Brown, F.A. Faculty

Babka (potato and egg casserole)

4 slices of bacon
2 large onions, diced
2 heaping tablespoons solid
   vegetable shortening
3 eggs

1 cup milk
5 large red skin potatoes,
   peeled
Salt and pepper to taste

Cut bacon into small slivers. In large skillet, sauté bacon and diced onions until onions are translucent. Add shortening. While onions are sautéing, blend milk and eggs together. Grate potatoes into egg mixture. Add the contents of skillet to contents of bowl, stirring continuously. Mix well and pour into casserole dish or pan 2½ to 3-inches high. Season to taste. Bake in preheated 375° oven for 30 minutes; reduce heat to 350° and bake additional 1 hour or until solid in the middle.

Emily Wetzel, Grandparent of Deanna and Duncan

Brunch Casserole

6 eggs
1 (5-ounce) can evaporated
   milk
2 cups grated sharp cheese

1 pound cooked sausage,
   drained (½ mild and ½ hot)
Chopped green and red
   pepper to taste
Chopped green onion to taste

Mix all ingredients. Pour into casserole dish. Bake in preheated 350° oven for 20 minutes. Cook until knife inserted in center comes out clean. Can be baked and frozen. Reheat covered.

Ruth Bowman, Grandparent of CoCo Smith

Egg Souffle

7 slices wheat bread
16 ounces sharp cheddar cheese, grated

2 cups milk
7 eggs

Remove crusts from bread and break into pieces. Put bread into buttered 9x13x2-inch glass casserole. Add cheese and mix with bread. In blender, mix milk and eggs. Pour over bread and cheese. Cover with foil and refrigerate overnight. Bake covered in preheated 350° oven for 35 to 40 minutes; remove foil and bake for 20 to 25 minutes more.

Irma Smith, Parent of Coco

Sausage Breakfast Casserole

6 slices white bread
2 cups sharp cheddar cheese, grated
1 pound cooked sausage, drained

1 (5-ounce) can evaporated milk
10 eggs
2 cups milk
Salt and pepper to taste

Lay bread in 9x13x2-inch greased pan. Sprinkle with sausage and cheese. Combine all other ingredients; pour over cheese. Refrigerate overnight. Bake in preheated 350° oven for 1 hour.

Beckie Bishop, F.A. Faculty, Parent of Jenna and Megan

Christmas Morning Brunch

2 pounds pork sausage
3 cups stuffing bread crumbs
3 cups grated sharp cheese,
    divided
1 jar mushroom pieces,
    drained
4 eggs

¾ teaspoon dry mustard
2 cups milk

Morning mixture:
1 can mushroom soup
½ cup milk

Brown and drain pork sausage; set aside. Place bread crumbs in greased 9x13x2-inch pan. Spread 2 cups cheese, mushrooms, and pork sausage on top of stuffing. Beat eggs, dry mustard, and milk. Pour over casserole. Refrigerate overnight.

Before baking, mix soup with milk; pour on casserole. Cover with foil and bake in preheated 325° oven for 45 minutes. Uncover, sprinkle with remaining cheese. Bake for 20 to 25 minutes.

Maggie Franzeen, F.A. Staff, Parent of Matthew

Apple Puff Pancake

1 cup milk
3 eggs at room temperature
¾ cup all-purpose flour
¼ cup + 2 tablespoons sugar,
    divided

3 apples, peeled, cored, and
    sliced ¼-inch thick
1½ tablespoons butter
½ teaspoon cinnamon
Powdered sugar

In mixing bowl, beat milk, eggs, flour and ¼ cup sugar until smooth; set aside. In 12-inch skillet with ovenproof handles, melt butter. Sauté apple slices 2 to 3 minutes over medium-high heat until slightly softened. Sprinkle with 2 tablespoons sugar and cinnamon. Remove from heat. Pour batter over apples in skillet and bake in preheated 375° oven for 30 to 40 minutes until pancake is puffed and lightly browned. Dust with powdered sugar. Serve immediately.

Ann Erteschik, Parent of Elaine

Cherry Crepes

Crepes:
1 cup flour
½ teaspoon baking powder
2 teaspoons sugar
¼ teaspoon salt
2 eggs
1 cup milk
2 tablespoons vegetable oil

Filling:
12 ounces cream-style cottage
   cheese
2 (3-ounce) packages cream
   cheese, softened
1 powdered egg
2 tablespoons sugar
½ teaspoon vanilla

Topping:
1 can cherry pie filling
½ teaspoon almond extract
Sour cream

Crepes: Combine dry ingredients; set aside. Beat eggs, milk, and oil. Add to dry ingredients and beat until smooth. Pour 3 tablespoons (gravy ladle) of batter into hot greased 6-inch skillet. Tilt and rotate pan to spread batter. Cook, then flip to cook other side. Stack crepes between squares of waxed paper.

Filling: In small bowl, beat cottage cheese and cream cheese until smooth. Stir in powdered egg, sugar, and vanilla. Spoon 2 to 3 tablespoons filling down center of each crepe. Turn ends in and roll crepes. Melt margarine in large skillet and heat 3 to 4 crepes at a time. Keep warm by putting crepes in cake pan in 200° oven.

Topping: Heat pie filling and almond extract. Can be thinned with water. Serve over crepes and top with sour cream.

Jo Harbert, Grandparent of Tracey Brooks '99

Blueberry French Toast

12 slices white bread
2 (8-ounce) packages cream
  cheese
1 cup blueberries, rinsed and
  drained
12 eggs
2 cups milk
⅓ cup maple syrup

Sauce:
1 cup sugar
2 tablespoons corn starch
1 cup water
1 cup blueberries, rinsed and
  drained
1 tablespoon butter

Trim crust from bread and cut into 1-inch cubes. Place half in 9x13x2-inch greased baking dish. Cut cream cheese into ½-inch cubes and place over bread. Top with blueberries and remaining bread. In large bowl, beat eggs; add milk and syrup. Mix well. Pour over bread mixture. Cover and chill overnight. Remove from refrigerator 30 minutes before baking.

Cover and bake in preheated 350° oven for 30 minutes; uncover and bake 25 to 30 minutes until brown and center is set. Serve with maple syrup or blueberry sauce.

Blueberry sauce: Combine sugar and corn starch; add water. Bring to boil for 3 minutes, stirring constantly. Stir in blueberries. Reduce heat and simmer 8 to 10 minutes until berries burst. Stir in butter. Serve over french toast.

Tricia Brooks, Parent of Tracey '99

Macadamia Nut French Toast

4 eggs, lightly beaten
¼ cup sugar
¼ teaspoon ground nutmeg
⅔ cup orange juice
⅓ cup milk
½ teaspoon vanilla extract

1 (16-ounce) loaf Italian bread,
  cut into 1-inch slices
⅔ cup butter or margarine,
  melted
½ cup macadamia nuts,
  chopped and toasted
Maple syrup

Combine eggs, sugar, nutmeg, juice, milk, and vanilla in bowl, stirring well. Place bread slices in single layer in lightly greased 9x13x2-inch baking dish. Pour egg mixture over bread slices; cover and chill overnight, turning bread once.

Pour melted butter in 10x15x1-inch jellyroll pan. Place bread slices in single layer in pan. Bake in preheated 400° oven for 10 minutes. Sprinkle nuts evenly over toast and bake another 10 minutes. Serve immediately with maple syrup. Serves 6.

Chris Kastner, Parent of Brian and Laura

Soups
and
Salads

Soups and Salads

Soups

Taco Soup

1½ to 2 pounds ground beef
  or turkey
1 medium onion, chopped
1 (4-ounce) can chopped
  green chiles
1 teaspoon salt
½ teaspoon black pepper
1 package taco seasoning mix

1 package ranch dressing mix
1 (15½-ounce) can whole
  kernel corn, drained
3 (16-ounce) cans stewed
  tomatoes, puréed if desired
1 (16-ounce) can kidney beans
1 (16-ounce) can chili beans
1½ cups water

Brown ground beef/turkey with onions. Drain off fat. Add green chiles. Transfer meat, onion, and chile mixture to large soup pot. Stir in remaining ingredients and cook for 30 minutes on low heat. Serve with sour cream and grated cheddar cheese. Serves 8 to 10.

Susan Barnes, Parent of Zack
Bernice Oswalt, Grandparent of Jennifer and Allison

Potato Soup

3 cups cubed potatoes
½ cup chopped onions
3 cups water
1 cup sour cream
⅓ cup all-purpose flour
1 teaspoon salt
¼ teaspoon pepper

2 cups milk (½ evaporated
  milk or half-and-half makes
  it creamier)
2 chicken bouillon cubes
2 tablespoons butter
¾ cup chopped celery
  (optional)

In large pot, cook potatoes and onions in water for 20 minutes. Mix sour cream, flour, salt and pepper. Add sour cream mixture, milk, bouillon cubes, butter, and celery to potatoes and onions. Cook over medium heat for 10 minutes, stirring frequently. Lower heat and cook 5 to 10 minutes more. Makes 2½ quarts.

Note: Very good served with cheese toast.

Vivian Bishop, Grandmother of Jenna and Megan

Oyster Spinach Soup

1 (8-ounce) can oysters with liquid
1 (12-ounce) package spinach soufflé, thawed

1 can cream of chicken soup
1 cup milk
1 tablespoon lemon juice
Dash pepper

Drain oysters; add water to liquid to make ¾ cup. Stir soufflé, soup, and oyster liquid together in sauce pan. Add milk; blend. Add oysters, lemon juice, and pepper. Heat until oysters plump. <u>Do not boil.</u> Serves 4 to 6.

Christopher White '97

Hamburger Vegetable Soup

1½ pounds ground chuck, browned and drained
2 onions, chopped
1 (16-ounce) can okra, undrained
1 (16-ounce) can white corn, undrained
1 (16-ounce) can small butter beans, undrained

1 (16-ounce) can tomatoes, puréed
2 cans tomato soup
1¾ cups water
Salt and pepper to taste
Pinch garlic salt
1 tablespoon chili powder
½ teaspoon ground oregano
½ teaspoon sugar

Combine all ingredients in soup pot. Simmer 2 to 3 hours. Serves 6 to 8.

Ann Hux, Parent of Susanne '77,
Grandparent of Caroline and Claire Long

Corn Chowder

2 (16-ounce) cans whole kernel corn
2 (16-ounce) cans creamed corn
½ cup butter or margarine
1 medium onion, diced

6 medium potatoes, diced
4 cups milk
Salt and pepper to taste
6 slices bacon, cooked and crumbled

Mix all ingredients, except bacon, in a pot. Cook until potatoes are done. Sprinkle with crumbled bacon and serve. Serves 4 to 6.

Lois Hochstatter, Grandparent of Brooke, Garrett, Megan and Seth Ebel

Alina's Tomato Soup

1½ cups chopped onion
3 cloves garlic, crushed
1 tablespoon butter
1 tablespoon olive oil
1 teaspoon dill weed
¼ teaspoon black pepper

1 (28-ounce) can crushed
  tomatoes with 2 cups water
  or 6 cups canned whole
  tomatoes, with liquid
1 tablespoon honey
¼ cup sour cream

In large saucepan, combine butter and olive oil. Add onions and garlic; cook 5 minutes or until onion is translucent. Add dill, pepper, tomatoes, and honey. Cover and simmer for 1 hour. Purée in blender. Before serving, add sour cream. Serves 4.

Note: Optional toppings include yogurt, parsley, and scallions.

Alina Myers, Great-great cousin of Mario Martinez

Minnesota Wild Rice Soup

1½ pounds ground beef,
  browned and drained
½ teaspoon salt
½ teaspoon pepper
1 tablespoon Italian seasoning
1 cup cooked wild rice
4¾ cups water, divided

½ teaspoon hot sauce
2 teaspoons instant beef
  bouillon granules
1 cup chopped celery
2 large onions, chopped
3 cans mushroom soup

In large soup pot, combine ground beef, salt, pepper, Italian seasoning, wild rice, 1 cup water, hot sauce, bouillon, celery, and onions. Simmer covered for 30 minutes. Stir in soup and 3¾ cups water. Simmer 30 minutes more. Serves 8 to 10.

Note: This is also very good with chicken in place of the hamburger, and chicken bouillon in place of the beef bouillon.

Harriette Sandeen, Grandparent of Matthew Franzeen

Danbo's Favorite Chicken Gumbo

2 tablespoons flour
½ cup vegetable oil
1 slice bacon, diced
1 onion, chopped
½ green pepper, chopped
1 clove garlic, minced
1 teaspoon soy sauce
1 tablespoon Worcestershire
  sauce
Dash hot sauce
1 teaspoon salt
Dash pepper
1 (16-ounce) can tomatoes,
  chopped
4 chicken breasts
2 to 3 cups water
1 cup frozen okra
1½ teaspoons filé powder

Combine flour and oil in large pot. Stir over medium heat until light brown. Stir in bacon; cook 1 minute. Stir in onion, green pepper, and garlic. Cook until onion is soft. Add sauces, salt, pepper, tomatoes, chicken, and water; simmer 45 minutes or until chicken is tender. Remove chicken; chop and return to pot. Add okra and cook 10 minutes more. Stir in filé powder just before serving. Serve over rice. Serves 6 to 8.

Maureen McNeill, Trustee, Parent of Dan

Baked Potato Soup

4 large baking potatoes
⅔ cup margarine
⅔ cup all-purpose flour
6 cups milk
¾ teaspoon salt
½ teaspoon black pepper
2 green onions, chopped
6 slices bacon, cooked and
  crumbled
¾ cup shredded cheddar
  cheese
1 (8-ounce) carton sour cream

Wash potatoes; prick several times and bake in preheated 350° oven for 45 minutes or until done. Cool potatoes; scoop out pulp. Melt margarine in large heavy pot over low heat; add flour, stirring until smooth. Cook 1 minute, stirring constantly. Gradually add milk; cook over medium heat, stirring constantly until thick and bubbly. Add potato pulp, salt, pepper, onion, bacon, and cheese. Cook until thoroughly heated. Stir in sour cream. Add extra milk if needed for desired consistency. Serve grated cheese and bacon on top. Serves 10.

Jane White, Grandparent of Robert DeGaetano

Cream Vichyssoise Glacee

4 leeks, white part only, thinly
  sliced
1 medium onion, thinly sliced
2 tablespoons butter
5 medium potatoes, thinly
  sliced
4 cups chicken broth

1 tablespoon salt
2 cups milk
2 cups whipping cream
Salt and pepper
1 cup heavy cream
Chopped chives

Sauté leeks and onion in butter until lightly browned; add potatoes. Stir in broth and salt. Boil gently 35 to 40 minutes. Crush and rub through fine strainer or whirl in blender. Return to heat; add milk and whipping cream. Season to taste with salt and pepper; bring to boil. Cool and then rub through very fine strainer. When soup is cold, add heavy cream. Chill thoroughly before serving. Garnish with finely chopped chives. Serves 8.

Lee Vieta, Parent of Kathryn '89, Amy '91, Laura '95, Paul '94

Zucchini Soup

1 small onion, chopped
1 tablespoon butter
2 cups chicken broth
2 tablespoons chopped green
  chiles
½ teaspoon salt
⅛ teaspoon pepper
2 small zucchini, chopped

1 (8¾-ounce) can whole kernel
  corn, drained
1 cup milk
2 ounces Monterey Jack
  cheese, cut into ¼-inch
  cubes
Ground nutmeg
Snipped parsley

Cook and stir onion in butter until tender. Stir in broth, chiles, salt, pepper, zucchini, and corn. Heat to boiling; reduce heat. Cover and cook for 5 minutes. Stir in milk. Heat just until hot; do not boil. Add cheese. Sprinkle with nutmeg and parsley. Serves 5.

Note: 150 calories per serving.

Sharon Kropp, Parent of Kathryn

Chicken Tortilla Soup

4 quarts chicken stock
1 quart vegetables, puréed
   (carrots, celery, onion)
4 ounces garlic, chopped
54 ounces crushed tomatoes

1 (48-ounce) can diced chiles
5 grilled chicken breasts,
   cut up
½ tablespoon white pepper

Boil stock and vegetables for 10 minutes. Add all other ingredients; cook on low heat for 40 to 45 minutes. (There are no tortillas in this soup, just flavor!) Serves 40 to 50.

Huske Hardware House Brewing Company

Broccoli and Cheddar Soup

3 bunches broccoli
4 quarts chicken stock
4 cups shredded cheddar
   cheese

1 quart heavy cream
1 quart roux (1 quart water
   mixed with 16 ounces corn
   starch)
½ tablespoon white pepper

Trim and purée broccoli stalks (save florets). Boil purée mix in chicken stock for 1 hour. Add heavy cream and when hot, add roux. Add cheese, stirring briskly. Add florets and pepper and cook on low heat until broccoli is tender. Serves 40 to 50.

Huske Hardware House Brewing Company

White Chicken Chili

1 pound chicken breasts or
   tenders, cubed
⅓ cup finely chopped onion
1 clove garlic, minced
½ teaspoon cumin
2 tablespoons oil
1 can cream of chicken soup

1 can cheddar cheese soup
1¼ cups milk
1 (16-ounce) can great
   northern beans
1 (4-ounce) can chopped
   green chiles
Chili powder to taste

Sauté chicken, onion, garlic, and cumin in oil until chicken is thoroughly cooked and onion is transparent. Add soups, milk, beans, and chiles. Season with chili powder. Simmer 10 minutes or longer.

Susan Williams, Parent of Catherine and Sam

Chicken Chili

2 tablespoons olive oil
1 medium onion, chopped
2 large garlic cloves, chopped
1½ pounds skinless, boneless
   chicken breast, cut up
4 teaspoons chili powder
1 tablespoon ground cumin
2 teaspoons oregano
1½ cups chicken stock
1 (28-ounce) can chopped
   tomatoes with juice

2 jalapeño peppers, seeds and
   ribs removed, chopped
   (optional)
Salt and freshly ground pepper
1 (15-ounce) can pinto beans,
   rinsed and drained
2 (15-ounce) cans black
   beans, rinsed and drained
Cilantro
Lime wedges
Hot sauce

In large non-aluminum sauce pan, heat oil. Add onion and garlic; cook over moderately low heat until barely tender. Add chicken and cook over medium heat until no longer pink, about 3 minutes. Stir in chili powder, cumin, and oregano. Add stock, tomatoes with juice, and peppers, if desired. Season with salt and pepper. Bring to boil. Cover; reduce heat and simmer on low for 15 minutes. Stir in beans and simmer, uncovered, over medium-low heat until thickened, about 15 minutes longer. Serve with cilantro, lime wedges, and hot sauce on the side.

Sharon Kropp, Parent of Kathryn

Rick's Chili

1 pound ground beef
1 pound hot bulk pork sausage
1 medium onion, chopped
1 (15-ounce) can pinto beans
1 (15-ounce) can kidney beans

1 (15-ounce) can whole
   tomatoes
1 (8-ounce) can tomato sauce
Red pepper to taste
8 shakes chili powder or to
   taste

Brown ground beef and sausage. Add onion and sauté until soft. Drain off excess fat. In large pot, mix beans, tomatoes, and tomato sauce. Add meat and red pepper; bring to boil. Reduce heat to simmer. Add chili powder; cover and cook for 45 minutes to 1 hour. Serves 6.

Rick Carter, Parent of Richard

Chili Con Carne

This recipe was used in my food service class when I was a home economics teacher. It was done in one 55-minute period. Any time I used ground beef, after browning it, I placed it in a colander, washed the meat with hot water and dried it with paper towels. Practically all fat from meat is removed this way.

1 pound lean ground beef
1 cup chopped onion
2 cups tomatoes, chopped
   (1-pound can)
1 (8-ounce) can tomato sauce

1 teaspoon salt
2 teaspoons chili powder
1 bay leaf (optional)
1 (15-ounce) can kidney beans

Brown meat with onions in pressure cooker. Add remaining ingredients (except beans). Cover; set control and cook 10 minutes after control jiggles. Reduce pressure normally for 5 minutes, then place under faucet to reduce pressure. Open.

Note: If a pressure cooker is not used, cook all ingredients except beans over low heat 40-45 minutes.

Add beans and simmer for 7 minutes. Remove bay leaf and serve.

Mary Frederick, Parent of Elizabeth '78 and Susan '78,
Grandparent of Richard Carter

Low-Fat Chili

1 green pepper, chopped
1 medium onion, chopped
2 tablespoons butter
1 (48-ounce) can tomato juice
   or tomato-vegetable juice
   cocktail

1 (15-ounce) can kidney beans
1 (14-ounce) can bean sprouts
½ pound ground beef,
   browned and cooled
Chili powder to taste
Salt and pepper to taste

In large pot, sauté green peppers and onions in butter for 5 minutes. Add tomato juice, beans, bean sprouts, and ground beef. Add chili powder, salt, and pepper to taste. Cook until well blended.

Pat Williford, F.A. Staff, Parent of Jerri Ann '94 and Patrice '99

Rita's Chili

2 pounds ground beef
1 medium onion, chopped
¼ teaspoon garlic powder
1 teaspoon salt
½ teaspoon pepper
½ teaspoon oregano
½ teaspoon cumin

3 to 4 teaspoons chili powder
Dash cayenne pepper
4 (8-ounce) cans tomato
  sauce
1 (6-ounce) can tomato paste
2 (15-ounce) cans kidney
  beans

In large pot, brown beef with onions. Add remaining ingredients and simmer for 45 minutes to 1 hour. Add water as needed. May be put into crock pot after beef is browned; cook on high setting for 2 to 3 hours or low setting for 5 to 6 hours. Serve with crackers and green salad. May top with shredded cheddar cheese, green onions, and sour cream. Serves 8.

Julia Tingler, Parent of Lauren

Brunswick Stew

3 to 4 chicken breasts or 1
  small whole chicken
3 (10 ¾-ounce) cans
  succotash

2 (16-ounce) cans of whole
  stewed tomatoes, squeeze
  until pulpy
1 (10 ¾-ounce) can tomatoes
  and okra

Cover chicken in salted water in Dutch oven. Boil until chicken is tender. Cool and pull chicken off bones. To approximately 1 gallon of stock, add chicken and canned vegetables. Cook uncovered over low heat for approximately 2 hours. This will reduce to thick stew. Serve with rolls for complete meal.

Billie Hankins, F.A. Faculty

Macaroni Beef Stew

2 tablespoons oil
1 pound beef stew meat, cut
   into cubes
1 cup sliced celery
½ cup sliced onion
1 (14½-ounce) can whole
   tomatoes, undrained

2½ cups water
1 teaspoon salt
1 teaspoon paprika
½ teaspoon chili powder
1 cup elbow macaroni,
   uncooked

Heat oil in Dutch oven over medium-high heat until hot. Add beef; cook and stir until browned. Add celery, onion, tomatoes, water, salt, paprika, and chili powder; mix well. Cover and simmer 2 hours or until beef is tender. Stir in macaroni. Cook uncovered over medium heat for 8 to 10 minutes or until macaroni is tender, stirring occasionally. Serves 4.

Florence Alvarez, Parent of Sean '79,
Grandparent of Jamie '94 and Ryan '98 Johnson, and Kristin Wellons

Dear Abby's Stew

2 pounds boneless beef stew
   meat, cut into 1½-inch
   cubes
1 can cream of mushroom
   soup

1 package dry onion soup mix
1¼ cups water
6 to 8 ounces wide noodles
2 tablespoons butter

In 3-quart casserole, combine meat, mushroom soup, onion soup mix, and water. Mix well. Cover and bake in preheated 300° oven for 3 hours. Prepare noodles according to package instructions. Drain and toss with butter. To serve, spread noodles on a large serving plate and top with stew. Serves 4 to 6.

Cornelia Hilburn, Parent of Amanda and Ben

Main Dish Salads
Won Ton Chicken Salad

½ package won ton wrappers
2 tablespoons sesame oil
¼ cup peanut oil
Sugar
4 chicken breasts, cooked and
  shredded
½ head lettuce, torn into
  pieces
6 green onions, chopped
¼ cup sliced almonds

Dressing:
1 teaspoon salt
1 teaspoon pepper
¼ cup white vinegar
¼ cup sugar
¼ cup olive oil

Fry wrappers in oils. Drain and toss with sugar. Break into pieces. Combine chicken, onions, almonds, lettuce, and wrappers about 30 minutes before serving.

Combine dressing ingredients in bottle. Shake well. Add dressing to salad just before serving. Serves 8.

Maureen McNeill, Trustee, Parent of Dan

Oriental Salad

1 box of chicken flavored rice-
  vermicelli mix, cooked as
  directed
1 (8-ounce) jar artichokes,
  drained and chopped
1 (8-ounce) can water
  chestnuts, chopped

1 cup chopped black olives
1 bunch green onions,
  chopped
1 cup mayonnaise
3 (6-ounce) cans shrimp,
  rinsed and drained

Cook rice-vermicelli mix as directed on box. Cool completely. Add remaining ingredients. Refrigerate. Serves 5 to 6.

Mary Burnham, Grandparent of Mary Shoup

Mandarin Salad

Sauce:
1 green onion, minced
3 garlic cloves, minced
2 tablespoons soy sauce
¼ cup white vinegar
Dash of seasoned salt flavor
  enhancer
¼ to ½ cup sugar
1½ tablespoons sesame oil

Salad:
1 to 2 cucumbers, peeled and
  cut into julienne strips
1 stalk celery, slivered
1 carrot, slivered
½ teaspoon salt
Water
½ package bean threads
1 medium green pepper,
  slivered
2 or 3 fried eggs, slivered
2 chicken breasts, cooked and
  slivered

Mix together sauce ingredients; set aside. Combine cucumbers, celery, and carrot; sprinkle with salt. Let stand ½ hour. Drain liquid. In small saucepan, bring water to a boil. Boil bean threads for 10 seconds; separate while boiling. Drain and cut into 2-inch lengths. Layer all ingredients. Pour sauce over; mix well. Serves 4.

Note: Bean threads can be found in the oriental food section.

Nina Godwin, Grandparent of Harry, Lacy, and Laura

Spring Chicken Salad

4 cups cooked and cubed
  chicken
1 cup chopped celery
1½ cups halved seedless
  green grapes

1 teaspoon salt
¼ teaspoon pepper
¾ cup mayonnaise
¼ cup sour cream
1 cup cocktail peanuts

Combine chicken, celery, and grapes in large bowl. Sprinkle with salt and pepper. Add mayonnaise and sour cream. Mix thoroughly. Toss in peanuts. Serves 6 to 8.

Barbara Appel, Parent of Eric '98 and Chris

Chinese Chicken Salad

3 cooked chicken breasts,
  shredded
¼ cup sesame seeds, toasted
½ cup sliced almonds, toasted
1 large head cabbage, thinly
  sliced
2 (3-ounce) packages ramen
  noodles, uncooked
4 green onions, thinly sliced

Dressing:
¼ cup sugar
1 cup canola oil
½ teaspoon salt
2 tablespoons sesame oil
¼ teaspoon cayenne pepper
½ cup seasoned rice wine
  vinegar

Combine chicken, sesame seeds, almonds, cabbage, ramen noodles, and onions. Blend dressing; toss with all other ingredients. Serves 6.

Beth Bradford Davis '84, Parent of Brawley and Dottie

Dilled Chicken Salad

1 (16-ounce) package spiral
  pasta, cooked and drained
2 cups cooked and cubed
  chicken
1 cup chopped celery
⅓ cup chopped onion
1 (10-ounce) package frozen
  peas, thawed

Dressing:
1 envelope ranch salad
  dressing mix
2 cups sour cream
1 cup mayonnaise
1 cup milk
3 tablespoons minced fresh
  dill or 1 tablespoon dill
  weed
½ teaspoon garlic salt

Combine pasta, chicken, celery, onion, and peas in large bowl. Mix well. Combine dressing ingredients; whisk until smooth. Pour over salad; toss to coat. Cover and refrigerate for at least 2 hours. Serves 10 to 14.

Gloria Bownas, Parent of Briggen

Fruited Chicken Salad

3 cups cooked and cubed
  chicken
1½ cups diced celery
3 tablespoons lemon juice
¾ cup slivered almonds
1½ cups purple seedless
  grapes, halved

Dressing:
1 cup mayonnaise
1 (8-ounce) can pineapple
  tidbits with juice
Salt and pepper to taste

Combine chicken, celery and lemon juice. Add almonds and grapes. Mix dressing ingredients; toss with chicken mixture. Chill at least 1 hour before serving.

Beth Ray, F.A. Faculty

Tuna/Potato Shoestring Salad

1 (12-ounce) can albacore
  tuna, drained
1 cup shredded carrots

1 cup diced apple
1 cup mayonnaise
1 (8-ounce) can shoestring
  potatoes

Combine tuna, carrots, apple, and mayonnaise. Before serving, add shoestring potatoes. Serves 4 to 6.

Diane Glanville, F.A. Faculty, Parent of Lee '91

Shrimp Macaroni Salad

1 pound shrimp, cooked and
shelled
1½ cups macaroni shells,
cooked and drained
4 ounces American or
cheddar cheese, cubed
½ cup chopped celery
¼ cup chopped green pepper

1 or 2 tablespoons chopped
onion
½ cup mayonnaise
½ cup sour cream
3 tablespoons apple cider
vinegar
¾ teaspoon salt
Dash hot pepper sauce

Cut shrimp in halves or quarters, depending on size of shrimp. Toss with macaroni, cheese, celery, pepper and onion. Blend remaining ingredients. Combine with shrimp mixture. Cover and chill. Stir before serving. Serves 6.

Judy Lennon, Parent of Hannah '95, Evan '98 and Ben

Six-Layer Tuna Salad

1¼ cups ranch dressing,
divided
2 (6½-ounce) cans tuna,
drained and flaked
3 tablespoons finely sliced
green onions
2 tomatoes, chopped

2 (2¼-ounce) cans sliced
black olives, drained
½ pound bacon, cooked crisp
and crumbled
1 avocado, thinly sliced
2 cups shredded lettuce,
divided

Combine 1 cup ranch dressing, tuna, and onions; mix until dressing is thoroughly absorbed. Combine tomatoes and olives. Combine bacon and avocado slices. In large salad bowl, layer 1 cup shredded lettuce, tomato mixture, ½ tuna mixture and avocado mixture. Repeat layering with remaining lettuce and tuna mixture. Drizzle remaining ¼ cup ranch dressing over salad. Serves 4 to 5.

Prima Yoshimoto, Parent of Brendan

Vegetable Salads
Blue Cheese Dressing

2 cups sour cream
1 (4-ounce) package blue
  cheese

Juice of 1 lemon
2 tablespoons Italian dressing

Mix all ingredients well. This can also be used as a dip.

Happy Bleecker '96

Broccoli Salad

1 large head broccoli (about
  1½ pounds)
10 slices bacon, cooked crisp
  and crumbled
5 green onions, sliced thin or
  ½ cup thinly-sliced purple
  onion
½ cup raisins
1 cup mayonnaise
2 tablespoons apple cider
  vinegar
¼ cup sugar

Optional Ingredients:
¼ cup sesame seeds, toasted
1 to 2 cups green or red
  grapes, cut in half
⅓ cup peanuts
1 apple, chopped
½ cup shredded cheese
¾ cup sunflower seeds

Wash and cut broccoli into bite-size pieces. Add bacon, green onions, and raisins. In separate bowl, combine mayonnaise, vinegar, and sugar. Pour over broccoli mixture; toss gently. Cover and refrigerate 2 to 3 hours.

Note: Any of the optional ingredients can also be added.

Low-fat hints: Use turkey bacon, low-fat mayonnaise, and omit sunflower seeds.

Becky Frank, Parent of Rebecca '96
Kim Green, Parent of Mandy '99
Kelly Wills Sears '90

Cashew and Pea Salad

Dressing:
¾ cup vegetable oil
¼ cup apple cider vinegar
1 garlic clove, minced
2 to 3 teaspoons spicy
  mustard
1 teaspoon Worcestershire
  sauce
½ teaspoon salt
½ teaspoon lemon juice
¼ teaspoon pepper
¼ teaspoon sugar

Salad:
1 (10-ounce) package frozen
  peas, thawed
2 celery ribs, thinly sliced
2 green onions, thinly sliced
½ cup sour cream
4 bacon strips, cooked and
  crumbled
¾ cup chopped cashews

Combine dressing ingredients in small bowl; mix well. Cover and refrigerate 1 hour. In large bowl, combine peas, celery, and onions. Combine sour cream and 2 tablespoons of dressing; mix well. Fold into pea mixture. Just before serving, stir in bacon and cashews.

Note: Refrigerate any remaining dressing and use on green salad.

Edith Gobien, Grandparent of Jacqueline and Jeremy

Marinated Asparagus

1 (15-ounce) can asparagus,
  drained
¼ cup red wine vinegar
½ cup sugar
¼ cup water
½ teaspoon celery seed
1 cinnamon stick
3 whole cloves
½ teaspoon salt

Place asparagus in shallow dish. Combine remaining ingredients in small pot. Cook on medium heat for 5 minutes. Pour hot liquid over asparagus; cover. Refrigerate overnight. Remove cinnamon and cloves before serving. Serves 4.

Eleanor Ninestein, Parent of Edward

Crunchy Spinach Salad

2 (10-ounce) bags fresh
  spinach, washed thoroughly
  and torn
1 (16-ounce) can bean
  sprouts, drained or 2 cups
  fresh
1 (8-ounce) can sliced water
  chestnuts, drained
4 hard-boiled eggs, chopped
6 bacon strips, cooked and
  crumbled
1 small onion, thinly sliced

Dressing:
½ cup brown sugar, firmly
  packed
½ cup vegetable oil
⅓ cup apple cider vinegar
⅓ cup ketchup
1 tablespoon Worcestershire
  sauce

In large bowl, combine salad ingredients. In a bottle or jar, combine dressing ingredients. Cover and shake well to mix. Just before serving, pour dressing over salad; toss. Serves 8.

Diane Ginthner, Parent of Kyle and Matthew

Strawberry Spinach Salad

1 pound spinach, washed
  thoroughly, stems trimmed
1 pint strawberries, hulled and
  sliced

Dressing:
¼ cup sugar
1½ teaspoons minced Vidalia
  onion
¼ teaspoon Worcestershire
  sauce
¼ teaspoon paprika
½ cup oil
¼ cup apple cider vinegar

Place spinach and strawberries in bowl. In separate container, mix dressing ingredients. Pour over spinach and strawberries. Toss.

Rosemary Rocconi, Parent of Dominic and Mario

Black Bean and Corn Salad

Dressing:
⅓ cup apple cider vinegar
⅔ cup olive oil
1 tablespoon dried basil
1 teaspoon dried thyme
½ cup Dijon mustard
¼ to ⅓ cup sugar
1 teaspoon sesame oil
2 teaspoons coarse black
  pepper

Salad:
½ pound dried black beans
1 pound yellow corn, cooked
  and cooled
1 small purple onion, diced
2 ribs celery, diced
1 small red pepper, diced
1 jalapeño pepper, seeded and
  diced
1 carrot, diced and blanched

In food processor, blend dressing ingredients until smooth. Add more mustard to emulsify if necessary. Cook beans until done; do not overcook. Drain and rinse well. Add remaining vegetables; mix. Combine dressing and vegetables; refrigerate overnight. Serves 8.

Note: If using fresh ingredients, prepare the beans and corn a day ahead. You can substitute canned black beans if you are making this dish with limited time. When cooking dried black beans, rinse beans thoroughly in colander. Soak in 3 to 4 times as much water as amount of beans. Remove beans that float. Soak overnight. Bring beans to a slow boil in the water they were soaked in and simmer until done. (To test if done, blow on a few beans in a spoon; if the skins burst, they are ready.)

Megg Potter Rader '79
Sarah Moorman, Wife of Frank '79

German Potato Salad

2 pounds potatoes
1 pound bacon
1 tablespoon parsley
¼ cup apple cider vinegar

1 onion, chopped
½ teaspoon salt
½ cup chicken broth

Boil potatoes with peels until done. Fry bacon until crisp; reserve drippings. Crumble bacon and set aside. In small bowl, mix parsley, vinegar, reserved bacon drippings, onion, salt, and broth. Microwave until very hot. When potatoes are cool enough to handle, peel and thinly slice. Add sauce and bacon. Serve hot.

Burglinde Walker, Parent of Morris

Yellow Squash Salad

5 medium yellow squash,
thinly sliced
½ cup sliced onion
⅓ cup salad oil
⅔ cup apple cider vinegar
1 teaspoon salt

½ cup sliced celery
⅓ cup chopped green pepper
1 teaspoon black pepper
¼ cup sugar
1 clove garlic, crushed

Mix squash and onion in serving bowl. Blend together remaining ingredients; pour over squash and onion. Chill at least 12 hours. Toss well, and either drain or serve with a slotted spoon.

Note: This keeps well for at least 7 days in refrigerator.

Linda Tillman, Parent of Scott '98

Not Just Cold Slaw

1½ to 2 packages slivered almonds
½ package (or more) sunflower seeds
16 ounces shredded cabbage
4 green onions, chopped
2 (3-ounce) packages ramen chicken noodles

Dressing:
1 cup safflower oil
½ cup apple cider vinegar
¾ cup sugar
1 tablespoon soy sauce
¼ teaspoon garlic powder

Toast almonds and sunflower seeds for 1 minute under broiler; don't overcook. Mix cabbage and onions; chill. Just before serving, add almonds, seeds, and noodles. Mix dressing before pouring. Toss together; serve.

Teresa Lindsley Dobson '80
Connie Koonce, F.A. Faculty

Pea Salad

2 (10-ounce) packages frozen green peas, thawed
1 cup dry-roasted peanuts
½ cup sour cream

½ cup mayonnaise
1 green onion, sliced
Salt and pepper to taste
⅓ to ½ cup bacon bits

Mix all ingredients together. Chill at least 2 hours. Serve.

Marcia Kinlaw, Parent of Grey '98 and Zach

Pasta Salads
Spaghetti Salad

1 (16-ounce) package thin
  spaghetti
Salt and pepper
Garlic powder
1 (2.62-ounce) bottle
  McCormick's Salad Supreme
2 large tomatoes, cubed and
  seeds removed
2 cucumbers, chopped, with
  seeds and pulp removed

1 bunch green onions, finely
  chopped
2 green peppers, finely
  chopped
2 to 3 stalks celery, finely
  chopped
1 (16-ounce) bottle Italian
  salad dressing

Cook spaghetti according to package directions, adding salt, pepper, and garlic powder to taste to the water. Drain, rinse, and cool. In large bowl, combine cooled spaghetti, seasoning, and vegetables. Stir in salad dressing. Refrigerate several hours before serving. Serves 8.

Note: Vegetables can vary according to preference. Low-calorie or fat-free dressing may be used. Serves 8.

Linda Lewis, Parent of Richard '81, Hardy '83, Frank, and David

Pasta Salad Dressing

¼ cup lemon juice
¼ cup apple cider vinegar
¼ cup apple juice
⅛ teaspoon thyme
⅛ teaspoon rosemary

½ teaspoon oregano
½ teaspoon dry mustard
½ teaspoon onion powder
½ teaspoon basil
2 cloves garlic, minced

Combine all dressing ingredients and blend well. Pour over 16 ounces of your favorite cooked pasta and toss. Serves 6 to 8.

Teri Mascia Williams '80, Wife of Stuart '80, Parent of Jared and Justin

Pasta Salad

1 pound pasta twists, cooked and drained
1 (8-ounce) jar zesty Italian dressing
1 (2.62-ounce) bottle McCormick's Salad Supreme
2 to 3 cucumbers, seeds removed and chopped
6 small green onions, chopped
2 small tomatoes, chopped
½ cup Parmesan cheese

Combine all ingredients. Chill before serving.

Ruth Bowman, Grandparent of CoCo Smith

Pizza Salad

This is great for a picnic because there is no mayonnaise!

½ cup salad oil
¼ cup vinegar
1 teaspoon oregano
2 teaspoons salt
¼ teaspoon pepper
1 garlic clove, crushed
8 ounces macaroni
3 tomatoes, chopped
1 pound Swiss cheese, cubed
1 red onion, sliced thin and separated into rings
½ cup freshly grated Parmesan cheese, divided

Mix salad oil, vinegar, oregano, salt, pepper, and garlic. Cook macaroni according to package direction. Cool. Add tomatoes, Swiss cheese, and onion rings; toss to mix. Pour vinegar mixture and ¼ cup Paremesan cheese over macaroni mixture. Mix well. Sprinkle with remaining Parmesan. Chill until ready to serve. Serves 8.

Tobie Little, F.A. Staff

Better Than Salad

3 cups cooked rice, cooled
½ cup chopped onion
1 cup mayonnaise
1 teaspoon mustard
2 hard-boiled eggs, chopped
¼ cup sweet pickle relish
Salt and pepper

Combine all ingredients; chill. Serves 8.

Barbara Gobien, Parent of Jacqueline and Jeremy

Fruit Salads

Frozen Pineapple Salad

1 (8-ounce) package cream
  cheese, softened
¼ cup sugar
¼ cup firmly packed brown
  sugar

2 cups pineapple or orange
  yogurt
1 (15-ounce) can crushed
  pineapple, drained
Pecans, chopped
Maraschino cherries, chopped

Mix cream cheese and sugars. Add yogurt and pineapple. Spoon mixture into serving bowl or individual cupcake cups; sprinkle with pecans and cherries. Remove from freezer ½ hour before serving. Serves 12.

Jane Buryk, Parent of Peter '99 and Anna

Five Cup Salad

1 cup mandarin oranges,
  drained
1 cup crushed pineapple,
  drained

1 cup shredded coconut
1 cup miniature marshmallows
1 cup sour cream

Mix all ingredients together. Chill and serve. Serves 6.

Dixie Moores, Grandparent of Brittany

Frozen Fruit Salad

1 (14-ounce) can sweetened
  condensed milk
1 can cherry pie filling
1 (11-ounce) can mandarin
  oranges, drained

1 (20-ounce) can crushed
  pineapple, drained
⅔ cup chopped pecans
1 (8-ounce) container frozen
  nondairy whipped topping,
  thawed

In large bowl, combine milk and pie filling. Add oranges, pineapple, and pecans; mix well. Gently fold in whipped topping. Spread in 9x13x2-inch pan. Cover and freeze. Remove from freezer 15 minutes before serving. Serve with spoon or cut into squares.

Linda Blair, Trustee, Parent of Jennifer '96,
Ashley '98, Emily '99, and Amanda

Fruit Compote

Garnish this lovely salad to match the season. At Christmas, garnish with red and green cherries and mint. At Easter, garnish with oranges or other seasonal fruits.

1 (8½-ounce) can fruit cocktail
1 (16-ounce) can pears, diced
1 (15-ounce) can pineapple
  chunks
1 (10-ounce) package frozen
  strawberries, thawed

1 (6-ounce) jar maraschino
  cherries, drained
2 apples, cubed
2 bananas, sliced
1 (3½-ounce) package instant
  vanilla pudding mix

Put all fruit with juice in large serving bowl. Sprinkle dry pudding over fruit; mix gently until all pudding is blended and dissolved. Cover and refrigerate at least 4 hours or overnight.

Mary Joan Fredette, Parent of Chris '94 and Jon

Assorted Melon and Berries with Bourbon Creme Anglaise

2 cups milk
1 teaspoon vanilla
4 egg yolks
4 teaspoons sugar
4 teaspoons Bourbon (or
  liqueur of choice)

Cantalope
Honeydew melon
Blueberries
Raspberries
Blackberries
Mint sprigs

In small saucepan, bring milk to boil. Set aside. Combine vanilla, egg yolks, and sugar in top of double boiler and beat until thickened and pale lemon colored. Slowly add hot milk to egg yolk mixture, stirring 8 minutes or until mixture thickens. Remove and strain through fine sieve into small bowl. Mix in Bourbon. Cover with plastic wrap and chill.

Thinly slice melons. Rinse and drain berries. Arrange melon slices on individual plates and sprinkle with berries. Top with Bourbon Crème Anglaise. Garnish with mint sprig.

Tobie Little, F.A. Staff

Congealed Salads

Cranberry "Red Stuff"

2 (3-ounce) packages cherry gelatin
2 cups boiling water, divided
1 (8-ounce) can cranberry sauce, divided
1 (8-ounce) package cream cheese, softened
1 (20-ounce) can crushed pineapple, drained
1 cup chopped pecans (optional)
1 (8-ounce) container frozen nondairy whipped topping, thawed

Mix 1 package gelatin with 1 cup boiling water. Blend in ½ can cranberry sauce. Place in refrigerator until set. Mix cream cheese, pineapple, nuts and whipped topping. Spread on top of gelatin. Mix other package of gelatin with boiling water. Blend with other ½ cranberry sauce. Cool. Spread on top of other mixture before gelatin sets. Sprinkle with pecans, if desired. Serves 8 to 10.

Donna McCormick, Former Faculty, Former Trustee, Parent of Keith '87

Blueberry Salad

2 (3-ounce) boxes grape gelatin
2 cups boiling water
1 can blueberry pie filling
1 (20-ounce) can crushed pineapple, drained
1 (8-ounce) container frozen nondairy whipped topping, thawed
½ cup chopped pecans

Dissolve gelatin in boiling water. Mix gelatin, pie filling, and pineapple and pour into a 9x13x2-inch dish. Chill until firm. Spread with whipped topping. Sprinkle with pecans. Serves 12 or more.

Charlotte Ingram '81

Grape or Cherry Gelatin Salad

2 cups boiling water
2 (3-ounce) packages grape or
  cherry gelatin
1 (20-ounce) can crushed
  pineapple
1 can blueberry pie filling

Topping:
1 (8-ounce) cream cheese,
  softened
½ cup sour cream
½ cup sugar
1 teaspoon vanilla
¾ cup chopped walnuts or
  pecans

Dissolve gelatin in boiling water. Stir in pineapple and blueberry pie filling. Place in refrigerator until congealed. Beat cream cheese, sour cream, sugar, and vanilla until smooth. Spread over congealed salad. Sprinkle nuts on top. Refrigerate until ready to serve. Serves 12 to 15.

Donna White, Parent of Robert
Beckie Bishop, F.A. Faculty, Parent of Jenna and Megan
Christine Holden, Grandparent of Candace

Easy and Good Salad

1 (6-ounce) package peach
  gelatin
2 (8-ounce) cans crushed
  pineapple

2 cups buttermilk
1 (8-ounce) container frozen
  nondairy whipped topping

In saucepan, combine dry gelatin and pineapple; heat to dissolve gelatin. Remove from heat. Add buttermilk and whipped topping. Mix, refrigerate to congeal. Serves 10.

Robin Tinney, Wife of Darren '84, Parent of Ashley

Mom's Fancy Gelatin

1 (3-ounce) package
  strawberry or peach gelatin
1 cup boiling water

1 can pie filling (matching
  gelatin flavor)

Dissolve gelatin in boiling water. Let cool. Combine with pie filling and pour into serving bowl. Refrigerate to congeal. Serve with whipped cream.

Teresa Kolander, Aunt of Matthew Franzeen

Strawberry Salad

3 (3-ounce) packages
  strawberry gelatin
1 cup boiling water
1 (20-ounce) can crushed
  pineapple, undrained

3 medium bananas, mashed
1 (10-ounce) box frozen
  strawberries, sliced
1 cup chopped pecans
2 cups sour cream

Dissolve strawberry gelatin in boiling water. Add pineapple, bananas, strawberries and pecans. Pour half of mixture into glass container. Spread sour cream over mixture. Pour remaining half of mixture over sour cream. Refrigerate to congeal. Serves 14 to 16.

Debbie Steadman, Parent of Adam, Cameron,
Caroline, and Grant

Cranberry Sauce Salad

1 (3-ounce) package raspberry
  gelatin
1 cup boiling water
1 (16-ounce) can whole-berry
  cranberry sauce

1 (8-ounce) can crushed
  pineapple
½ cup chopped nuts

In mixing bowl, dissolve gelatin in boiling water. Add cranberry sauce and blend well. Stir in pineapple and nuts. Pour into 1-quart casserole or bowl; chill until set.

Susan Williams, Parent of Catherine and Sam

Seafood
Entrees

Seafood Entrees

Seafood

Crab Cakes

½ cup chopped onion
½ cup chopped celery
½ cup chopped green pepper
2 cloves garlic, minced
1 tablespoon butter
3 cups soft bread crumbs, divided
3 eggs
3 teaspoons chopped parsley
1 teaspoon horseradish
1 teaspoon Worcestershire sauce
½ teaspoon salt
½ teaspoon pepper
1 pound claw crab meat, drained, rinsed, and flaked
¾ cup olive oil

Sauté onion, celery, green pepper, and garlic in butter until tender. Combine sautéed vegetable mix with 2 cups bread crumbs, eggs, parsley, horseradish, Worcestershire sauce, salt, pepper, and crab meat, mixing well. Shape into 6 big or 12 small patties. Coat patties in remaining 1 cup bread crumbs. In hot olive oil, fry until crab cakes are golden brown. Serves 6.

Gwen Barnum Melton, Parent of Kurston

Barbeque Shrimp

3 pounds shrimp, with shells
1 teaspoon vinegar
1 tablespoon salt
¾ cup olive oil
1 tablespoon Creole seasoning or cayenne pepper
6 cloves garlic, coarsely chopped
1 teaspoon oregano
1 cup white wine

Wash shrimp well and drain. While draining, pour vinegar over shrimp; add salt. Heat olive oil over medium-high heat. Add Creole seasoning or cayenne pepper, garlic, and oregano. Add shrimp to olive oil mixture. When shrimp turn pink, add wine. Shrimp are ready when shells shrivel from the skin.

Joyce Barnum, Grandparent of Kurston Melton

Linguine with Clam and Caper Sauce

6 tablespoons olive oil
½ small onion, chopped
2 cloves garlic, chopped
¼ cup dry white wine
2 dozen small clams, scrubbed or 1 (10-ounce) can whole clams, drained
1 (6½-ounce) can chopped clams, undrained

1 tablespoon fresh lemon juice
1 teaspoon anchovy paste
1 pound dried linguine
3 tablespoons chopped fresh Italian parsley
1 tablespoon capers, drained
Additional olive oil

Heat oil in heavy large skillet over medium-low heat. Add onion and garlic; sauté until tender, about 7 minutes. Add wine and bring to simmer. Add fresh clams. Cover and steam until clams open, about 5 minutes. Discard any clams that do not open. Stir in canned clams with juices, lemon juice and anchovy paste; simmer for 1 minute. Cook linguine in boiling salted water until just tender but still firm to bite. Drain. Add parsley and capers to sauce. Mound pasta on platter. Drizzle with olive oil. Spoon sauce over and serve. Serves 4.

Vallie Rosner, Parent of Regina

Clam Linguine

2 tablespoons butter
1 clove garlic, minced
2 tablespoons all-purpose flour
1 tablespoon oregano
2 (10-ounce) cans whole clams, undrained

½ cup dry white wine
¼ cup whipping cream
8 ounces linguine, cooked and drained
¼ cup grated Parmesan cheese

Melt butter in large skillet over medium heat; add garlic and sauté for 1 minute. Add flour and oregano; cook, stirring constantly for 1 minute. Stir in clams and wine; cook, stirring frequently for 8 minutes or until mixture reduces slightly. Remove from heat. Stir in whipping cream and cook over low heat until thoroughly heated. Spoon over hot linguine. Sprinkle with Parmesan cheese. Serves 2 to 4.

Tracy Altman Spooner '84

Crab Shrimp Casserole

1 pound crab meat
1 pound shrimp, peeled and
  deveined
2 cups chopped celery
1 medium onion, chopped
1 (8-ounce) can sliced water
  chestnuts
1 (4½-ounce) can mushrooms

1 cup sliced almonds
1½ cups mayonnaise (regular
  or light)
2 teaspoons Worcestershire
  sauce
1 teaspoon salt
Italian bread crumbs

Combine all ingredients except Italian bread crumbs. Pour into greased casserole dish. Sprinkle with bread crumbs. Bake in preheated 350° oven for 30 minutes. Serves 12.

Ruth Bowman, Grandparent of CoCo Smith

Shrimp Gibson

1 pound medium to large
  shrimp, peeled and shells
  reserved
3 tablespoons olive oil,
  divided
1 can chicken broth
1 teaspoon thyme
¼ cup brandy or white wine

4 garlic cloves, minced
1 (6-ounce) can tomato paste
½ cup whipping cream
8 ounces smoked sausage or
  kielbasa, diced
1 medium onion, diced
1 stalk celery, diced
Pepper to taste

Sauté shrimp shells in 1 tablespoon oil until browned. Add broth, thyme, brandy, garlic, and tomato paste; simmer 15 minutes or until thickened. Strain and discard shells. Add cream and simmer until thickened again.

Sauté shrimp, sausage, onion, and celery in remaining oil until shrimp is pink. Add to shrimp cream sauce. Heat and serve over rice. Serves 4.

Ruth Ruppe, Grandparent of Charles Smith

Ben's Bait (Shrimp Scampi)

As a part-time salt water angler and a full-time gourmet seafood diner, the Headmaster has learned from years of experience that while the fish were biting yesterday, and they will be biting tomorrow, today they are not biting! What to do? The following recipe for shrimp is the answer. In fact, you don't even need to go fishing!

2 pounds medium to large shrimp
6 tablespoons butter, melted
½ cup olive oil
⅓ cup chopped fresh parsley
2 to 3 cloves garlic, minced
Juice of 1 lemon, freshly squeezed

Shell and clean shrimp. In large bowl, combine butter and olive oil. Mix in parsley and garlic. Add lemon juice; mix well. Put shrimp into sauce mixture and mix thoroughly carefully coating shrimp. Allow shrimp to marinate for 1 to 8 hours in refrigerator. Broil shrimp for 2 to 3 minutes; turn shrimp and broil for 2 to 3 more minutes. Serves 6 to 8.

P.S. So far no fish have been caught on the leftover shrimp scampi!

Ben Crabtree, Headmaster

Jersey Shore Salmon

1 pound salmon fillet, with skin
Corn flake crumbs
1 tablespoon margarine

Cover flesh side of salmon with corn flake crumbs. Turn salmon over and cover skin side with corn flake crumbs. Using 2 layers of aluminum foil make a foil pan slightly larger than salmon. Preheat grill or broiler. Melt margarine in foil pan. Put salmon in pan, skin side up. Cook 8 minutes. Turn salmon and cook another 8 minutes (cooking time varies with thickness of salmon). Serve flesh side up with garnish. Serves 3.

Mal Buchner, Grandparent of Gordon McCambridge

Thin Spaghetti with White Clam Sauce

3 cloves garlic, cut in half
⅔ cup olive oil
1 cup bottled clam juice
¼ teaspoon salt
Pepper to taste
½ teaspoon oregano
3 (7½-ounce) cans minced or
  whole baby clams, undrained
½ cup chopped green onions
½ cup chopped fresh parsley
1 pound thin spaghetti,
  cooked
Parmesan cheese, freshly
  grated
Steamed fresh clams for
  garnish

Sauté garlic in oil, mashing as it cooks. Add clam juice, salt, pepper, and oregano. Simmer 5 minutes. Add canned clams with juice; cook uncovered so liquid will reduce. Add onions and fresh parsley; cook 10 minutes longer. Toss ½ sauce with hot spaghetti and Parmesan cheese to taste. Pour remaining sauce on top of spaghetti, and arrange freshly steamed clams around sides of dish. Serve with additional Parmesan cheese. Serves 4 to 6.

Joyce Sorensen, Parent of Blake '95

Nana's Crab Imperial

4 tablespoons butter
2 tablespoons all-purpose
  flour
⅔ cup milk
1 pound lump crab meat
2 teaspoons lemon juice
1 tablespoon chopped parsley
2 hard-boiled eggs, chopped
1 teaspoon mustard
1 teaspoon salt
½ teaspoon horseradish
Worcestershire sauce to taste
Mayonnaise

Over low heat, melt butter in small saucepan. Add flour and cook, stirring constantly for 1 to 2 minutes. Slowly add milk, whisking constantly until mixture is smooth and thickened. Combine crab meat, lemon juice, parsley, eggs, mustard, salt, horseradish, and Worcestershire sauce in bowl. Mix with milk sauce. Spoon mixture into large clam shells, individual ramekins, or a pie plate. Spread a thin layer of mayonnaise over crab mixture. Broil until mayonnaise is golden and crab mixture is hot. Serves 4 to 6.

Mal Buchner, Grandparent of Gordon McCambridge

Charleston Deviled Crabs

¼ cup butter
1½ cups chopped onion
1 cup chopped green pepper
1 can cream of mushroom
 soup
¾ cup water
1 tablespoon Worcestershire
 sauce

Lemon juice
½ teaspoon red pepper
½ teaspoon black pepper
1 pound white crabmeat
3 cups round buttery cracker
 crumbs

Melt butter in heavy saucepan over low heat; add onion and green pepper. Cook until tender but not brown. Mix soup and water. Add diluted soup, Worcestershire sauce, lemon juice to taste, red, and black pepper; stir until well mixed. Add crabmeat; cook 5 minutes. Add cracker crumbs. Mixture should be the consistency of soft bread dressing. Spoon into crab shells or individual ramekins. Dot with more butter and brown in preheated 375° oven for 15 to 20 minutes. Serves 4.

Linda Knight, Parent of Lauren '99

Crabmeat Casserole

3 tablespoons melted butter
1 cup finely chopped celery
½ cup finely chopped green
 pepper
⅓ cup chopped pimento
⅔ cup herb-seasoned stuffing
 mix
1 cup mayonnaise
1 cup milk
3 eggs, beaten
Salt and pepper to taste

1 pound crabmeat
½ teaspoon hot pepper sauce
1 tablespoon Worcestershire
 sauce

Topping:
1 cup herb-seasoned stuffing
 mix
1 cup grated sharp cheddar
 cheese
1 teaspoon paprika

Sauté celery and green pepper in butter until tender. Add pimento, stuffing mix, mayonnaise, milk, eggs, salt, and pepper. Stir in crab meat; add hot pepper sauce and Worcestershire sauce. Pour into greased 2-quart casserole. Mix topping ingredients and sprinkle on top of casserole. Bake uncovered in preheated 350° oven for 30 to 40 minutes. Serves 6 to 8.

Hazel Simpson, Grandparent of Anastasia Rave

Don's Softshell Crabs

2 cloves garlic, finely chopped
1 teaspoon olive oil
¼ cup butter
¼ cup finely chopped fresh
  parsley
2 eggs
2 cups milk
1 cup all-purpose flour

Salt and pepper to taste
8 softshell crabs, cleaned,
  fresh
Sherry wine (not cooking
  sherry)
White bread slices, toasted
  and cut diagonally

Sauté garlic in olive oil. Add butter and melt. Add parsley. Beat eggs and milk together in bowl. Combine flour, salt, and pepper. Dip crabs in milk-egg mixture; dredge in flour mixture. Pan fry crabs turning once. Sprinkle with sherry after first turn. Serve on white toast points. Serves 4.

Don Latella, Parent of Liza '94 and Leah

Bay Scallops Claiborne

1 pound bay scallops
Salt
Freshly ground pepper
5 tablespoons olive oil, divided
3 tablespoons finely chopped
  shallots

½ cup peeled, seeded, cubed
  tomatoes
2 teaspoons white wine vinegar
1½ tablespoons chopped
  parsley

Sprinkle scallops with salt and pepper. In small saucepan, combine 3 tablespoons of olive oil, shallots, tomatoes and vinegar. Let simmer 2 minutes. Heat remaining oil in skillet; add scallops in one layer. Cook, turning them about lightly in pan until scallops turn opaque and are heated through. Spoon scallops into 4 small serving dishes; pour equal portions tomato sauce over scallops. Sprinkle with parsley. Serve over rice. Serves 4.

Nina Godwin, Grandparent of Harry, Lacy, and Laura

Lemon Fish

2 pounds Orange Roughy
¾ cup dry white wine
1 (8-ounce) container low-fat
   lemon yogurt

¼ teaspoon dill weed
¼ teaspoon grated lemon peel
¼ teaspoon minced garlic

Place fish in shallow baking dish. Mix remaining ingredients and pour over fish. Bake covered in preheated 350° oven for approximately 20 minutes. Uncover. Broil 5 to 10 minutes or until lightly brown. Serves 4.

Kathy Hodges, F.A. Staff, Parent of Alison and Andrew

Mock Lobster Tail

3 cups water
1 tablespoon white vinegar
1 teaspoon paprika
½ teaspoon red pepper

Salt to taste
1 bay leaf
1 pound Haddock filet
Melted butter

Bring water to boil. Add vinegar, paprika, pepper, salt, and bay leaf. Add fish; boil for 15 minutes. Remove from water with slotted spoon. Serve with melted butter for dipping. Serves 4.

Ursula LeFevre, Grandparent of Jordan Ethington

Salmon Patties

1 (15-ounce) can pink salmon,
   flaked and drained
1 egg
⅓ cup minced onion

¼ cup all-purpose flour
1½ cups shortening
½ cup cornmeal

Mix salmon, egg and onions. Stir in flour. Form into small patties. Heat shortening in frying pan. Roll patties in cornmeal; fry 5 minutes or until golden brown. Serves 4.

Betty Russell, Grandparent of Katie

Shrimp Hurry Curry

¼ cup butter
¾ cup finely chopped onion
2 garlic cloves, minced
3 tablespoons all-purpose
  flour
2 tablespoons curry powder
½ teaspoon ginger
1 cup chicken broth
1 cup whipping cream

1 pound medium shrimp,
  cooked and peeled
2 tablespoons fresh lemon
  juice
Cooked rice
Peanuts, chopped and toasted
Shredded coconut
Dried currants
Chutney

Melt butter in large skillet over medium heat. Add onion and garlic; sauté until tender. Stir in flour, curry powder, and ginger; cook 3 minutes. Slowly add broth and cream. Stir until thickened, about 5 minutes. Add shrimp and lemon juice; cook 2 minutes or until heated through. Serve shrimp mixture over rice. Offer peanuts, shredded coconut, currants, and chutney as garnish. Serves 4.

Diane Ginthner, Parent of Kyle and Matthew

Shrimp Creole

3 slices bacon
½ cup chopped celery
½ cup chopped onion
2 (16-ounce) cans chopped
  tomatoes
1½ teaspoons salt

3 tablespoons ketchup
1 tablespoon Worcestershire
  sauce
2 pounds shrimp, cleaned
1 tablespoon sugar
Hot cooked rice

Fry bacon. Remove from pan, crumble, and set aside. Drain all but 1 tablespoon of drippings from pan. Sauté celery and onion in drippings. Add tomatoes, salt, ketchup, Worcestershire sauce, and bacon. Simmer uncovered on low heat for 1 hour. Add shrimp and sugar; simmer 15 more minutes. Serve over rice. Serves 4 to 6.

Pam Little, F.A. Faculty

"Hot" Shrimp

1 (2-pound) bag frozen,
cooked shrimp
1 tablespoon paprika
2½ teaspoons salt
1 teaspoon onion powder

1 teaspoon cayenne pepper
¾ teaspoon white pepper
½ teaspoon dried thyme
½ teaspoon oregano
½ cup unsalted butter, divided

Thaw and rinse all shrimp. Put paprika, salt, onion powder, peppers, thyme, and oregano in gallon-size plastic zipper bag. Add shrimp. Add ¼ cup melted butter. Distribute evenly. Marinate overnight. Cook shrimp on hot grill or pour into hot cast iron skillet with ¼ cup butter. Stir until combined and well heated. Serves 3.

Victoria Thomas, Parent of Katie, Megan, and Michael

Company Tuna Bake

1 (3-ounce) package cream
cheese, softened
1 can cream of mushroom
soup
1 cup tuna, drained and flaked
1½ tablespoons chopped
pimento
1 tablespoon chopped onion

1 tablespoon mustard
¼ cup milk
1 cup macaroni, cooked and
drained
½ cup dry bread crumbs
2 tablespoons butter or
margarine, melted

Blend cream cheese and soup until smooth. Stir in tuna, pimento, onion, mustard and milk. Add macaroni and blend well. Put mixture in 1½-quart baking dish. Mix crumbs and butter; sprinkle over top. Bake in preheated 375° oven for 20 to 25 minutes or until thoroughly heated. Serves 5 to 6.

Carolyn Snow, Grandparent of Hannah '95, Evan '98, and Ben Lennon

Mountain Barbequed Shrimp

Despite its numerous ingredients, it is easy to make this delicious shrimp. I grill the shrimp over charcoal and serve with rice, green salad, and crusty rolls for a main course for 6.

Remoulade Sauce:
½ cup mayonnaise
¼ cup finely diced celery
2 tablespoons finely chopped green onion
2 tablespoons finely chopped fresh parsley
2 tablespoons mustard
2 tablespoons horseradish
2 tablespoons ketchup
2 teaspoons lemon juice
2 teaspoons white wine vinegar
1 teaspoon Worcestershire sauce
2 to 3 drops hot pepper sauce
½ teaspoon finely minced garlic
½ teaspoon salt
¼ teaspoon dry mustard
¼ teaspoon paprika
1 anchovy filet, drained and finely chopped

Spice Mixture:
1 tablespoon mild chili powder
1 teaspoon ground cumin
1 teaspoon sugar
1 teaspoon salt
½ teaspoon dry mustard
½ teaspoon thyme
½ teaspoon freshly ground black pepper
½ teaspoon curry powder
¼ teaspoon cayenne pepper
2 tablespoons extra-virgin olive oil

Shrimp:
2½ pounds large shrimp (about 20 per pound), peeled and deveined
Olive oil for brushing the grill or skillet

Mix all sauce ingredients together in bowl, pressing with spoon to mash onion, garlic, and anchovy. Cover with plastic wrap; chill at least 1 hour (best flavor after 24 hours).

Pat shrimp dry with paper towels. Combine spice mixture ingredients in large bowl. Add shrimp; toss evenly to coat. Cover and marinate in refrigerator 30 minutes. Heat grill or heavy skillet. Brush with olive oil; cook shrimp until just barely opaque in the center, 1 to 2 minutes on each side. Arrange on warm platter or plates and serve the remoulade sauce in cup for dipping. The shrimp are also good cold. Serves 6.

*Linda Blair, Trustee, Parent of Jennifer '96,
Ashley '98, Emily '99, and Amanda*

To Die for Scalloped Oysters

2 cups saltine cracker crumbs
½ cup butter, melted
½ teaspoon salt
1 quart oysters, drained, liquid reserved
½ teaspoon Old Bay seasoning
Pepper to taste
¾ cup light cream
1 teaspoon Worcestershire sauce

Combine cracker crumbs with butter and salt. Spread ½ of cracker mixture in bottom of buttered casserole dish. Cover with oysters crowded closely together. Sprinkle with seasoning and pepper. In small bowl, combine cream, reserved oyster liquid, and Worcestershire sauce. Pour over oysters. Top with remaining cracker mixture. (Cracker mix should completely cover oysters.) Bake in preheated 350° oven for 1 hour or until lightly browned and bubbly.

Suzanne Coates Bullard '82

Mahi Mahi in Macadamia Crust

4 (5-ounce) mahi mahi fillets
⅓ cup fresh lime juice
2 tablespoons olive oil
2 teaspoons finely grated ginger root
1 cup Macadamia nuts
¼ cup all-purpose flour
Dash of salt and pepper
1 egg
2 tablespoons milk

Place fish in glass dish. Combine lime juice, olive oil, and ginger root; pour over fish. Place in refrigerator and marinate for 30 to 60 minutes, turning to coat completely. Finely grind nuts in food processor or blender until coarse cornmeal consistency. Place nuts in shallow bowl; set aside. In small mixing bowl, combine flour, salt, and pepper. In third bowl, beat egg and milk together with a fork. Remove fish from marinade and drain. Dip each fillet in flour mixture and shake off excess. Dip in egg mixture; roll in nuts until evenly coated. Place on greased baking sheet or shallow pan. Bake in preheated 500° oven for 6 to 8 minutes or until fish is opaque.

Chris Kastner, Parent of Brian and Laura

Shrimp Curry

½ cup minced onion
5 tablespoons butter
6 tablespoons all-purpose
  flour
2½ teaspoons curry powder
1¼ teaspoons salt
1½ teaspoons sugar

¼ teaspoon ginger
1 cup chicken broth
2 cups milk
2½ pounds shrimp
1 teaspoon lemon juice
6 cups cooked rice

In top of double boiler, sauté onion in butter until tender. Stir in flour, curry powder, salt, sugar, and ginger. Add chicken broth and milk. Cook, stirring constantly, until thickened. Add shrimp and lemon juice. Heat well; serve with rice. Serves 4.

Note: Suggested toppings to serve with shrimp curry are: chopped nuts, crumbled bacon, chutney, chopped hard-boiled eggs, India relish, coconut, and chopped celery.

Libbie Crabtree, Wife of Headmaster Ben Crabtree

Scallops and Red Pepper

4 tablespoons olive oil
1 pound bay scallops
1 clove garlic, finely minced
½ teaspoon oregano
⅛ teaspoon black pepper
1 (7-ounce) jar chopped
  roasted peppers

3 tablespoons chopped fresh
  parsley
4 tablespoons Italian style
  bread crumbs, divided
1 tablespoon lemon juice

In large skillet, heat olive oil until hot. Add scallops, garlic, oregano, and pepper. Sauté over high heat for 3 minutes. Remove from heat. Add roasted peppers, parsley, 2 tablespoons bread crumbs, and lemon juice; mix well. Place in buttered casserole dish. Sprinkle with remaining bread crumbs. Broil until lightly browned. Serve over hot pasta. Serves 4.

Annette Rhoads, Aunt of Brian and Laura Kastner

Baked Shrimp

¼ cup butter
1 (8-ounce) bottle Italian salad
   dressing
Juice of 2 lemons

¼ teaspoon freshly ground
   pepper
3 pounds large shrimp, peeled
   with tails intact

Melt butter in 9x13x2-inch baking dish. Add Italian dressing, lemon juice, and pepper. Add shrimp to sauce; mix well. Bake in preheated 325° oven for 25 to 30 minutes, stirring several times. Serves 6 to 8.

Tobie Little, F.A. Staff

Salmon with Pineapple Salsa

1½ to 2 pounds salmon fillets
¾ cup soy sauce (lite or
   regular)

Pineapple Salsa:
1½ cups chopped fresh
   pineapple
½ cup chopped red pepper
¼ cup chopped fresh cilantro
¼ cup chopped onion
2 tablespoons lime juice

Place salmon fillets and soy sauce in zippered plastic bag; marinate 4 to 6 hours. Combine salsa ingredients in nonmetal bowl and mix well. Grill salmon 10 to 16 minutes or until fish flakes easily with fork. Top salmon with salsa. Salsa will keep in refrigerator up to 1 week.

Chris Kastner, Parent of Brian and Laura

Carolina Crab Cakes

3 tablespoons butter, divided
1 garlic clove, pressed
2 tablespoons finely chopped red pepper
1 green onion, finely chopped
Cayenne pepper to taste
1 tablespoon Dijon mustard
3 tablespoons heavy cream
1 egg, beaten
1 teaspoon minced fresh basil
1 teaspoon minced fresh parsley
1 cup bread crumbs, divided
1 pound fresh lump crabmeat, rinsed and shells removed
½ cup grated Parmesan cheese
2 tablespoons oil

In large skillet, melt 1 tablespoon butter. Sauté onion, garlic, and red pepper 2 minutes or until wilted. Add cayenne, mustard, and cream. Cool slightly. Add beaten egg, basil, parsley, ½ cup bread crumbs, and crabmeat. Mix lightly. Mold into 16 2-inch wide patties.

Combine remaining bread crumbs and Parmesan cheese in shallow dish. Roll patties in crumbs and cheese mixture. Chill at least 1 hour.

In large skillet, combine oil and remaining butter over medium heat. Sauté crabcakes 3 minutes on each side. Serve with tartar or cocktail sauce.

Tobie Little, F.A. Staff

Cocktail Sauce

1 cup mayonnaise
1 tablespoon lemon juice
3 tablespoons ketchup
3 tablespoons chili sauce
2 tablespoons horseradish (optional)
2 tablespoon heavy cream
Hot sauce to taste

Mix ingredients. Serve with cold boiled shrimp or crab cakes.

Tobie Little, F.A. Staff

Low Country Shrimp Casserole

½ pound sliced mushrooms
2 tablespoons butter
2 tomatoes, chopped
1 onion, finely chopped
½ cup half and half
2 tablespoons flour
¼ cup sherry

1 tablespoon Worcestershire sauce
Salt, pepper, and paprika to taste
3 pounds shrimp, cooked and peeled
¼ cup buttered bread crumbs

Sauté mushrooms in butter. Add tomatoes and onion; simmer for 10 minutes. Blend half and half and flour; add to mushrooms. Add sherry, Worcestershire sauce, salt, pepper, and paprika. Add shrimp and place in large buttered casserole dish. Top with bread crumbs. Bake in preheated 350° oven for 20 minutes or until brown. Serve over rice. Serves 8.

Tobie Little, F.A. Staff

Poultry
Entrees

Poultry Entrees

Chicken and Sausage Casserole

2 pounds chicken, cooked
  with broth reserved
1 (6-ounce) package long
  grain wild rice with herbs
1 pound bulk pork sausage
1 (8-ounce) can mushrooms,
  drained

1 can cream of mushroom
  soup
1 cup chicken broth
Salt and pepper to taste
1 (4-ounce) package
  herb-seasoned stuffing mix
½ cup margarine, melted

Remove chicken from bone; cut into small pieces and place in 2-quart casserole dish. Prepare rice according to package directions. Brown sausage, drain, and crumble. Combine sausage, mushrooms, soup, broth, salt, pepper, and cooked rice; mix well. Pour mixture over chicken. Sprinkle with stuffing. Top with melted margarine. Bake in preheated 350° oven for 25 minutes. Serves 8.

Teri Mascia Williams '80, Parent of Jared and Justin

"Bride and Groom" Chicken Casserole

4 to 6 cups cooked and cubed
  chicken
1 cup chicken broth
½ cup chopped onions
¾ cup chopped celery
2 tablespoons vegetable oil

1 cup sour cream
1 can cream of chicken soup
½ cup butter
1 (8-ounce) package
  herb-seasoned stuffing mix
½ teaspoon poultry seasoning

Layer chicken in greased 9x13x2-inch casserole dish. Pour broth over chicken. Sauté onion and celery in vegetable oil; pour over chicken. Mix sour cream and soup; pour over onion and celery. Melt butter; mix with stuffing and seasoning. Spread over top of casserole. Bake in preheated 325° oven for 25 minutes. Serves 6 to 8.

Donna McCormick, Former Faculty, Former Trustee, Parent of Keith '87

Very Little Mess, Very Little Time Lemon Asparagus Chicken

4 boneless, skinless chicken
  breasts (about 1 pound)
Lemon pepper
Cooking spray or
  1 tablespoon vegetable oil
1 can cream of asparagus
  soup
¼ cup milk

3 tablespoons lemon juice,
  divided
4 cups cooked rice or linguine
20 to 30 asparagus spears
1 teaspoon butter or
  margarine (optional)
Lemon slices for garnish

Liberally sprinkle chicken with lemon pepper. Coat skillet with cooking spray; heat over medium heat. Brown chicken on both sides (about 10 minutes). Remove; drain excess fat. In same skillet, combine soup, milk, 2 tablespoons lemon juice, and dash more lemon pepper. Heat to boiling, stirring often. Return chicken to skillet. Cover; reduce heat to low and cook until chicken is done (5 to 10 minutes). Stir occasionally. Steam asparagus in water, remaining lemon juice, and butter. Serve chicken over rice or linguine with asparagus on the side. Garnish with lemon slices. Serves 4.

CarraLee Koonce Spain '87

Cranberry Chicken

6 chicken breasts
1 (15-ounce) can whole-berry
  cranberry sauce

1 (8-ounce) bottle of fat free
  Catalina salad dressing
1 package dry onion soup mix

Place chicken in baking pan. Mix together remaining ingredients; pour over chicken. Bake in preheated 400° oven for 1 hour and 30 minutes or until chicken is done. Serve over white rice. Serves 6.

June Pugliese, Grandparent of Kimberly Sansverie

Poulet Saute Au Citron
(Chicken with Lemon Cream Sauce)

1 (4-pound) chicken, cut up or
    4 to 6 boneless chicken
    breasts
½ cup butter
1 tablespoon sherry
1 tablespoon white wine

1 large lemon, juiced and peel
    grated
1 small orange, peel grated
Salt and pepper to taste
1 cup half and half
¼ cup grated cheese

Heat butter in skillet and brown chicken. Cover and continue sautéing over low heat until nearly cooked. Remove chicken; stir sherry and white wine into pan. Add lemon rind, orange rind, lemon juice, salt, and pepper. Turn up heat to medium and slowly stir in half and half. Return chicken to pan and continue cooking just long enough to get chicken completely heated through. Remove chicken from pan and arrange on oven-safe serving dish. Pour sauce over chicken. Sprinkle with grated cheese. Place several slices of lemon on top of chicken and dot with butter. Brown under broiler and serve immediately. Serves 4 to 6.

Kelli Koba, F.A. Faculty

Yankee Chicken

1 egg, beaten
1 cup vegetable oil
2 cups apple cider vinegar
2 tablespoons salt

1 tablespoon poultry seasoning
1 teaspoon pepper
4 to 5 pounds chicken parts,
    cut up

Beat egg with oil. Add vinegar and stir. Stir in salt, poultry seasoning, and pepper. Marinate chicken in mixture for 4 to 6 hours or overnight in covered container in refrigerator.

Heat grill to approximately 350°. Place chicken pieces over hot coals. Watch carefully and turn frequently to avoid flare-ups. Baste chicken between turns. Cook for 20 to 30 minutes. Serve immediately. Serves 6 to 8.

Dick Kells, Parent of Rich '97 and John

Grilled Margarita Chicken

½ cup nonalcoholic margarita
  mix
1 clove garlic, minced

3 tablespoons lemon juice
3 to 4 chicken breasts

Combine margarita mix, lemon juice, and garlic in resealable heavy-duty plastic bag. Add chicken; seal bag. Turn to coat chicken in marinade. Refrigerate 1 to 24 hours, turning bag occasionally. Heat grill to 325°; cook chicken 20 to 25 minutes or until done. Serves 3 to 4.

Jeanne Harbison, Parent of Vicki

Chicken Enzo

1 pound Italian sausage, cut
  into bite-size pieces
4 skinless, boneless chicken
  breasts cut into bite-size
  pieces
1 onion, diced
4 to 6 cloves garlic, minced
2½ cups chicken broth

1½ cups white wine
1 (6-ounce) can tomato sauce
2 tablespoons parsley
2 tablespoons oregano
2 tablespoons basil
3 tablespoons corn starch
Angel hair pasta

In large skillet, fry sausage until done. Remove from skillet and set aside. Leave 1 to 2 tablespoons of grease in skillet and add chicken. Sauté until done. Remove chicken from skillet. Add onion and garlic; sauté for 3 to 4 minutes to soften and release flavor. Return chicken and sausage to skillet; add broth, wine, and tomato sauce. Bring to boil; lower heat to simmer until liquid is reduced to half. Add herbs and thicken sauce with corn starch. Serve over angel hair pasta. Serves 8 to 10.

Kitty Proctor, Parent of Jamie

Boursin Chicken

4 skinless, boneless chicken
 breasts
Salt and pepper
Juice of 1 lemon

1 round Boursin cheese
2 eggs, beaten
Bread crumbs
¾ cup butter

Pound chicken breasts with meat mallet until about ¼-inch thick. Season with salt and pepper. Sprinkle with lemon juice. Cut round of Boursin cheese into quarters and roll like a finger. Place finger of cheese horizontally across each flattened chicken breast. Roll chicken, tucking in sides so it is snug. (You may have to use toothpicks to make chicken stay rolled.) Dip chicken roll in beaten egg and roll well in bread crumbs. In frying pan over medium-high heat, melt butter. Add chicken and cook 10 to 15 minutes on each side. Serves 4.

Ginny Lee Starke '73

Creamy Chicken Breasts

8 skinless, boneless chicken
 breasts
8 (4x4-inch) slices Swiss
 cheese
1 can cream of chicken soup

¼ cup water, white wine or
 milk
1 cup herb-seasoned stuffing
 mix

Arrange chicken breasts in 9x13x2-inch baking dish. Top with cheese slices. Combine soup and water; spoon evenly over chicken. Sprinkle with stuffing mix. Bake in preheated 350° oven for 1 hour. Serves 8.

Dot Ray, Parent of Beth Ray (F.A. Faculty)
Christopher White '97
Michelle Caviness, F.A. Faculty

Southern Fried Chicken

1 whole chicken, cut up
2 cups buttermilk
1 to 1½ cups all-purpose flour
1 to 2 tablespoons salt
1 to 2 tablespoons pepper

1 to 2 tablespoons paprika
6 tablespoons butter
Solid vegetable shortening or
   vegetable oil

Soak chicken pieces in salted water 6 to 8 hours or overnight. Dry and soak pieces in buttermilk for 1 to 2 hours. Mix flour, salt, pepper, and paprika in large paper bag. Shake 1 to 2 pieces of chicken at a time until completely covered in flour mixture. If time allows, do this 30 minutes before cooking. Place chicken on cooling rack. (This helps the coating stay on the chicken during cooking.) In electric skillet or iron skillet on medium-high to high heat, melt butter and enough shortening or oil so that it is 1½-inches deep in pan. Put dark meat pieces in pan first, then white meat. Keep skillet covered. Turn chicken after 10 to 15 minutes. Lower temperature to medium; cook on other side an additional 10 to 15 minutes. Take out white meat first and lay on a brown paper bag to drain. Then remove dark pieces.

Mary Frederick, Parent of Elizabeth '78 and Susan '78,
Grandparent of Richard Carter

Honey Curry Chicken

¼ cup butter, melted
¼ cup honey
¼ cup mustard
¼ teaspoon salt

½ to 1 teaspoon curry powder
2 to 3 pounds chicken pieces,
   skinned
Parsley sprigs (optional)

Combine butter, honey, mustard, salt, and curry powder; stir well. Dip chicken into honey sauce coating all sides. Place chicken in greased 9x13x2-inch dish. Reserve remaining sauce. Bake uncovered in preheated 375° oven for 45 minutes to 1 hour, basting occasionally with remaining sauce. Garnish with parsley. Serve with rice.

Diane Ginthner, Parent of Kyle and Matthew

Presbytery Chicken

1 cup light mayonnaise
½ cup butter, melted
3 tablespoons Dijon mustard

3 pounds skinless, boneless
   chicken breasts
1 (16-ounce) package
   herb-seasoned stuffing mix

Mix mayonnaise, butter, and mustard. Put stuffing mix in blender or food processor; process into crumbs. Dip chicken in mayonnaise mixture and roll in herb stuffing mix. Place in shallow baking dish. Cover with foil; bake in preheated 350° oven for 50 minutes. Remove foil. Return to oven and bake additional 10 minutes to brown chicken. Serves 8 to 10.

Susan Frederick Flanagan '78

Chicken Paprika

4 skinless, boneless chicken
   breasts
Bacon drippings or cooking
   oil
1 small onion, chopped
1 cup chicken stock or broth

2 bay leaves
2 whole cloves
2 teaspoons paprika
1 cup sour cream
½ teaspoon Worcestershire
   sauce

Sauté chicken in bacon drippings or oil until brown. Remove chicken; add onion and sauté until soft. Return chicken to pan; add chicken stock, bay leaves, cloves, and paprika. Simmer covered for 30 minutes or until chicken is tender. Add sour cream and Worcestershire sauce. Heat thoroughly but do not allow to boil. Serve over rice. Serves 4.

Lee Vieta, Parent of Kathryn '89, Amy '91, Laura '95, and Paul '94

Chicken Lasagna

½ pound fresh mushrooms, sliced
7 tablespoons butter, divided
1¼ cups dry white wine, divided
4 tablespoons all-purpose flour
4 cups half and half
¼ teaspoon tarragon
Salt and pepper
1 (8-ounce) package lasagna noodles, cooked
5 cups cooked and shredded chicken
2 cups Swiss or Gruyere cheese

Sauté mushrooms in 3 tablespoons butter for 3 minutes. Add 1 cup wine; cook until almost evaporated. In small saucepan, melt remaining butter; stir in flour. Gradually add half and half, stirring until thick. Add mushrooms, remaining wine, tarragon, salt, and pepper. Simmer 3 minutes. In 9x13x2-inch buttered dish, layer noodles, chicken, wine sauce and cheese. Repeat several times, ending with cheese. Bake in preheated 350° oven for 40 minutes. Serves 8.

Ginny Lee Starke '73

Chicken Parmesan

2 jars Paul Newman's Venetian spaghetti sauce
2 jars Paul Newman's Sockarooni sauce
8 to 10 skinless, boneless chicken breasts
1 egg, beaten
2 cups milk
Italian and plain bread crumbs
Cooking oil
2 (8-ounce) packages Italian 6-cheese blend shredded cheese

Mix spaghetti sauce and sockarooni sauce; set aside. Pound chicken flat. Combine egg and milk; mix well. Combine bread crumbs. Dip chicken in egg mixture; dredge in bread crumbs, covering well. Fry chicken in cooking oil until done. Remove chicken from pan and lay on cookie sheet. Cover with sauce. Heavily sprinkle cheese on top of chicken and sauce. Place in oven and broil long enough to melt cheese. Serves 8 to 10.

Tina Martindale Estes '76, Parent of Chris '99 and Stephan

Roasted Chicken

1 tablespoon butter
1 whole (4-pound) chicken
⅛ teaspoon onion salt
¼ teaspoon rosemary

⅛ teaspoon pepper
8 to 10 whole garlic cloves
1 medium onion, cut in
   wedges

Melt butter; season chicken with spices. Place breast side down in deep cast iron roasting pan with lid. Surround chicken with garlic cloves and onions (put some inside cavity). Bake in preheated 350° oven for 30 minutes. Turn chicken over to breast side up; bake 40 more minutes. Remove from oven and let rest for 5 minutes before serving. Serves 4.

Rhonda Dees, Board of Trustees Chair, Parent of Sarah

Hot Chicken Salad

2 cups cooked and diced
   chicken
2 cups finely chopped celery
½ cup slivered almonds,
   toasted
½ teaspoon salt
2 tablespoons finely chopped
   onion
½ cup mayonnaise

1 tablespoon chopped green
   pepper
2 tablespoons chopped
   pimiento
½ cup cream of chicken soup
2 tablespoons lemon juice
1½ cups crushed potato chips
½ cup grated cheddar cheese

Mix all ingredients together except potato chips and cheese. Place in greased 2-quart casserole dish; sprinkle chips and cheese on top. Bake in preheated 350° oven for 20 to 25 minutes or until thoroughly heated. Serves 8.

Note: The amount of chicken can be increased. Add more soup accordingly. This recipe can also be baked in individual baking dishes at the same temperature for 10 minutes.

Janet Robinson, Parent of Courtney and Hillary

Chicken Cacciatore

½ cup all-purpose flour
1½ teaspoons salt, divided
4 skinless, boneless chicken
   breasts, cubed
½ cup oil
¼ cup chopped onions
1 clove garlic, finely chopped
1 bay leaf

1 (12½-ounce) can tomatoes,
   drained
¼ teaspoon pepper
1 (15-ounce) can peas or
   1 (10-ounce) box frozen
   peas
Parsley

Mix flour with ½ teaspoon salt; dredge chicken in flour mix. Over medium heat, sauté chicken in oil until brown; remove chicken to covered dish to keep warm. In the same oil, sauté onions and garlic. Add bay leaf and tomatoes to onion and garlic; season with 1 teaspoon salt and pepper. Simmer for 20 to 25 minutes. Put chicken breasts in sauce; cook until heated through. Add peas during the last 15 minutes of heating. Serve over noodles. Garnish with parsley. Serves 4 to 5.

Jean Wychock, Grandparent of Jack McDaniel

Chicken, Cheese & Rice

1 can cream of chicken soup
½ cup water
1½ tablespoons
   Worcestershire sauce

4 skinless, boneless chicken
   breasts
1 (8-ounce) package shredded
   cheddar cheese
4 cups cooked white rice

Simmer soup in saucepan. Stir water into soup; heat until soup liquefies. Add Worcestershire sauce. Place chicken breasts in greased baking pan. Pour mixture over top of chicken breasts. Sprinkle cheese over chicken. Bake in preheated 400° oven for 35 minutes. Serve over cooked white rice. Serves 4.

Martha Till Cade '90

Chicken Spaghetti

1 cup chopped onion	1 can cream of chicken soup
1 cup chopped celery	1 (2-ounce) jar chopped
1 tablespoon butter	pimentos, drained
1 (7-ounce) package vermicelli	½ red pepper, chopped
3 cups cooked and cubed	½ green pepper, chopped
chicken	8 ounces cheddar cheese,
1 (4-ounce) jar mushrooms	shredded
1 can cream of mushroom	1 teaspoon chili powder
soup	Salt and pepper to taste

Sauté onion and celery in butter until tender but not brown. Cook vermicelli according to package directions; drain. Mix onion, celery, vermicelli, chicken, mushrooms, soups, pimento, peppers, cheese, chili powder, salt, and pepper. Put mixture in greased 9x13x2-inch casserole dish. Cover and bake in preheated 350° oven for 30 to 35 minutes. Serves 10 to 12.

Note: You can divide this recipe into two 8x8-inch casseroles and freeze one. Pour 1 can of chicken broth over casserole destined for the freezer so it won't be dry when baked.

Elizabeth Frederick Carter '78, F.A. Staff, Parent of Richard

Chicken and Black Beans on Rice

1 (16-ounce) can black beans,	⅓ cup provolone cheese,
drained and rinsed	grated or sliced
⅓ cup medium picanté sauce	1½ cups cooked and diced
2 tablespoons water	chicken
	3 cups cooked rice

Combine black beans, picanté sauce, water and provolone cheese in saucepan. Stir over medium heat until cheese melts. Add chicken. Stir until chicken is warm. Serve over rice. Serves 4.

Nancy and Jim Collier, Parents of Ty and Coca

Pasta with Chicken, Peas, and Sun-dried Tomatoes

¼ cup olive oil
2 garlic cloves, finely chopped
½ pound skinless, boneless chicken breasts, cut into wide strips
¾ cup frozen peas, thawed
¾ cup oil-packed sun-dried tomatoes, drained and thinly sliced
2 teaspoons chopped fresh basil
Pinch crushed red pepper flakes
Salt and pepper to taste
¼ cup dry white wine
¾ cup chicken broth or stock
1 tablespoon butter or margarine
8 ounces penne or rigatoni pasta, cooked and drained
½ cup grated Parmesan cheese

In large skillet, heat oil over medium heat. Sauté garlic until golden, stirring constantly. Add chicken strips and sauté until almost completely cooked. Add peas, tomatoes, basil, pepper flakes, salt, and pepper. Stir in wine, broth, and butter. Cook 3 to 5 minutes, stirring occasionally. Toss chicken and sauce with pasta and Parmesan cheese. Serves 4.

Mary Flagg Haugh, Parent of Jamie Haugh

Mexican Salsa Chicken

4 skinless, boneless chicken breasts
½ cup all-purpose flour
⅛ teaspoon garlic powder
⅛ teaspoon paprika
⅛ teaspoon chili powder
3 tablespoons olive oil
¼ cup salsa
4 to 6 ounces Monterey Jack cheese, grated

Place chicken breasts between waxed paper; pound with rolling pin or mallet until ¼-inch thick. In shallow dish, combine flour, garlic, paprika, and chili powder. Coat chicken with flour mixture. Heat oil in skillet over medium-high heat. Cook chicken 3 to 4 minutes per side or until lightly brown. Reduce heat; spoon 1 tablespoon salsa on center of each chicken breast. Sprinkle with cheese. Cover. Cook until cheese melts. Serves 4.

Tracy Altman Spooner '84

Chicken and Wine

1 whole chicken, cut up
½ cup sliced onion
¼ cup chopped green pepper
½ pound fresh mushrooms,
  sliced

1 can cream of celery soup
1 tablespoon soy sauce
Salt and pepper
¼ cup white wine

Brown chicken pieces in cooking oil over medium-high heat. Remove chicken to casserole dish. Brown onion, green pepper, and mushrooms; add to chicken. Add soup, soy sauce, salt, and pepper; add to chicken. Pour wine over chicken; cover. Bake in preheated 375° oven for 45 minutes. Remove lid. Bake for 10 to 15 minutes more. Serve with rice or egg noodles. Serves 4 to 6.

Tracy Altman Spooner '84

Quick Chicken and Rice

1 can cream of mushroom
  soup
1 can cream of chicken soup
2½ cups water
1 package onion soup mix

1¼ cups uncooked rice
  (not instant)
6 skinless, boneless chicken
  breast halves
Salt and pepper to taste

Combine soups, water, soup mix, and rice. Pour ½ into 9x13x2-inch baking dish. Place chicken in dish; salt and pepper to taste. Cover with remaining soup and rice mixture. Cover and bake in preheated 350° oven 1 hour. Serves 5 to 6.

Beth Ray, F.A. Faculty
Catharine Brown, Parent of Bucky and Bobby

Chicken Casserole

4 to 5 cups cooked and diced chicken
2 cups diced celery
1 (8-ounce) can water chestnuts, drained and sliced thin
¾ cup mayonnaise
1 cup cream of mushroom soup
1 cup cream of chicken soup
1 teaspoon seasoned salt flavor enhancer
1 tablespoon grated onion
½ teaspoon pepper
2 tablespoons lemon juice
1 cup grated sharp cheddar cheese
½ cup butter or margarine, melted
1 (8-ounce) bag cornbread stuffing mix

Place chicken, celery, and water chestnuts in greased 9x13x2-inch baking dish. Combine mayonnaise, soups, seasoned salt, onion, pepper, and lemon juice; pour over chicken. Top with cheese. Cover and store in refrigerator overnight to blend flavors. Before baking, mix butter and stuffing mix. Sprinkle over casserole. Bake in preheated 350° oven for 45 minutes. Serves 8.

Robena Keatley, Grandparent of Caitlin, Rachel and Will Keeton

Chicken and Rice Casserole

2 cups cooked and diced chicken
1 cup cooked rice
1 can cream of chicken soup
2 tablespoons chopped onion
1 cup chopped celery, sautéed
½ cup mayonnaise
1 tablespoon slivered almonds, slightly browned in butter or margarine
¼ cup butter or margarine
1 cup crushed cornflakes cereal

Mix chicken, rice, soup, onion, celery, mayonnaise, and almonds; spread in greased 9x13x2-inch baking dish. Bake in preheated 350° oven for 30 minutes. Melt butter; add cornflakes and spread over casserole. Reduce oven heat to 300° and bake for additional 30 minutes.

R. B. Spell, Grandparent of Laura Caroline

Chicken Fajitas

¼ cup white wine vinegar
¼ cup lime juice
2 tablespoons Worcestershire sauce
2 tablespoons chopped onion
2 cloves garlic, minced

1 tablespoon oregano
¼ teaspoon ground cumin
1 to 1½ pounds of skinless, boneless chicken breasts
Flour tortillas

Mix all ingredients except tortillas. Marinate chicken breasts overnight. Grill chicken. Slice chicken into ½-inch wide strips. Fill tortillas.

Note: When serving fajitas, serve sautéed onions and red peppers along with sour cream, grated cheese, and whatever else you like. The chicken can also be served on a green salad.

Chris Kastner, Parent of Brian and Laura

Susie's Chicken Enchiladas

1 (4½-ounce) can chopped green chiles
1 can cream of mushroom soup
1 can cream of chicken soup
1 cup sour cream
½ teaspoon oregano
1 teaspoon chili powder
3 tablespoons grated onion
Garlic salt to taste

3 tablespoons Worcestershire sauce
8 to 10 frozen flour tortillas
1 large chicken, boiled, deboned and chopped or 5 skinless, boneless, cooked and diced chicken breasts
2 cups Monterey Jack cheese
2 cups grated medium cheddar cheese

Mix all ingredients except tortillas, chicken, and cheese. In 9x13x2-inch casserole dish layer tortillas, chicken, soup mixture, and cheese. Repeat layering twice. Top with cheese. Bake in preheated 350° oven for 25 minutes or until bubbly. Serves 6.

Susie Brown, F.A. Faculty

Tricia's Chicken Enchiladas

1 tablespoon butter or margarine	3½ cups cooked and chopped chicken breast
1 medium onion, chopped	8 (8-inch) flour tortillas
1 (4½-ounce) can chopped green chiles, drained	1 (16-ounce) package Monterey Jack cheese, shredded
1 (8-ounce) package cream cheese, cubed	2 cups heavy whipping cream

Melt butter in large skillet over medium heat; add onion and sauté 5 minutes. Add drained green chiles; sauté 1 minute. Stir cream cheese into heated mixture; add chicken. Stir until cream cheese melts. Spoon 2 to 3 tablespoons chicken mixture down center of each tortilla. Roll up tortillas and place, seam side down, into lightly greased 9x13x2-inch baking dish. Sprinkle with cheese. Pour cream over tortillas (it will form a sauce with the cheese). Bake in preheated 350° oven for 45 minutes. Serves 4 to 5.

Tricia Brooks, Parent of Tracey '99

Chicken Enchilada Casserole

1 can cream of chicken soup	3 (6-ounce) cans white chicken chunks
1 (10-ounce) can tomatoes with green chiles	1 (12-ounce) package tortilla chips
1 (5-ounce) can evaporated milk	2 cups shredded cheddar cheese
1 medium onion, chopped	

Combine soup, tomatoes, milk, onion and chicken in bowl; mix well. Layer tortilla chips, chicken mixture and cheese, ½ at a time, in 9x13x2-inch baking dish. Bake in preheated 350° oven until bubbly, about 20 to 30 minutes. Serve over additional tortilla chips. Serves 8.

Emily Schaefer, Wife of Dickson '84

Blair's Chicken Enchiladas

Chicken mixture:
1 cup chopped onion
½ cup chopped green pepper
2 tablespoons butter or
  margarine
4 cup cooked and diced
  chicken or turkey
1 (4½-ounce) can green chile
  peppers, rinsed, seeded and
  chopped

Sauce:
3 tablespoons butter or
  margarine
¼ cup all-purpose flour
1 teaspoon ground coriander
¾ teaspoon salt
2½ cups chicken broth
1 cup sour cream
1½ cups shredded Monterey
  Jack cheese, divided
12 (6-inch) tortillas

In large saucepan, cook onion and green pepper in butter until tender. Remove from heat. Combine with chicken and green chili peppers; set aside. Melt butter in saucepan; stir in flour, coriander, and salt. Add chicken broth; stir constantly until thickened and bubbly. Continue to cook for 1 to 2 minutes more. Remove from heat; stir in sour cream and ½ cup of cheese. Fill each tortilla with ¼ cup of chicken mixture. Roll up tortillas. Place in 9x13x2-inch baking dish. Pour sauce over tortillas. Sprinkle with remaining cheese. Bake in preheated 350° oven for 25 minutes. Serves 6.

Blair Broadfoot Knowlton '84

Chicken Tortillas

3 chicken breasts, cooked and
  diced
1 can cream of celery soup,
  divided
1 (4½-ounce) can green chiles

1 cup sour cream, divided
8 ounces grated sharp
  cheddar cheese
8 flour tortillas

Mix ½ can soup, ½ cup sour cream, and chiles. Put 2 tablespoons of soup mixture, 4 tablespoons diced chicken, and 2 tablespoons of cheese in center of each tortilla. Roll up. Place rolled tortilla, seam side down, into greased baking pan. Mix remaining soup and sour cream; spread over rolled tortillas. Sprinkle remaining cheese over soup mixture. Bake in preheated 350° oven for 30 minutes. Serves 5 to 6.

Judy Lennon, Parent of Hannah '95, Evan '98, and Ben

Sour Cream Chicken Enchiladas

2 large chicken breasts
6 tablespoons butter, divided
1 onion, chopped
1 garlic clove, minced
1 (16-ounce) can tomatoes, diced
1 (8-ounce) can tomato sauce
1 (4½-ounce) can green chiles, drained
1 teaspoon sugar

1 teaspoon cumin
½ teaspoon salt
½ teaspoon oregano
½ teaspoon basil
1 teaspoon chili powder
12 flour tortillas
¾ cup sour cream
2½ cups grated Monterey Jack cheese

In preheated 350° oven, bake chicken breasts in 4 tablespoons butter for 1 hour. Remove skin and bones; cut into 12 strips and set aside. Cook onion and garlic in 2 tablespoons butter until soft. Add tomatoes, tomato sauce, chiles, sugar, cumin, salt, oregano, basil, and chili powder; heat to boil. Reduce heat; simmer covered 20 minutes. Remove from heat. Dip each tortilla in tomato mixture to soften. Place 1 piece of chicken and 2 tablespoons cheese on each tortilla. Roll up and place seam side down in 9x13x2-inch baking dish. Stir sour cream into sauce mixture; pour over tortillas. Sprinkle with remaining cheese. Bake in preheated 350° oven for 45 minutes. Serves 6.

Paulette Banks, Parent of James

Chicken and Broccoli Casserole

4 to 6 chicken breasts
2 (10-ounce) boxes frozen broccoli spears
2 cans cream of mushroom soup

1 cup mayonnaise
4 teaspoons lemon juice
1 cup shredded cheddar cheese

Boil chicken for 1 hour; cool and shred. Steam or microwave broccoli just to separate. Mix together soup, mayonnaise, and lemon juice; set aside. Layer broccoli in bottom of 9x13x2-inch casserole dish. Add ½ of sauce, all shredded chicken, and remaining sauce. Top with cheese. Cover with foil and bake in preheated 350° oven for 30 to 40 minutes. Serve over rice. Serves 4 to 6.

Robin Wade, Parent of Bryan

Savory Chicken Pie

Crust:
1 cup sour cream
1 egg
½ cup butter, softened
1 teaspoon salt
1 teaspoon baking powder
1 cup flour
½ teaspoon ground thyme

Filling:
2 tablespoons butter, melted
½ cup chopped onion
½ cup chopped celery or
   green pepper
½ cup sliced carrots
½ cup chopped pimento
½ cup sliced mushrooms
2 cups cooked and diced
   chicken or turkey
1 can cream of chicken soup
1 cup grated cheddar cheese

Cream sour cream, egg, and butter. Add salt, baking powder, flour, and thyme; blend well. Spread mixture over bottom and sides of 9-inch pie plate. Sauté onion, celery or green pepper, and carrots in melted butter. Add pimento, mushrooms, chicken, and soup. Mix well; spoon filling into crust and sprinkle with shredded cheese. Bake in preheated 400° oven for 25 to 30 minutes. Serves 6 to 8.

Ann Hux, Parent of Susanne '77,
Grandparent of Caroline and Claire Long

Two Step Chicken Broccoli Divan

1 pound fresh broccoli, cut
   into spears, or 1 (10-ounce)
   package frozen broccoli
   spears, cooked and drained
1½ cups cooked and cubed
   chicken or turkey
1 can cream of broccoli soup

⅓ cup milk
½ cup shredded cheddar
   cheese
1 tablespoon butter, melted
2 tablespoons dry bread
   crumbs

In 9-inch pie plate or shallow casserole dish, arrange broccoli; top with chicken. Combine soup and milk; pour over chicken. Sprinkle with cheese. Combine butter and bread crumbs; sprinkle over cheese. Bake in preheated 450° oven for 15 minutes or until hot. *OR* cover with waxed paper; microwave on high for 6 minutes or until hot; rotating halfway though heating. Serves 4.

Mary Ksanznak, Grandparent of Karen Pittman

Doves with Wild Rice

8 dove breasts
½ cup butter
2 cups sliced mushrooms
1 green onion, chopped

1 cup dry white wine
2 tablespoons lemon juice
Salt and pepper to taste

In heavy pan, brown dove breasts in butter. Remove and set aside. In same pan, sauté mushrooms and onions. Place doves, mushrooms, and onions in shallow baking dish and cover with foil. Combine wine, lemon juice, salt, and pepper. Set aside. Bake in preheated 350° oven for 1 hour. Remove foil and baste frequently with wine mixture 15 minutes or until tender. Serve on bed of wild rice (recipe below).

Wild Rice

1½ cups wild rice or long
   grain and wild rice
4 cans undiluted boullion or
   beef broth
1 cup chopped onion

1 cup chopped green pepper
1 cup sliced mushrooms
¼ cup butter
1 cup heavy cream
Salt and pepper to taste

Wash rice; cook in boullion until most liquid has been absorbed, about 20 to 25 minutes. Drain. Sauté onion, green pepper, and mushrooms in butter. Add cream, salt, and pepper. Stir in rice and place in 9x13x2-inch baking dish. Bake in preheated 350° oven for 20 to 25 minutes. Serves 8.

Janice McDaniel, Parent of Greg '76,
Grandparent of Jack

Turkey Teriyaki

4 whole turkey wings
Vegetable oil
⅔ cup soy sauce
¼ cup cream sherry

2 tablespoons minced ginger
2 large cloves garlic, minced
1 tablespoon grated orange
rind

Cut off wing tips. Cut remaining wing at joint into 2 portions. Brush with oil. Place wings in shallow baking pan (wings need to fit pan with no extra space). Roast wings uncovered in preheated 375° oven for 45 minutes. Stir together soy sauce, sherry, ginger, garlic, and orange rind; pour over wings. Cover tightly with foil. Continue to roast at 375° until tender, about 45 minutes longer. Serves 4.

Beverly Brooks, Grandparent of Tracey '99

Meatloaf Florentine

2 pounds ground turkey
1 envelope meatloaf
   seasoning mix
1 egg, lightly beaten
1 (10-ounce) package frozen
   chopped spinach, thawed
   and drained

3 tablespoons chopped onion
2 slices uncooked bacon,
   chopped
½ cup ketchup
2 tablespoons Worcestershire
   sauce

Combine ground turkey, seasoning mix and egg. Pat ½ in bottom of 9x5-inch loaf pan. Combine spinach with onion and bacon. Spread over meat. Top with remaining meat, sealing well. Bake in preheated 350° oven for 50 minutes. Pour off excess fat. Mix ketchup and Worcestershire sauce and spread on top. Serves 6 to 8.

Irma Smith, Parent of CoCo

Dr. E. C. Bennett's Chicken Barbeque Sauce

Dr. Bennett, Miss Lambert's grandfather, was a longtime physician in Elizabethtown, N.C. He was well-known for his love of cooking.

½ pound butter, melted
½ cup Worcestershire sauce
2 teaspoons hot pepper sauce
½ cup apple cider vinegar
1 quart tomato juice

1 (24-ounce) bottle ketchup
1 teaspoon sugar
3 teaspoons chili powder
1 to 2 teaspoons "hot stuff"

Combine all ingredients. Baste chicken with sauce at frequent intervals. May be made in large quantities and frozen.

Barbara E. Lambert '76, F.A. Staff

The Best Marinade for Chicken

1½ cups vegetable oil
2 tablespoons dry mustard
¾ cup soy sauce
¼ cup Worcestershire sauce
2¼ teaspoon salt

1 tablespoon black pepper
½ cup wine vinegar
1½ teaspoons dried parsley
1 teaspoon garlic powder
⅓ cup fresh lemon juice

Combine all ingredients; mix well. Marinade can be drained from the meat for a second time. Store in tightly covered jar in refrigerator for up to 1 week.

Nancy Moore, Grandparent of Hampton and Kirkland

Meat and Vegetarian Entrees

Meat/Vegetarian Entrees

Beef
French Beef with Burgundy

6 strips bacon, cut into ½-inch pieces
3 pounds beef chuck, cut into 1½-inch cubes
1 large carrot, sliced
1 medium onion, sliced
1 teaspoon salt
¼ teaspoon pepper
3 tablespoons + ¼ cup all-purpose flour, divided

2 cans beef broth, divided
2 cups red Burgundy wine
1 tablespoon tomato paste
1 bay leaf
5 tablespoons butter, divided
2 tablespoons vegetable oil
1 quart mushrooms, quartered
1 pound small whole white onions

In Dutch oven, cook bacon until crisp; remove. Brown beef in same pot; remove. In drippings, brown carrot and onion. Spoon off fat; return bacon and beef to pan. Season with salt and pepper. Stir in 3 tablespoons flour. Reserve ½ cup beef broth; add remainder to stew. Add wine, tomato paste and bay leaf. Cover; simmer 3 hours. Sauté mushrooms in 3 tablespoons butter and oil 5 minutes; lift out. Add small onions and brown. Add reserved broth; simmer covered until tender, about 10 minutes. Skim fat from stew. Cream ¼ cup flour and 2 tablespoons butter; roll into pea-size balls and drop into stew. Stir over very low heat till thickened. Add mushrooms and onions; bring to boil. Serves 8 to 10.

Evelyn Cima, Grandparent of Brooke Forbis

Olive Stuffed Roast

1 (4- to 5-pound) sirloin tip roast
1 (10-ounce) jar pimento-stuffed olives

1 envelope garlic salad dressing mix

With sharp knife, make 10 to 12 cross-shaped cuts on both sides of roast. Push olives all the way into roast. Roll roast in salad dressing mix. Bake in preheated 325° oven for 15 to 25 minutes per pound.

Susanne Hux Long '77, Parent of Caroline and Claire

Bul Go Gi (Korean Barbequed Beef)

1 pound top round beef, sliced
  into very thin strips
3 tablespoons brown sugar
½ cup soy sauce
Salt and pepper to taste
4 tablespoons sesame oil

1 garlic clove, crushed
2 scallions, sliced, green tops
  only
½ teaspoon MSG
2 tablespoons sesame seeds

Mix beef, sugar, soy sauce, salt, and pepper. Add sesame oil, garlic, scallions, and MSG. Set aside at room temperature for 2 hours, basting and turning meat occasionally. Preheat grill to hot (approximately 400°). Lay beef strips on grate and cook until evenly browned on both sides, turning once. Remove from heat. Sprinkle with sesame seeds and serve immediately. Serves 4.

Aeran Lee Dela Cerna, Parent of Joonho '99 and Taeree Lee

Hillsville Pot Roast

1 can golden mushroom soup
1 can cream of mushroom
  soup
¾ to 1 cup water
2 to 3 pounds rump roast

4 to 5 potatoes, cut into
  chunks
7 to 8 carrots, cut into 2-inch
  pieces
1 large onion, peeled and
  sliced

Mix soups and water; pour into large baking dish. Add roast and surround with potatoes and carrots. Top with sliced onions. Cover and bake in preheated 325° oven 4 hours or until meat is fork tender. Serves 6 to 8.

Sheila Frazier, Aunt of Lindsay '98 and Carlin Williford

Tate Brisket

1 (5-pound) beef brisket
2 tablespoons liquid smoke
1 tablespoon garlic salt
1 tablespoon onion salt
2 teaspoons celery seed
1½ teaspoons salt
2 teaspoons pepper
2 tablespoons Worcestershire
sauce
1 (24-ounce) jar picanté sauce

Mix all ingredients and marinate brisket at least 24 hours in refrigerator. Put brisket in roasting pan and cover well with foil. Bake in preheated 225° oven for 9 hours. Smoke for 2 hours with foil open; baste frequently.

Emily Tate, Aunt of Matthew Franzeen

Chinese Pepper Steak

1 pound round steak, cut into
thin strips
1 onion, chopped
½ cup diced celery
Vegetable oil or bacon
drippings for browning
⅛ teaspoon pepper
½ teaspoon sugar
1½ cups water
1 beef bouillon cube or 1
teaspoon beef bouillon
granules
1 green pepper, cut in thin
strips
1½ tablespoons corn starch,
mixed with a little water to
resemble paste
1½ tablespoons soy sauce
Chinese noodles

Brown steak, onion, and celery in hot fat. Add pepper, sugar, water, and bouillon cube. Cover; reduce heat and simmer 1 hour. Add green pepper and cook 10 minutes longer. Blend corn starch paste with soy sauce. Add, stirring until thickened. Serve over rice; top with Chinese noodles. Serves 4 to 6.

Nancy Moore, Grandparent of Hampton and Kirkland

Flank Steak

1½ to 2 pounds flank steak	2 tablespoons ginger
1½ cups beer	1½ teaspoons red pepper
5 scallions, chopped	flakes
⅓ cup oil	1 teaspoon salt
3 tablespoons soy sauce	2 cloves garlic, chopped
2 tablespoons brown sugar	

Combine all ingredients. Marinate flank steak for 24 hours. Take steak out of marinade and place on medium-hot grill. Grill for approximately 5 minutes on each side. (Grilling time depends on thickness of steak.) Serves 4.

Rosemary Rocconi, Parent of Dominic and Mario

Rouladen

4 (½-inch thick) slices London Broil or beef top round	½ cup mustard
	3 stalks celery, finely chopped
⅓ cup sweet pickle relish (optional)	1 tablespoon mayonnaise
	1 pound bacon, diced
Carrots, grated	4 packages mushroom gravy
3 onions, finely chopped	mix

Put relish, carrots, onion, celery, and bacon into bowl. Add mustard and mayonnaise. Mix all ingredients well. Pound thinly sliced London Broil to tenderize. Spread 1 tablespoon relish mixture on each slice of London Broil. Roll up and secure with toothpicks. Bake in preheated 350° oven. Keep checking until browned, then turn and bake until done. Mix broth from meat (and water as necessary) with 4 packages of mushroom gravy mix and pour over Rouladen. Serves 4.

Burglinde Walker, Parent of Morris

Beef Burgundy

3 pounds beef stew meat
3 tablespoons oil
1 package French onion soup
   mix

2 cans mushroom soup
½ pound fresh mushrooms,
   sliced
¾ cup Burgundy wine

In large pot or Dutch oven, brown meat in oil. Add soup mix, mushroom soup, mushrooms, and wine. Cover; simmer 2 to 3 hours. Remove lid last half hour to thicken juices. Serve over noodles or rice. Serves 6 to 8.

Morgan Anderson '94

Sour Cream Hamburger Casserole

1½ pounds ground beef
2 tablespoons butter
Dash garlic salt
1 teaspoon salt
½ teaspoon pepper
1 tablespoon sugar
2 (8-ounce) cans tomato
   sauce

1 (3-ounce) package cream
   cheese, softened
1 cup sour cream
1 small onion, chopped
1 (8-ounce) package noodles,
   cooked and drained
½ cup grated cheddar cheese

Sauté ground beef with butter, garlic salt, salt, pepper, and sugar. Add tomato sauce and simmer 20 minutes. In separate bowl, blend cream cheese and sour cream; add onion. Put meat, cream cheese mixture, and noodles into casserole dish. Top with grated cheese. Bake in preheated 350° oven for 20 minutes. Serves 8 to 10.

Sweetie Stewart, Parent of Whitner '96, Anne '99, and Katie

Santa Fe Casserole

1 pound ground beef
1 package taco seasoning mix
2 cups chicken broth
¼ cup all-purpose flour
1 cup sour cream
1 (7-ounce) can diced green
  chiles

1 (11-ounce) package corn or
  tortilla chips
2 (8-ounce) packages grated
  Monterey Jack or cheddar
  cheese
½ cup sliced green onions

In medium skillet, brown meat and stir until crumbly; drain excess fat. Add seasoning mix; blend well. In small bowl, combine broth and flour. Add to meat mixture; bring to boil to slightly thicken liquid. Stir in sour cream and chiles; blend well. In 9x13x2-inch lightly greased glass baking dish, layer ½ chips, ½ beef and sauce mixture, ½ cheese, and ½ green onions. Layer again with remaining ingredients, ending with green onions. Bake in preheated 375° oven for 20 minutes. Let stand 5 minutes before cutting. Serves 6.

Kelley Ebel, F.A. Staff,
Parent of Brooke, Garrett, Megan, and Seth

Cheeseburger Pie

1 pound ground beef
1½ cups chopped onion
½ teaspoon salt
¼ teaspoon pepper

1 cup shredded cheese
1 cup milk
½ cup biscuit/baking mix
2 eggs

Lightly grease 9-inch pie pan. Brown beef and onion; sauté for 5 minutes. Drain off excess fat. Add salt and pepper. Spread mixture in pie pan. Sprinkle with cheese. Beat milk, biscuit/baking mix, and eggs on high speed for 1 minute. Pour over cheese. Bake in preheated 400° oven for 25 to 30 minutes or until golden brown and knife inserted near center comes out clean. Let stand 3 to 5 minutes before slicing. Serves 6 to 8.

Robin Tinney, Wife of Darren '84, Parent of Ashley

Farmer's Pie

Meat mixture:
½ cup tomato sauce
¾ cup bread crumbs
1 pound ground beef
¼ cup chopped onion
¼ cup chopped green pepper
1 teaspoon salt
Dash of pepper

Rice Filling:
1½ cups instant rice
1 cup water
1½ cups tomato sauce
½ teaspoon salt
1 cup grated cheddar cheese,
  divided

Combine all ingredients for meat mixture and pat into greased 9-inch pie plate. Combine rice, water, tomato sauce, salt, and ½ cheese. Place rice mixture over meat mixture; cover with foil. Bake in preheated 350° oven for 25 minutes. Remove from oven and sprinkle with remaining cheese. Return to oven and bake uncovered for additional 15 minutes. Serves 4.

Betty Russell, Grandparent of Katie

Yumasetta (Amish Casserole)

2 pounds ground beef
½ medium onion, chopped
3 tablespoons brown sugar
Salt and pepper to taste

1 can tomato soup
1 (6-ounce) package noodles
1 can cream of chicken soup
1 cup grated cheddar cheese

Combine ground beef, onion, brown sugar, salt, and pepper in skillet. Cook until meat browns and onions are soft. Drain off excess fat; add tomato soup. Set aside. Cook and drain noodles. Add cream of chicken soup to noodles. Layer noodle mixture, cheese, and meat mixture in large casserole dish. Bake in preheated 350° oven for 30 minutes.

Eileen Haefele, Grandparent of Trey Bright

Cabbage and Hamburger

1 large onion, chopped
1 green pepper, chopped
2 to 3 tablespoons butter or
    margarine

1 pound lean ground beef
Salt and pepper to taste
1 medium cabbage, shredded
1 can tomato soup, undiluted

In saucepan, sauté onion and green pepper in butter for 4 minutes. Add beef and brown lightly. Drain off fat. Season mixture with salt and pepper. Place ½ cabbage in casserole dish; add meat mixture. Cover with remaining cabbage. Pour soup on top. Cover and bake in preheated 375° oven for 1 hour. Serves 4 to 6.

Carolyn Snow, Grandparent of Hannah '95, Evan '98, and Ben Lennon

Spinach Fandango

1 medium onion, chopped
2 pounds ground beef
1 (7-ounce) can mushrooms
1 clove garlic, crushed
1 tablespoon oregano
Salt and pepper to taste

2 (10-ounce) packages frozen
    chopped spinach
1 can cream of celery soup
1 cup sour cream
Mozzarella cheese, sliced or
    grated

In large saucepan, combine onion, ground beef, mushrooms, garlic, oregano, salt, and pepper. Sauté until meat is completely brown. Place frozen spinach on top of browned beef. Simmer until spinach thaws and is mixable with other ingredients. In medium-sized casserole dish, mix soup and sour cream well. Add hot meat mixture and stir to mix. Top with cheese. Bake uncovered in preheated 350° oven for 15 to 20 minutes.

Judy Waggoner, Parent of Christopher and Ryan

Mock Chow Mein

1 cup rice
2½ cups boiling water
1 pound ground beef
2 teaspoons brown sugar

½ cup chopped celery
3 ounces soy sauce
1 (4-ounce) can mushrooms

In 2-quart casserole, pour boiling water on rice and let stand. Brown ground beef; drain excess fat. Add beef and remaining ingredients to rice. Mix well. Bake in preheated 350° oven for 1 hour.

Maggie Franzeen, F.A. Staff, Parent of Matthew

Chow Mein

1 pound beef, cut into thin slices
1 pound pork, sliced thinly (optional)
1 large onion, diced
1 package onion mushroom soup mix (optional)

2 tablespoons oil
1 cup diagonally sliced celery
1 (16-ounce) can bean sprouts or oriental vegetables
1 (7-ounce) can mushrooms, drained

In large frying pan, sauté beef, pork, onion, and soup mix in oil. Set aside. In smaller pan, sauté celery, bean sprouts, and mushrooms until tender. Mix with meat. Serve with rice.

Mrs. Cloyd Strand, Grandparent of Jessica Hanson '99

Ground Beef Chop Suey

1½ pounds lean ground beef
1 large onion, cut in 6 wedges
3 medium celery ribs, cut in
   1-inch pieces
2 cups beef broth
2 tablespoons soy sauce

1 (16-ounce) can bean
   sprouts, rinsed and drained
2 tablespoons corn starch
   mixed with ¼ cup water
Hot cooked rice
Chow mein noodles

In large skillet, brown meat, stirring to break up pieces. Add onion, celery, broth, and soy sauce. Cook over low heat, stirring occasionally, 15 minutes or until onion and celery are crisp-tender. Add bean sprouts and cook 3 minutes or until just heated through. Stir in corn starch mixture; cook and stir until thickened. Serve over rice with additional soy sauce and chow mein noodles. Serves 6.

Sharon Young, Parent of Allison and Stephanie

Sweet and Sour Meatloaf

Meatloaf:
2 pounds ground chuck
1 small onion, chopped
8 round buttery crackers,
   crushed (approximately
   ¼ cup)
Salt and pepper
1 egg, lightly beaten

Sauce:
1 (16-ounce) can tomato
   sauce
¾ cup brown sugar
   (adjust to taste)
¼ cup apple cider vinegar
1 teaspoon mustard

Mix meatloaf ingredients; set aside. Mix sauce ingredients. Add ½ cup sauce mixture to meat. Put meat in loaf pan. Bake in preheated 400° oven for 30 minutes. Remove from oven and pour off excess fat. Pour remaining sauce over loaf and return to oven for 30 more minutes at 400° or lower oven to 375° and bake for 40 minutes.

Lucy Jones, Trustee, Parent of Lee '99, Jordan, and Rosanne

Swedish Meatballs

Meatball mixture:
1 cup fine bread crumbs
⅓ cup milk
¼ cup minced onion
1 pound ground beef
1 egg, lightly beaten
1½ teaspoons salt
⅛ teaspoon pepper
½ teaspoon nutmeg
2 tablespoons butter

Sauce:
2 teaspoons flour
1 cup hot water
1 bouillon cube or 1 teaspoon
   bouillon granules
½ cup milk
½ cup light cream

Soak bread crumbs in ⅓ cup milk. Add onion, ground beef, egg, salt, pepper, and nutmeg. Mix thoroughly. Shape into 1-inch balls. In large skillet, sauté meatballs in butter until lightly browned on all sides. Remove meatballs. Add flour to skillet and blend. Add water, bouillon, ½ cup milk, and cream. Cook and stir over medium heat until sauce is smooth and thickened, about 2 minutes. Add meatballs; cover and simmer 15 minutes. Serves 6.

Harriette Sandeen, Grandparent of Matthew Franzeen

Meatballs

1 pound ground beef
¼ pound ground pork
¼ pound ground veal
1 onion, chopped
½ cup saltine cracker crumbs
1 clove garlic, chopped
2 tablespoons minced parsley

1 tablespoon chopped basil
½ teaspoon salt
¼ teaspoon pepper
2 tablespoons milk
1 egg, beaten
Vegetable oil

Combine all ingredients except oil in large bowl. Mix thoroughly and shape into 1-inch balls. Heat vegetable oil in large frying pan. Brown meatballs lightly on all sides. Drain on paper towels. Meatballs can be added to either tomato sauce or brown gravy. Serves 8 to 10.

Sharon McDaniel, Wife of Greg '76, Parent of Jack

Sweet and Sour Meatballs

1 can tomato soup
2 teaspoons Worcestershire
   sauce
Hot pepper sauce (optional)
1¼ cups water
Juice of 1 lemon
1 onion, chopped

Salt and pepper to taste
3 heaping tablespoons brown
   sugar
¾ to 1 cup ketchup
1½ pounds ground beef
Bread crumbs

Bring all ingredients except hamburger and bread crumbs to boil. Reduce heat to simmer and cook for at least 45 minutes. (Sauce is better if simmered longer.) If liquid is too thin, add corn starch dissolved in water to thicken.

Mix hamburger, salt, pepper, and a few bread crumbs together; form into 1-inch balls. Brown meatballs and add to sauce. Serve over white rice. Serves 6.

Barbara Appel, Parent of Eric '98 and Chris

Sloppy Joes

1 pound ground beef
1 onion, chopped
2 cans chicken gumbo soup

1 tablespoon mustard
1 tablespoon ketchup

In large skillet, brown beef and onion. Add remaining ingredients and simmer for 20 minutes. Serve over hamburger buns.

Elyse Arthur, F.A. Faculty,
Parent of Janene '99, Jacqueline and Cara

Sloppy Joes for a Crowd

5 pounds ground beef
1 cup dry onions
¼ cup sugar
2 teaspoons dry mustard

Salt and pepper
⅓ cup white vinegar
7 cups ketchup
1 cup water

Brown hamburger. Mix remaining ingredients with browned beef; heat thoroughly. Serve on hamburger or sandwich buns. Serves approximately 40. (Perfect in a crock pot.)

Maggie Franzeen, F.A. Staff, Parent of Matthew

Meat Boats (Stuffed Zucchini)

6 zucchini, medium to large
1½ pounds lean ground beef
 or ground chuck
1 medium onion, chopped
Italian spices to taste (garlic,
 oregano, thyme, basil, red
 pepper flakes)

1 recipe homemade marinara
 sauce *(below)* or
1 (26-ounce) jar marinara
 sauce
Grated mozzarella cheese
Parmesan cheese
Fresh chopped parsley

Clean zucchini and cut off stems. Slice in ½ lengthwise and scoop out pulp, leaving at least ¼-inch boat or shell all around. Brown meat and onion in large frying pan. Drain off excess fat. Add zucchini pulp along with desired Italian spices; continue cooking until meat is no longer pink and pulp is blended in. Stir in marinara sauce and simmer 20 minutes to blend flavors. In large baking pan, arrange zucchini boats in single layer and fill with meat mixture. Pour additional sauce over and around boats. Sprinkle with cheeses and bake in preheated 350° oven for 30 to 45 minutes. Sprinkle with parsley before serving. Serves 4 to 6.

Mary Joan Fredette, Parent of Chris '94 and Jon

Homemade Marinara Sauce

1½ to 2 pounds ground beef
2 (12-ounce) cans tomato
 sauce
2 (6-ounce) cans tomato paste
1 large onion, chopped
1 small green pepper,
 chopped (optional)

1 to 2 cloves garlic, minced or
 1 teaspoon garlic salt
½ teaspoon thyme
½ teaspoon sage
½ teaspoon oregano
1 tablespoon parsley
Salt and pepper to taste
Red pepper flakes (optional)

Brown ground beef. Add remaining ingredients and simmer for 1 hour to blend flavors.

Mary Joan Fredette, Parent of Chris '94 and Jon

Lasagna

Meat mixture:
1½ pounds ground beef
1 tablespoon olive oil
1 clove garlic, minced
1 tablespoon parsley
1 tablespoon basil
2 teaspoons salt
Pinch oregano
1 (16-ounce) can tomatoes
1 (6-ounce) can tomato paste

Cheese mixture:
1 (24-ounce) container cottage cheese
2 eggs, beaten
2 teaspoons salt
½ teaspoon pepper
½ cup Parmesan cheese
1 to 2 tablespoons parsley
2 cups shredded mozzarella or cheddar cheese
1 (16-ounce) package of lasagna noodles

Brown meat in olive oil. Add remaining ingredients for meat mixture and simmer 1 hour. In bowl, combine ingredients for cheese mixture (except noodles). Cook lasagna noodles according to package directions. Grease 9x13x2-inch pan. On bottom of pan, layer ½ noodles, cheese mixture and meat mixture. Repeat. Top with more cheese and bake in preheated 325° oven for 50 to 60 minutes or until cheese is golden. Serves 6 to 8.

Mary Lyn Maulden Morgan '81

Irish-Italian Spaghetti

1 onion, chopped
2 tablespoons oil
1 pound lean ground beef
1 teaspoon salt
¼ teaspoon black pepper
Dash of red pepper
½ teaspoon chili powder
½ teaspoon hot sauce
1 can mushroom soup
1 can tomato soup
½ cup Parmesan cheese
8 ounces spaghetti noodles

Brown onion in hot oil; add meat and seasonings; brown lightly. Cover and simmer 10 minutes. Add soups; cover and simmer 45 minutes. Cook spaghetti noodles in boiling salted water until tender. Drain and rinse with hot water. Arrange on hot platter. Pour sauce over spaghetti and sprinkle with cheese. Serves 4 to 6.

Maggie Franzeen, F.A. Staff, Parent of Matthew

Mexican Lasagna

1 pound lean ground beef
1 (16-ounce) can refried beans
2 teaspoons oregano
1 teaspoon ground cumin
¾ teaspoon garlic powder
12 uncooked lasagna noodles
2½ cups water

2½ cups picanté sauce
2 cups sour cream
¾ cup sliced green onions
1 (2.2-ounce) can sliced black
   olives, drained
4 ounces Monterey Jack
   cheese, shredded

Combine beef, beans, oregano, cumin, and garlic powder. Place 4 uncooked noodles in bottom of 9x13x2-inch baking pan. Spread ½ beef mixture over noodles. Top with layer of 4 noodles and remaining beef mixture. Combine water and picanté sauce. Pour over all. Cover tightly with foil; bake in preheated 350° oven for 1 hour and 30 minutes or until noodles are tender. Combine sour cream, onions, and olives. Spoon over casserole; top with cheese. Bake uncovered until cheese is melted, about 5 minutes. Serves 12.

Beverly Brooks, Grandparent of Tracey '99

Harry's Favorite Spaghetti Sauce

1 medium white onion, finely
   chopped
1 clove garlic, minced
1 tablespoon olive oil
2 (15-ounce) cans tomato
   sauce

1 pound ground beef,
   browned and drained
1 tablespoon brown sugar
1 teaspoon Italian seasoning

Sauté onion and garlic in olive oil until soft. Add tomato sauce, ground beef, brown sugar, and Italian seasoning. Simmer at least 1 hour. Serve over pasta. Serves 6.

Betty Dumas, Grandparent of Harry and Lacy Godwin

Manicotti

1 egg
1 (8-ounce) container cottage
  cheese
Salt and pepper to taste
1 cup shredded sharp cheddar
  cheese
2 cups shredded mozzarella
  cheese
Pinch of diced onions

Pinch diced green pepper
Manicotti noodles
1 to 1½ pounds pork sausage
  or ground beef, browned
  (optional)
1 (26-ounce) jar of spaghetti
  sauce with mushrooms
¼ cup grated Parmesan
  cheese

Combine egg, cottage cheese, salt, and pepper; mix well. Add shredded cheeses, onion, and green pepper; mix well and set aside. Cook noodles according to package directions; cool. Stuff noodles with cheese mixture or, if desired, stuff shells with browned meat. Spread ½ cup spaghetti sauce on bottom of well greased 9x13x2-inch pan. Arrange stuffed shells in single layer over sauce. Pour remaining sauce over shells, covering shells completely. Sprinkle evenly with Parmesan cheese. Cover and bake in preheated 350° oven 15 to 20 minutes or until thoroughly heated. Serves 8.

Lee Holmes Zettel '75

"My Mother-in-Law's" Spaghetti Sauce

Sauce mixture:
1 (15-ounce) can tomato
  sauce
2 (12-ounce) cans tomato
  puree
2 (6-ounce) cans tomato paste
Salt to taste
7 to 8 bay leaves
3 tablespoons oregano

1 large onion, diced
1 tablespoon minced garlic

Meat mixture:
1½ pounds ground beef
1 tablespoon diced onion
1 teaspoon minced garlic
Salt to taste

In large pot, mix sauce ingredients; simmer 2 hours. Combine meat mixture ingredients in skillet and sauté until ground beef is browned. Add meat mixture to sauce and continue to cook on simmer for 3 to 4 hours. Serves "a bunch!"

Judy Waggoner, Parent of Christopher and Ryan

Pork
Peppered Pork Chops with Molasses Butter

¼ cup butter, softened
1 tablespoon molasses
½ teaspoon freshly squeezed
  lemon juice

4 tablespoons cracked black
  pepper (or coarsely ground)
4 (1½-inch thick, 6-ounce)
  boneless center-cut loin
  pork chops

Cream together butter, molasses, and lemon juice; set aside. Rub pork chops evenly with pepper on both sides. Grill over medium coals for 12 to 15 minutes or until done, turning once. Top with molasses butter and serve. Serves 4.

Charlie Stewart '77

Smothered Pork Chops

6 to 8 center-cut pork chops
Seasoned salt
Garlic powder
Black pepper
All-purpose flour

Vegetable oil
½ green pepper
1 medium onion
½ cup water

Trim excess fat from pork chops. Season pork chops with seasoned salt, garlic powder and black pepper on both sides. Flour one side of pork chops. In just enough oil to cover bottom of large frying pan, fry pork chops for 3 to 4 minutes, turning once; remove from frying pan to 10-inch frying pan or 3- to 4-quart pot, making sure chops are in single layer. If more area is needed for chops, reserve remaining chops for second layer. Slice green pepper into ¼-inch strips. Cut onion in ½ and slice into ¼-inch strips. Cover pork chops with onions and green peppers. If necessary, put another layer of chops; cover with more onions and green peppers. Add ½ cup water and let chops simmer for 30 to 45 minutes until onions and green peppers are nice and tender. Enjoy!

Norman Barnum III, Grandparent of Kurston Melton

Pork Chop Rice Casserole

4 thick pork chops
4 tablespoons butter, divided
1 box beef-flavored rice
vermicelli mix

2 cups hot water
1 (16-ounce) can tomatoes,
chopped

In large skillet, brown chops on both sides in 2 tablespoons butter. Remove from pan. Add 2 tablespoons of butter and rice mix to same skillet; cook until golden. Add 2 cups hot water, seasoning package, and canned tomatoes. Bring to simmer. Place chops on top of rice mixture and simmer 20 more minutes. Serves 4.

Irma Smith, Parent of CoCo

Garlic and Rosemary Roasted Pork

½ cup olive oil
¼ cup balsamic vinegar
2 tablespoons apple cider
vinegar
2 tablespoons honey
3 cloves garlic, minced

1 tablespoon chopped fresh
rosemary or 2 teaspoons
dried rosemary
1 tablespoon Dijon mustard
1 (14- to 16-ounce) pork
tenderloin

Blend olive oil, balsamic vinegar, apple cider vinegar, honey, garlic, rosemary, and Dijon mustard in processor or blender until rosemary and garlic are finely chopped. Place pork in heavy zippered plastic bag. Pour ½ marinade over pork (refrigerate remaining marinade for another use). Seal bag and refrigerate overnight, turning occasionally.

Drain pork; discard marinade. Place pork in small roasting pan. Roast in preheated 375° oven until meat thermometer inserted into center registers 150°, about 25 minutes. Slice thinly and serve. Serves 4.

Prima Yoshimoto, Parent of Brendan

Roast Pork

8 cloves garlic	2 tablespoons apple cider
8 peppercorns	vinegar
2 teaspoons oregano	6 pounds pork roast
2 tablespoons olive oil	Salt

Crush garlic, peppercorns and oregano. Add olive oil and vinegar. Marinate meat and salt it. Bake in preheated 350° oven 35 minutes per pound. Slice thin.

Elyse Arthur, F.A. Faculty, Parent of Janene '99, Jacqueline and Cara Allison

Filet de pore Normande
(Pork tenderloin with mushrooms)

1½ pounds pork tenderloin	2 tablespoons butter
4 tablespoons all-purpose	2 tablespoons Calvados or
flour	brandy
Salt and pepper	⅔ cup heavy cream
1¼ cups white wine	2 tablespoons fresh parsley,
½ pound button mushrooms,	chopped
sliced	

Slice pork into thin medallions. Blend flour with salt and pepper. Dredge medallions in flour; shake off excess. Pour wine into saucepan; add mushrooms. Cover and simmer gently for 10 minutes. Melt butter in large frying pan; add pork and fry quickly until pork is browned. Spoon Calvados or brandy over medallions; ignite. When flames die down, add wine and mushrooms. Simmer gently for 5 minutes. Add cream and heat gently without boiling. Spoon into serving dish. Sprinkle with parsley and serve. Serves 4.

Sharon Kropp, Parent of Kathryn

Pork Tenderloin

1 (2-pound) package contain-
　ing 2 pork tenderloin strips
⅓ cup soy sauce
½ teaspoon ginger

5 cloves garlic, halved
2 tablespoons brown sugar
3 tablespoons honey
2 teaspoons oil

Cut pork tenderloins down the center, lengthwise, to within ¼-inch of other side. Place in zippered plastic bag. Mix soy sauce, ginger, and garlic; pour into bag. Refrigerate at least 3 hours or overnight. In saucepan over low heat, mix sugar, honey, and oil until sugar dissolves. Drain meat. Heat grill. Place meat on grill. Baste meat with sugar mixture frequently (keep the sugar mixture on the grill to keep it liquid). Serves 4 to 6.

Diane Harrell, Parent of Greg and Steven

Baked Pork Tenderloin

½ cup all-purpose flour
1 teaspoon thyme leaves
1 teaspoon basil leaves
½ teaspoon rosemary
½ teaspoon oregano leaves
1 (2-pound) package contain-
　ing 2 pork tenderloin strips

4 tablespoons butter or
　margarine
2 cups chicken broth
Dash of Maggi seasoning
　(optional)
¼ to ½ cup white cooking wine
12 ounces fresh mushrooms,
　sliced

Mix flour, thyme, basil, rosemary, and oregano. Dredge pork tenderloin in flour mixture; brown in butter or margarine. Remove meat and place in baking dish. Make sauce with 3 tablespoons of seasoned flour and butter remaining in skillet. Add chicken broth. When sauce is cooked, add mushrooms and white wine. Pour over pork tenderloin. Cover with foil; bake in preheated 350° oven for 45 minutes. Remove foil and continue to bake 15 minutes more. Serves 6.

Note: Double the above recipe for 2 packages of tenderloins.

Janet Robinson, Parent of Courtney and Hillary

Roast Pork Tenderloin

2 to 3 pound pork tenderloin	1 teaspoon dried thyme
½ cup butter, divided	1 teaspoon paprika
1 large onion, chopped	½ teaspoon dried marjoram
2 cloves garlic, minced	Salt and pepper
1¾ cups beef broth	½ cup white wine

Brown pork tenderloin on all sides in ¼ cup butter. Place tenderloin in long pan. Heat remaining butter in same skillet used to brown tenderloin. Add onion; sauté until soft. Add garlic and beef broth. Add thyme, paprika, marjoram, salt, and pepper. Add wine; simmer 10 minutes. Pour over tenderloin. Marinate 1 to 12 hours. Cover and bake in preheated 300° oven for 1 to 1½ hours basting every 20 minutes. Juices may be thickened to make gravy. Serves 4 to 6.

Sharon McDaniel, Wife of Greg '76, Parent of Jack

Pork Chop Schnitzel

6 lean pork chops	2 tablespoons all-purpose flour
Salt and pepper	¾ cup fine bread crumbs
Paprika	⅓ cup margarine
1 egg	1 lemon, cut into 6 slices
3 tablespoons milk	

Pound pork chops lightly with a meat mallet. Sprinkle with salt, pepper, and paprika. Combine egg and milk; beat to mix well. Coat with flour; dip into egg mixture. Roll in bread crumbs. Fry in hot margarine over medium heat 8 minutes on each side, turning only once. Arrange on platter; top each pork chop with 1 lemon slice. Serves 4 to 6.

Steffi Schnabel, Parent of Jason

Pork Chops a' la Orange

4 (1-inch thick) center-cut pork chops	1½ teaspoons corn starch
Salt and pepper to taste	¼ teaspoon salt
Paprika	¼ teaspoon cinnamon
1 cup orange juice, divided	10 whole cloves
5 tablespoons sugar	4 to 6 orange slices

Trim fat from pork chops. Render fat over low heat in skillet; discard fat but reserve drippings. Sprinkle pork chops with salt, pepper, and paprika. Cook over medium-high heat in drippings until browned on both sides. Reduce heat to low. Add ½ cup orange juice. Cover tightly. Simmer 45 minutes to 1 hour or until tender. In saucepan, combine sugar, corn starch, ¼ teaspoon salt, cinnamon, cloves, and ½ cup orange juice. Cook over medium heat until thick, stirring constantly. Arrange pork chops on platter. Pour orange sauce on top. Garnish with orange slices. Serves 4.

Mary Anne Ethington, Parent of Jordan

Souper Skillet Pork Chops

4 to 6 pork chops	1 can cream of mushroom soup
Dash of salt and pepper	¾ cup water
½ cup chopped onion	1 can French fried onion rings
1 can French style green beans, drained	

Season chops with salt and pepper. In frying pan, cook chops on low heat until brown on both sides. Remove chops from pan. Sauté onions. Add green beans; heat until slightly brown. Add soup and water; stir. Pour into large baking pan. Add pork chops. Sprinkle with onion rings to cover entire pan. Cover and bake in preheated 375° oven for 50 to 60 minutes. Serve with rice. Serves 4 to 6.

Teresa Lindsley Dobson '80

Barbequed Pork Chops

4 or 5 pork chops
¼ cup chopped onion
4 tablespoons sugar
⅛ teaspoon pepper
¼ cup ketchup

3 tablespoons apple cider
  vinegar
1 tablespoon Worcestershire
  sauce

Place pork chops in frying pan. Mix remaining ingredients; pour over pork chops. Simmer on low heat until done. Serves 4.

Joyce Smith, Grandparent of Jacqueline and Jeremy Gobien

Pork Chops with Onions and Balsamic Vinegar Sauce

4 (1-inch thick) center-cut pork
  chops
4 tablespoons extra virgin
  olive oil
1 teaspoon salt
½ teaspoon freshly ground
  pepper

2 medium onions, thinly sliced
1 tablespoon chopped garlic
1 tablespoon chopped fresh
  rosemary
½ cup chicken broth
¼ cup balsamic vinegar

Brush both sides of pork chops with oil. Sprinkle both sides with salt and pepper. In large skillet, cook 4 minutes per side. Transfer to plate. Sauté onion, garlic, and rosemary in same pan. Stir in broth and vinegar; boil 1 minute. Return pork chops to pan. Reduce heat to low; cover and cook 8 minutes until meat thermometer reaches 160°. Serve with mashed potatoes. Serves 4.

Tobie Little, F.A. Staff

Ham
Swiss Ham Ring Around

1 cup fresh or frozen broccoli
¼ cup chopped parsley or 2 tablespoons dry parsley flakes
2 tablespoons finely chopped onion
2 tablespoons mustard
1 tablespoon butter, softened

1 teaspoon lemon juice
¾ cup shredded Swiss cheese
1 (6-ounce) can ham, drained and separated
1 (8-ounce) can refrigerated crescent dough
Parmesan cheese, grated

Cook and drain broccoli. In large bowl, combine parsley, onion, mustard, butter, and lemon juice; blend well. Add cheese, broccoli, and ham. Mix lightly and set aside.

Separate crescent dough into 8 triangles. On greased baking sheet, arrange triangles, points toward outside in a circle with bases overlapping. (Center should be about 3-inches in diameter.) Spoon ham mixture evenly in ring over bases of triangles. Fold points over top of ham mixture. Bake in preheated 350° oven for 25 to 30 minutes until lightly brown. Serves 6.

Lee Holmes Zettel '75

Baked Feta Noodles with Tomatoes and Ham

12 ounces rigatoni, cooked and drained
8 ounces ham, diced
4 large plum tomatoes, chopped

1 cup crumbled feta cheese
1 cup grated mozzarella cheese
1 cup whipping cream
Salt and pepper

Mix pasta, ham, tomatoes, and cheese. Pour into greased 9x13x2-inch baking pan. Pour cream over pasta. Sprinkle with salt and pepper; toss to blend. Cover with foil. Bake in pre-heated 375° oven for 15 minutes. Uncover and stir. Cover and bake 30 minutes more. Serves 6.

Meredith McCambridge, Parent of Gordon

Spinach, Ham, and Tomato Pie

1 pie crust, unbaked	1 cup chopped frozen leaf
2 cups milk	spinach, thawed and
4 eggs	squeezed dry
1 cup shredded cheddar	½ cup sliced green onion
cheese, divided	½ teaspoon salt
1 cup ham, cooked and diced	2 small plum tomatoes,
	seeded, thinly sliced

Prick bottom of pie crust; place on baking sheet. Bake in preheated 400° oven for 8 minutes. Remove to wire rack. Whisk milk and eggs together in large bowl. Stir in ¾ cup cheese, ham, spinach, onion, and salt. Pour into crust; top with tomatoes and remaining cheese. Bake for 20 minutes. Reduce heat to 350° and bake 40 to 45 minutes. Let set 10 to 15 minutes before cutting. Serves 6.

Jane White, Grandparent of Robert DeGaetano

Ham Balls

2½ pounds ground ham	Sauce:
2 pounds ground pork	2 cans tomato soup
2 pounds ground beef	¾ cup white vinegar
3 cups graham cracker crumbs	2 cups brown sugar
2 cups milk	2 teaspoons dry mustard
3 eggs, lightly beaten	
1 teaspoon salt	

Grind meats together. Add cracker crumbs, milk, eggs, and salt. Mix well. Use ⅓ cup measuring cup to form balls. (Can freeze at this point.) In large roasting pan, mix sauce ingredients. Put meatballs into sauce and bake in preheated 350° oven for 1½ hours. After 45 minutes, turn ham balls over and cover. Serves 20.

Doris Johnson, Grandparent of Matthew Franzeen

Other Meats/Vegetarian

Rosemary Grilled Lamb Chops

¾ cup balsamic vinegar
6 tablespoons olive oil
3 tablespoons fresh lemon
juice
3 tablespoons minced fresh
rosemary or 3 teaspoons
dried

6 garlic cloves, minced
1 teaspoon pepper
12 (1-inch thick) loin lamb
chops
Fresh rosemary

Mix vinegar, olive oil, lemon juice, rosemary, garlic, and pepper in small bowl. Place lamb chops in single layer in 9x13x2-inch glass dish. Pour marinade over chops. Cover and refrigerate at least 4 hours, turning occasionally. Prepare grill. Use mesquite wood chips soaked in cold water for 1 hour to get a smoked flavor. When chips begin to smoke, place chops on grill. Cover. Grill chops to desired doneness, basting often with marinade, about 4 minutes per side for medium-rare. Place on platter. Garnish with fresh rosemary. Serves 4.

Joyce Sorensen, Parent of Blake '95

Veal Scallopini

2 pounds veal, cut in thin
strips
¼ cup all-purpose flour
½ teaspoon salt
½ teaspoon pepper
½ teaspoon paprika
4 tablespoons butter

3 to 4 shallots, chopped
1 cup sliced mushrooms
½ cup sweet white wine,
divided
1 tablespoon chopped parsley
Tarragon to taste

Mix flour, salt, pepper and paprika. Dredge veal in seasoned flour. Sauté slowly in butter. When browned, place in hot casserole to keep warm. To butter left in pan, add shallots and sauté 2 minutes. Add mushrooms; blend well. Add ¼ cup wine; cook until liquid is reduced. Add parsley and tarragon. Add another ¼ cup wine; bring to boil. Pour over veal. Place tight lid on casserole, and simmer 1 to 2 hours. Serves 6.

Nancy Moore, Grandparent of Hampton and Kirkland

Hey Hey's Chow Mein

¼ cup butter
1½ cups lean veal or cooked,
  diced chicken or turkey
1 cup chopped onions
1 teaspoon salt
1½ cups hot water
1½ cups canned mushrooms
1 cup bean sprouts, drained

Dash of pepper
2 cups finely chopped celery
2 tablespoons cold water
2 tablespoons corn starch
2 teaspoons soy sauce
1 teaspoon sugar
Water chestnuts (optional)
Bamboo shoots (optional)

Heat butter. Sear meat without browning. Add onions, celery, salt, and hot water. Cover and cook 5 to 6 minutes. Add mushrooms and bean sprouts. Mix thoroughly and bring to boil. Combine water, corn starch, soy sauce, and sugar; add to mixture. Mix lightly and cook 1 minute. If desired, add bamboo shoots and water chestnuts.

Harriette Sandeen, Grandparent of Matthew Franzeen

Chili Relleno Bake

8 eggs
3 tablespoons all-purpose
  flour
¾ cup milk
Salt and pepper to taste

6-8 cans (24-32 ounces) whole green chilies, drained and rinsed.

1 pound Monterey Jack
  cheese, shredded
1 pound cheddar cheese,
  shredded

Mix together eggs, flour, milk, salt and pepper. Grease 9x13x2-inch casserole dish. Layer chiles in bottom of casserole dish. Alternate layers of chiles and cheese (leave enough cheese for topping.) Pour egg mixture over layers and top with cheese. Bake in preheated 350° oven for 40 minutes.

Robin Wade, Parent of Bryan

City Chicken (which is not really chicken!)

½ pound pork	Bread crumbs (seasoned if
½ pound veal	you prefer)
1 egg, beaten	Butter
	1 cup milk

Cut pork and veal into 1-inch cubes. Thread on bamboo or wooden skewers, alternating chunks of pork and veal. Dip skewers in egg; coat with bread crumbs. Sauté in butter until browned. Put skewers in baking pan; add milk. Cover with foil. Bake in preheated 350° oven for about 1 hour.

Emily Wetzel, Grandparent of Deanna and Duncan

Pastalman Verde

2 tablespoons olive oil	4 ounces thinly sliced
1 cup finely chopped shallots	prosciutto, chopped
¼ teaspoon dried crushed red	⅔ cup grated asiago, divided
pepper	2 tablespoons fresh parsley,
½ cup vodka	chopped
¾ cup whipping cream	2 tablespoons chopped fresh
¾ cup tomato sauce	basil or 2 teaspoons dried
8 ounces rigatoni pasta,	basil
cooked	

Heat oil in large skillet over medium heat. Add shallots and red pepper; sauté until shallots are translucent, about 5 minutes. Add vodka and ignite with long match. Simmer until flames subside, about 2 minutes. Increase heat to high; add cream and boil until mixture thickens, about 3 minutes. Add tomato sauce; boil until sauce thickens and coats back of spoon, about 2 minutes. (Sauce can be made one day ahead.) Chill.

Bring sauce to simmer. Add pasta, prosciutto, ⅓ cup asiago, parsley, and basil to skillet. Toss to coat. Use remaining cheese to garnish plate. Serves 3 to 4.

Mary Green '93

Zucchini Lasagna

4 to 6 zucchini, approximately 9-inches long
2 cups part-skim ricotta cheese
2 cups part-skim shredded mozzarella cheese, divided
¼ cup grated Parmesan cheese
¼ cup chopped fresh parsley

2 eggs
¼ teaspoon ground black pepper
½ cup chopped onion
2 cloves garlic, crushed
1 (26-ounce) jar tomato and basil sauce
1 tablespoon sugar

Cut ends off zucchini; don't peel. Cut into 2-inch slices, lengthwise. Cook in boiling water for 5 minutes. Let cool; dry off. Mix together ricotta cheese, 1 cup mozzarella cheese, Parmesan cheese, parsley, eggs, and pepper. Mix together onion, garlic, tomato sauce, and sugar. Spread ¾ cup sauce on bottom of 9x13x2-inch pan. Arrange ⅓ zucchini on top. Spread ½ cheese mixture on zucchini, then ¾ cup sauce over cheese mixture. Repeat once, using ⅓ zucchini, other ½ cheese mixture, and ¾ cup sauce. Finish with last ⅓ zucchini and ¾ cup sauce. Top with 1 cup mozzarella cheese. Cover with foil. Bake in preheated 350° oven for 30 minutes or until hot and bubbly. Remove foil; bake 10 minutes longer. Let stand 10 minutes before cutting. Serves 6 to 8.

Mary Carini, Grandparent of Daniel Broussard

Eggplant–Zucchini Spaghetti Casserole

2 (8-ounce) cans tomato
  sauce
2 teaspoons Worcestershire
  sauce
Freshly ground black pepper
1 teaspoon oregano
½ teaspoon basil
½ teaspoon marjoram
2 cloves garlic, crushed
1 eggplant, peeled and cut
  into ¼-inch slices

2 zucchini, peeled and cut into
  ¼-inch slices
1 cup uncooked spaghetti,
  broken into pieces
3 stalks celery, chopped
1 onion, chopped
1 green pepper, chopped
8 ounces sliced mozzarella
  cheese, cut into 18 pieces
  2x3½-inches

Combine tomato sauce, Worcestershire sauce, pepper, oregano, basil, marjoram, and garlic; mix well. In 9x13x2-inch casserole dish, arrange ½ eggplant in a single layer, ½ spaghetti, ½ zucchini, ½ celery, onion, and green pepper. Spoon ½ tomato sauce mixture evenly over spaghetti and vegetables. Arrange 9 slices of cheese on top of tomato sauce mixture. Repeat layers (except for onion and green pepper). Bake, covered, in preheated 350° oven for 1 hour or until vegetables are tender. Serves 8.

Note: 260 calories per servings.

Libbie Crabtree, Wife of Headmaster Ben Crabtree

Pineapple Glaze

1 (8-ounce) can crushed
  pineapple
1 cup firmly packed brown
  sugar

1 tablespoon mustard
1 teaspoon dry mustard
Juice of 1 lemon

Drain syrup from pineapple and reserve. In blender, combine drained pineapple and remaining ingredients; blend until smooth. Add as much of the reserved syrup as necessary to have the mixture of good spreading consistency. Brush over meat during barbecuing. Makes 1½ cups.

Joyce Rhoads, Grandparent of Brian and Laura Kastner

Stromboli

1 loaf frozen bread dough, thawed or homemade bread dough
1 egg, beaten
1 teaspoon oregano
6 slices provolone cheese
1 (12-ounce) package pepperoni slices

On lightly floured surface, roll dough into 12x14-inch rectangle. (Mentally divide dough into 3 sections.) Beat egg and oregano together. Brush egg mixture in center of dough. Place provolone cheese slices down center; place pepperoni slices on top of cheese. Take right side of dough and fold over layers to the left. Repeat process of egg, cheese, and pepperoni. Take left side of dough, fold over to right. Tuck under loaf on side and top and bottom. Brush top with egg and bake in preheated 375° oven for 20 to 30 minutes. Cut into 2-inch slices. Makes 1 loaf.

Diane Discavage, Parent of Beth '97 and Sara

Grilled Marinated Leg of Lamb

4 cloves garlic, minced
⅔ cup lemon juice
⅓ cup dry white vermouth
1 teaspoon salt
1 teaspoon ground black pepper
1 tablespoon rosemary
¼ cup olive oil
¼ cup Worcestershire sauce
1 (6-pound) leg of lamb, butterflied
⅔ cup Dijon mustard

Combine garlic, lemon juice, vermouth, salt, pepper, rosemary, olive oil, and Worcestershire sauce for marinade. Place lamb in marinade for 24 hours in refrigerator, turning occasionally. Before putting lamb on grill, beat with a wooden mallet until meat is uniformly flat and less thick. Put on grill; brush with Dijon mustard and marinade. Cook 20 minutes. Turn; brush with mustard and marinade. Cook 20 minutes. If you prefer meat less rare, cook for a longer time. Take off grill. Slice and serve. Serves 6 to 8.

Nina Godwin, Grandparent of Harry, Lacy, and Laura

Pasta Carbonara

1 pound bacon, fried, drained
   and crumbled
1 cup heavy cream
Red or black pepper to taste
2 whole eggs

2 egg yolks
1 cup grated Parmesan cheese
1 pound of your favorite pasta

Save ½ of bacon drippings in pan; add cream. Add crumbled bacon and pepper. Bring to boil; simmer 6 minutes, stirring occasionally. Simmer until reduced to ½ its original amount. Remove from heat. In separate bowl, combine eggs, egg yolks, and cheese. Mix well; set aside.

Cook pasta as directed on package. Drain well and return to pot. Immediately add both mixtures. Mix well and serve promptly. Serves 6 to 8.

Gloria Bownas, Parent of Briggen

Barbara's Teriyaki Marinade

¼ cup cooking oil
¼ cup soy sauce
¼ cup dry sherry
2 tablespoons molasses or
   corn syrup

1 clove garlic, minced
1 tablespoon grated fresh
   ginger root or 1 teaspoon
   ground ginger

Combine all ingredients. Pour over chicken, pork or beef. Marinate for 4 to 6 hours. Drain; reserve marinade and use to baste meat. Heat marinade to boil to use as "au jus" over meat. Makes enough for 2 pounds of meat.

Barbara Gobien, Parent of Jacqueline and Jeremy

Chris's Teriyaki Marinade

½ cup soy sauce (lite or
regular)
¼ cup sherry
3 to 4 tablespoons brown
sugar

½ teaspoon ginger
1 garlic clove, crushed
1 pinch dry mustard

Mix all ingredients in advance to let flavors blend. Marinate flank steak or chicken overnight. Grill.

Chris Kastner, Parent of Brian and Laura

Spinach Lasagna

4 cloves garlic
1 small onion
4 tablespoons extra virgin
olive oil, divided
3 (12-ounce) cans tomato
sauce
2 (6-ounce) cans tomato paste
½ cup red wine
2 tablespoons brown sugar

1 tablespoon oregano
2 teaspoons basil
6 lasagna noodles,
cooked al dente
1½ pounds fresh baby
spinach, chopped
8 ounces ricotta cheese
8 ounces mozzarella cheese
16 ounces provolone cheese

Smash and mince garlic; mince onion. Heat 3 tablespoons oil on medium-low; add onion and garlic; stir until onion begins to turn transluscent (do not brown). Add tomato sauce, tomato paste, and wine; stir to mix. Add brown sugar, oregano, and basil. Simmer over low heat until reduced by ¼, about 30 to 40 minutes.

Coat 9x13x2-inch pan with 1 tablespoon olive oil. Using ⅓ of each ingredient, layer in this order: noodles, sauce, spinach, cheeses. Overlap noodles to keep sauce from leaking through. Repeat. Then make third complete layer in this order: noodles, spinach, sauce, cheeses, putting provolone on top. (Sauce keeps spinach from drying out.) Cover with aluminum foil, making a tent to keep it from sticking to cheese.

Bake in preheated 350° oven for 40 minutes. Uncover and bake 10 to 15 minutes or until cheese is brown. Remove and let stand 15 minutes before cutting.

Steve Shoup, Parent of Mary

Vegetarian Stir Fry

2 cups regular rice
2½ cups water
2 eggs, beaten
½ small onion
3 cloves garlic, smashed and minced
4 Thai peppers or other type pepper, chopped (optional)
¼ green pepper
⅛ teaspoon ginger
¼ cup frozen peas
6 medium, fresh mushrooms

¼ cup diced tomatoes
8 ounces firm tofu, cut in 1-inch squares
2 tablespoons fish sauce or 3 tablespoons soy sauce
⅛ cup chopped fresh cilantro
½ cup sliced cucumbers
⅛ cup chopped green onion
1 tablespoon sesame seeds
1 tablespoon sesame oil
Juice of ½ lemon

In medium saucepan cook rice in water just until firm in center; refrigerate overnight or until completely cooled.

Chop vegetables into thin slices, 1- to 2-inches long. In wok or large, heavy, high-sided skillet, heat 2 tablespoons oil on high. Scramble eggs just until soft; remove. Add remaining oil, onions, garlic, green pepper, ginger, rice, eggs, and peppers; stir continuously and smash ingredients with back of spatula 4 to 5 minutes. Add more oil by tablespoons if necessary to keep rice from sticking. Add peas, mushroom, tomato, and tofu. Stir without smashing until rice is tender, 3 to 4 minutes. Remove from heat; stir in fish or soy sauce. Garnish with cilantro, cucumbers, green onions, and sesame seeds. Drizzle sesame oil and lemon juice; serve immediately. Serves 4.

Note: You can also add carrots, bamboo shoots, fresh green beans, broccoli, water chestnuts, or any other firm vegetable. Chop in thin pieces, using ¼ to ⅓ cup of each. Also, any vegetable can be left out. If desired, add other soft vegetables with the mushroom, tomato, and tofu.

Steve Shoup, Parent of Mary

Accompaniments

Accompaniments

Pasta, Rice, and Beans

Fettuccine with Tomato-Basil Cream Sauce

2 tablespoons butter
2 tablespoons all-purpose flour
2 cloves garlic, chopped
2 cups heavy cream
Salt and pepper

1 cup fresh basil, shredded
1 pound fettuccine noodles, cooked al dente
2 large tomatoes, chopped
Fresh parsley, chopped
Parmesan cheese, grated

Heat butter. Add flour; mix until smooth. Add garlic; mix until smooth. Add cream; whisk until blended. Add salt, pepper, and basil. Add cooked fettuccine noodles and tomatoes. Heat thoroughly. Serve hot. Garnish with fresh parsley and Parmesan cheese.

Note: This is equally good with sautéed shrimp or chicken filet strips. Add to sauce before fettuccine noodles. Heat thoroughly then add noodles and tomatoes. Serves 4 to 6.

Megg Potter Rader '79

Halushki (a quick noodle dish)

1 package wide noodles
1 head cabbage
Butter

Water
Salt and pepper

Cook noodles; drain. Cut up cabbage. Add butter and water. Cook until cabbage is done, making sure no water remains (5 to 7 minutes). Pour cabbage over noodles; mix well. Add salt and pepper.

Note: The amount of ingredients you use depends on how much halushki you want to make. Experiment!

Emily Wetzel, Grandparent of Deanna and Duncan

Szechwan Noodles

12 to 14 garlic cloves
1-inch ginger root
½ cup rice vinegar
1 pound Chinese noodles or
 angel hair pasta
¼ cup peanut oil
1 to 2 teaspoons hot pepper
 flakes

1 teaspoon ground black
 pepper
5 tablespoons tahini
 (sesame paste)
1 cup soy sauce
2 teaspoons sugar
1 bunch scallions, chopped

Peel and mince garlic and ginger root. Mash to smooth paste in food processor. Put in large bowl with vinegar; stir and set aside. Bring 6 quarts water to rapid boil; add noodles and cook according to directions on package. Drain well and toss with peanut oil. Add pepper flakes, pepper, tahini, soy sauce, and sugar to garlic-ginger mixture. Toss with noodles until they glisten with sauce. Add chopped scallions. This is best served chilled, but is also good warm.

Note: Tahini is available in oriental section of grocery stores.

Linda Blair, Trustee, Parent of Jennifer '96,
Ashley '98, Emily '99, and Amanda

Bean and Cheese Enchiladas

1 large onion, chopped
1 teaspoon vegetable oil
2 (15-ounce) cans kidney
  beans
3 tablespoons chili powder,
  divided
¾ teaspoon garlic powder,
  divided

11 ounces taco or enchilada
  sauce, divided
½ cup cottage cheese
8 large corn tortillas
¾ teaspoon onion powder
4 ounces grated cheddar
  cheese

Sauté onion in oil until soft. Drain beans; mash and add to onions. Add 2 tablespoons chili powder, ½ teaspoon garlic powder, 3 tablespoons taco sauce, and cottage cheese; mix well.

If tortillas are brittle, steam until soft. Place 3 tablespoons mixture on each tortilla; roll up. Place seam side down in 9x13x2-inch baking dish. In small bowl, combine remaining sauce, garlic powder, chili powder, and onion powder. Stir; pour over enchiladas. Sprinkle with cheese. Cover and bake in preheated 350° oven for 25 minutes.

Julia Tingler, Parent of Lauren

Easy Black Beans and Rice

1 clove garlic, minced
2 to 3 tablespoons chopped
  green pepper
2 to 3 tablespoons chopped
  onion

1 to 2 tablespoons olive oil
1 (15-ounce) can black beans
1 bay leaf
1 tablespoon vinegar
1 cup cooked rice

Sauté garlic, green pepper, and onion in olive oil. Add black beans and bay leaf; simmer 4 to 5 minutes. Just before serving, add vinegar. Serve over rice. Serves 2.

Betty Campbell, Grandparent of Janene '99,
Cara, and Jacqueline Allison

Neighborhood Baked Beans

1 medium onion, chopped
1 (15-ounce) can baked beans
   in tomato sauce
1 (15-ounce) can kidney
   beans, drained
1 (15-ounce) can lima or
   garbanzo beans, drained

¼ pound sharp cheddar
   cheese, cubed
2 tablespoons brown sugar
2 teaspoons Worcestershire
   sauce
¼ cup ketchup
1 teaspoon mustard

Mix all ingredients together. Bake in preheated 350° oven for 1 hour. Serves 6 to 8.

Note: If desired, browned and drained ground beef may be added.

Betty Southard, Grandparent of Peter '99 and Anna Buryk

Fiesta Baked Beans

6 strips bacon
1 medium onion, chopped
½ green pepper, chopped
½ pound boiled ham, cubed
2 (16-ounce) cans pork-and-
   beans
½ cup chili sauce

¼ cup brown sugar
1 tablespoon molasses
1 tablespoon Worcestershire
   sauce
½ teaspoon salt
¼ teaspoon pepper
2 to 3 drops liquid smoke

Cook bacon until crisp. Drain and crumble. Sauté onion and green pepper in 2 tablespoons drippings for 5 minutes. Add ham and sauté 5 minutes more. Combine with remaining ingredients in shallow 9x11-inch baking dish. Bake in pre-heated 350° oven for 45 minutes. Serves 8 to 10.

Note: For vegetarians, eliminate bacon and ham. Use vegetarian beans. Use vegetable oil to sauté onion and green pepper.

Caroline Withers, Parent of Katherine '97 and Jonathan

Fiesta Black Beans

1 (15-ounce) can tomatoes,
  drained (may use fresh
  chopped tomatoes)
1 (15-ounce) can black beans
1 teaspoon olive oil
2 teaspoons Creole
  seasoning, divided

1 (7-ounce) can whole chiles,
  coarsely chopped
1 cup frozen, whole kernel
  corn
2 tablespoons chopped fresh
  cilantro
½ to 1 cup shredded Mexican
  (or mild cheddar) cheese

Toss tomatoes, beans and olive oil; place in casserole dish. Sprinkle with 1 teaspoon Creole seasoning. Layer chiles, corn, and cilantro on top; sprinkle with remaining Creole seasoning. Top with shredded cheese. Cover and bake in preheated 350° oven for 20 to 30 minutes or on grill until heated thoroughly. Serves 4 to 6.

Linda Tillman, Parent of Scott '98

Rice with Mushrooms

1 cup rice, uncooked
1 cup chopped tomato
1 pound mushrooms, sliced
½ cup chopped onions
½ cup butter or margarine
3 cups chicken broth

½ cup red wine
1½ teaspoons salt
⅛ teaspoon pepper
1 cup green peas, cooked
¼ cup grated Parmesan
  cheese

In large skillet, cook rice, tomato, mushrooms, and onions in butter for 10 minutes, stirring occasionally. Add broth, wine, salt, and pepper. Mix well. Cover and simmer 45 minutes or until rice is tender and liquid is absorbed. Stir in peas. Heat and sprinkle with cheese. Serves 6.

Edith Gobien, Grandparent of Jacqueline and Jeremy

Dirty Rice

¼ cup margarine
1 medium onion, chopped
½ green pepper, chopped
  (optional)
1 can beef consommé
1¼ cups water

1 cup rice, uncooked
1 (4-ounce) can mushrooms
  with juice
2 teaspoons beef bouillon
1 (4-ounce) jar pimento
  (optional)

Melt margarine. Sauté onion and green pepper until tender. Add consommé, water, rice, mushrooms, and bouillon. Pour into greased 2-quart casserole or 9x13x2-inch baking dish. Bake in preheated 350° oven for 1 hour. Garnish with pimento.

Kay Boyette, Parent of Allison and Meredith

Spanish Rice

1 cup rice, uncooked
3 tablespoons bacon
  drippings
1 medium onion, finely
  chopped
1 garlic clove, minced
1½ cups canned tomatoes,
  diced

2 tablespoons minced green
  pepper
1 teaspoon cumin
2 tablespoons minced carrots
1 (10-ounce) can chicken
  broth

Brown rice well in hot bacon drippings. Add remaining ingredients. Cover and cook slowly until all liquid is absorbed, about 25 minutes.

Susan Barnes, Parent of Zack

Granny's Rice Pilaf

When I was a little girl, I lived next door to my grand-mother. It was a wonderful place where I could have tea parties with Granny and then fall asleep in her lap as she rocked me in her old wooden rocking chair. When I wasn't feeling well, Granny used to make this rice. It is mild enough that it sure tasted good on an upset tummy!

8 tablespoons butter, divided   1 cup chopped carrots
1½ cups rice, uncooked   1 cup chopped celery
¼ cup chopped onion   3 cups chicken broth

In large saucepan, melt 6 tablespoons butter; add rice and onion. Sauté 5 minutes; add carrots, celery, and broth. Bring to boil. Cover; reduce heat and simmer 15 minutes. Remove from heat; add 2 tablespoons butter. Fluff with fork.

Maggie Franzeen, F.A. Staff, Parent of Matthew

Bunny's Oyster Stuffing

1 pound bulk pork sausage   2 pints oysters with liquid
1 large green pepper, chopped   2 (16-ounce) packages herb-
1 large onion, chopped   seasoned bread crumbs
3 stalks celery, chopped   2 cans chicken broth
4 tablespoons vegetable oil

Brown pork sausage and set aside. Sauté green pepper, onion, and celery in vegetable oil until soft. Add oysters and oyster liquid; cook 5 to 8 minutes. Add bread crumbs 1 cup at a time, alternating with chicken broth. Mix until all broth and crumbs have been added. Add water for moister dressing.

Gwenesta Barnum Melton, Trustee, Parent of Kurston

Vegetables
Asparagus Casserole

Sliced potatoes	1 can cream of mushroom
Sliced onions	soup
1 (15-ounce) can asparagus	1¼ cups water

Using any size casserole dish, place one layer of sliced potatoes, about ⅛-inch thick in bottom of dish. Add one layer of sliced onions, about ⅛-inch thick. Add layer of asparagus. Thin soup with water; pour on top. Bake in preheated 325° oven for 20 to 30 minutes or until potatoes are tender. (Use a fork to check them.)

Note: You might need to add another cup of water; be sure there is enough liquid in casserole to maintain moisture.

Mary Lyn Maulden Morgan '81

Patsy's Asparagus

1 pound fresh trimmed	⅓ cup grated Parmesan
asparagus	cheese
4 tablespoons butter, divided	

Steam asparagus until just tender. Dot bottom of oven-proof casserole with butter. Arrange a single layer of asparagus and dot with butter. Sprinkle ½ cheese on top. Repeat layers until all ingredients are used. Bake in preheated 450° oven for 10 minutes until crusty and golden. Serves 4.

Patsy Welsher, Parent of Shana '99 and David

Barbequed Butter Beans

4 slices bacon
½ onion, chopped
1 clove garlic, mashed
2 tablespoons all-purpose
   flour
3 tablespoons vinegar
1½ cups tomato juice

¾ teaspoon dry mustard
½ teaspoon salt
3 tablespoons sugar
Dash pepper
3 cups tiny green butter
   beans, cooked

Cook bacon until crisp. Remove from pan. Cook onion and garlic in drippings until tender. Add remaining ingredients except butter beans. Cook 5 minutes, stirring until thickened and smooth. Add butter beans and pour into casserole dish. Stir crumbled bacon into mixture or sprinkle on top. Bake in preheated 350° oven for 35 minutes. Serves 6 to 8.

Judy Lennon, Parent of Hannah '95, Evan '98, and Ben

Broccoli with Balsamic Butter

1 large head broccoli, broken
   into florets
2 tablespoons balsamic
   vinegar

2 tablespoons dry red wine
6 tablespoons butter, cut into
   small pieces
Salt and pepper to taste

Steam broccoli in vegetable steamer until just tender. Combine vinegar and wine in small pan and boil until reduced by half. Remove pan from heat. Whisk butter in gradually until sauce becomes creamy. Season with salt and pepper to taste. Place broccoli in serving dish. Pour sauce over broccoli, tossing to coat well. Serve hot. Serves 4 to 6.

Patsy Welsher, Parent of Shana '99 and David

Cheese Scalloped Carrots

12 medium carrots, peeled and
   sliced
1 small onion, chopped
¼ cup butter
¼ cup all-purpose flour
1 teaspoon salt
¼ teaspoon dry mustard

2 cups milk
⅛ teaspoon pepper
¼ teaspoon celery salt
½ pound grated sharp
   cheddar cheese
2 cups fresh buttered bread
   crumbs

Cook carrots in boiling water until tender; drain. In sauce-pan, sauté onion in butter 2 to 3 minutes. Stir in flour, salt, mustard, and milk. Cook, stirring until smooth. Add pepper and celery salt. In casserole, layer carrots and cheese. Repeat, ending with carrots. Pour sauce over carrots and top with bread crumbs. Bake in preheated 350° oven for 35 to 45 minutes. Serves 6.

Rachael Squires, Grandparent of John and Margaret Lingle

Ginger Glazed Carrots

2 pounds carrots, peeled and
   sliced
½ cup butter
2 cups brown sugar

⅛ teaspoon nutmeg
½ teaspoon ginger
¼ cup white wine

Cook carrots in salted water. Melt butter; add brown sugar, nutmeg, ginger and wine. Put carrots in 1-quart casserole, pour sauce over carrots. Refrigerate overnight. Bake in preheated 350° oven for 15 to 20 minutes. Serves 6 to 8.

Sharon McDaniel, Wife of Greg '76, Parent of Jack

Corn Casserole

1 (12-ounce) can cream-style corn	1 tablespoon diced celery
¼ cup grated green pepper	1 teaspoon chopped onion
¼ cup grated carrots	½ teaspoon sugar
¼ cup evaporated milk	½ teaspoon salt
½ cup grated cheese	6 drops hot pepper sauce
2 eggs, beaten	½ cup crushed saltine crackers
	¼ cup melted butter

Combine all ingredients except crackers and butter. Pour into lightly greased casserole dish. Top with saltines and melted butter. Bake in preheated 350° oven for 35 minutes. Serves 6.

Rachael Squires, Grandparent of John and Margaret Lingle

Cornelia's Corn Pudding

¼ cup sugar	6 eggs
3 tablespoons all-purpose flour	2 cups whipping cream
	½ teaspoon butter
2 teaspoons baking powder	6 cups fresh corn kernels (or 6
2 teaspoons salt	cups frozen shoepeg corn)

Combine sugar, flour, baking powder, and salt. In large bowl, beat eggs with fork; stir in cream and butter. Gradually add sugar mixture, stirring until smooth. Stir in corn. Pour into greased 9x13x2-inch baking pan. Bake in preheated 350° oven for 45 minutes or until mixture is set. Let stand 5 minutes. Serves 8.

Cornelia Hilburn, Parent of Amanda and Ben

Summertime Cukes

4 to 5 medium cucumbers,
  peeled and thinly sliced
1 tablespoon salt
1 tablespoon vegetable oil
1 tablespoon white vinegar

2 teaspoons sugar
¼ teaspoon pepper
1 Vidalia onion or green
  onions, chopped
Paprika

Place sliced cucumbers in colander. Sprinkle with salt and let stand 20 to 30 minutes. Toss occasionally. Rinse and drain. Combine oil, vinegar, sugar, and pepper in bowl; add cucumbers and stir. Place onions on top and sprinkle with paprika. Refrigerate until serving or add a few ice cubes to chill.

Frances Bowyer, Former Trustee,
Parent of Robert '90 and Wendell '88

Daylily Stir Fry

1 cup daylily buds, chopped
  (pesticide free)
½ cup celery, sliced thinly on
  the diagonal
1 bunch green onions,
  chopped
1 head broccoli, cut into
  bite-size pieces

2 medium carrots, cut into
  thin rounds
½ head cauliflower, cut into
  florets
3 tablespoons oil
Toasted sesame seeds
Daylily petals

In large frying pan or wok, heat oil. Add broccoli, carrots and cauliflower; stir-fry 5 minutes, covering between frequent stirrings. Add celery, daylily buds, and green onions. Cook 5 more minutes, covering between frequent stirrings. Serve immediately or refrigerate and microwave as needed. Garnish with daylily petals and sesame seeds. Serves 4.

Winifred Jernigan Williams, Former Parent,
In Memory of Bettie Godwin Jernigan

Eggplant Parmesan

3 tablespoons butter or
   margarine
2 or 3 small eggplants
½ cup Parmesan cheese
½ cup bread crumbs

2 eggs
1 (16-ounce) can seasoned
   tomato sauce
1 (8-ounce) package shredded
   mozzarella cheese

Melt butter in 9x13x2-inch baking pan; set aside. Peel
eggplant and slice in circles ½-inch thick. Mix Parmesan
cheese and bread crumbs in small bowl and set aside. Beat
eggs. Dip each eggplant slice in egg, coating both sides. Then
dip in cheese-bread crumb mixture, coating both sides. Place
slices in single layer in prepared pan. Bake in preheated 375°
oven for 20 minutes. Turn each slice and bake 15 minutes
more. Pour seasoned tomato sauce over slices, then top with
mozzarella cheese. Return to oven for 5 more minutes or until
cheese is melted.

Susan Williams, Parent of Catherine and Sam

Fried Eggplant

2 pounds eggplant
2 cups rice flour
1 teaspoon red chili powder

1 teaspoon pepper
Salt to taste
4 tablespoons sesame seeds

Cut eggplant into ½-inch thick circles. Mix flour, red chili
powder, pepper, and salt; toss with eggplant slices. Sprinkle
sesame seeds over each slice and press so they stick. Deep
fry each slice and place on serving dish. Serves 4.

Huma Hyder-Haque, Parent of Imad

Kathie's Baked Eggplant

Since my twin sister and I don't have "twin names," our husbands do! They are Glenn and Ben. I believe that Glenn got the real homemaker. She bakes, cans, freezes, makes pickles and preserves ... I make the beds!

1 eggplant	Salt and pepper to taste
1 onion	¾ cup milk
2 eggs, beaten	1 tablespoon butter, melted
Dash hot sauce	2 cups shredded cheese
8 to 10 saltine crackers, crushed	

Peel and dice eggplant and onion. Slowly simmer in water 15 to 20 minutes or until tender. Drain well; set aside. Mix remaining ingredients. Gently stir into eggplant mixture. Spoon into well-greased 1½-quart casserole. Bake in preheated 350° oven for 30 minutes.

Kathie Smith, Libbie Crabtree's twin sister
(Libbie is the wife of Headmaster Ben Crabtree)

Green Bean Casserole

2 (9-ounce) frozen packages green beans, thawed or 2 (14-ounce) cans green beans, drained	¾ can milk
1 can cream of mushroom soup	1½ cups mild or sharp cheddar cheese, divided
1 (2.8-ounce) can French fried onion rings, divided	1 cup water chestnuts, chopped

Mix ingredients together, reserving ½ cup onion rings and ½ cup cheese. Pour into 2-quart casserole. Sprinkle top with remaining onion rings and cheese. Bake in preheated 350° oven for 30 minutes. Serves 4 to 6.

Rhonda Dees, Board of Trustees Chair, Parent of Sarah

Sesame Green Beans

1 pound fresh green beans,
cut julienne
3 tablespoons tamari or soy
sauce
1 tablespoon sesame oil

¼ teaspoon nutmeg
4 large mushrooms, sliced
¼ to ½ cup sesame seeds,
toasted

Steam beans until crisp-tender, about 10 minutes. Combine tamari sauce, oil, and nutmeg in large skillet over low to medium heat. Add mushrooms and sauté just until tender. Add beans and toss lightly. Add sesame seeds and toss again. Serve immediately. Serves 6.

Janice McDaniel, Parent of Greg '76
Grandparent of Jack

Meredith's Mushroom Pie

3 tablespoons butter
1 large onion, thinly sliced
1½ pounds mushrooms, sliced
1 teaspoon salt
Dash pepper
½ teaspoon Worcestershire
sauce

1 tablespoon lemon juice
½ pound Swiss cheese, grated
1 pie crust, plus lattice strips
(made from second frozen
crust, if you want)

Sauté onion in butter for 3 minutes or until tender. Add mushrooms, salt, pepper, Worcestershire sauce, and lemon juice; cook 5 to 7 minutes, stirring often. Drain. Stir in cheese. Fill crust and weave lattice top. Bake in preheated 375° oven for 35 to 40 minutes. Allow to stand 10 minutes before serving.

Meredith McCambridge, Parent of Gordon

Janice's Mushroom Pie

2 to 2½ pounds fresh
  mushrooms
6 tablespoons butter, divided
2 shallots or green onions,
  minced
Salt and pepper
Juice of 2 lemons

4 tablespoons all-purpose
  flour
1½ cups chicken stock
½ cup Madeira wine
½ cup whipping cream, heated
1 pie crust mix
1 egg, beaten

Wash, dry, and trim mushrooms. Slice thickly, leaving very small ones whole. Heat 4 tablespoons butter in large, non-aluminum skillet; add mushrooms, shallots and lemon juice. Sprinkle with salt and pepper. Cook 10 minutes, stirring occasionally. Place mushrooms in center of 2-quart casserole. Add remaining butter to juices in pan; stir in flour and stock. Cook stirring constantly until sauce is thickened. Add wine and hot cream; adjust seasoning. Pour sauce over mushrooms and cover with pie crust made according to directions. Brush with beaten egg and cut slits in top to release steam. Bake in preheated 450° oven for 15 minutes; reduce heat to 300° and bake 15 minutes more.

Janice McDaniel, Parent of Greg '76
Grandparent of Jack

Sandra's Vidalia Onion Pie

2 pounds Vidalia onions, thinly
  sliced
½ cup butter
3 eggs, well beaten
1 cup sour cream

¼ teaspoon salt
½ teaspoon white pepper
Dash of hot pepper sauce
1 pastry shell, unbaked
Grated Parmesan cheese

Sauté onion in butter. Combine eggs and sour cream. Add to onion mixture. Season with salt, pepper, and hot pepper sauce; pour in pastry shell. Top with cheese. Bake in preheated 450° oven for 20 minutes; reduce heat to 325° for 20 more minutes.

Sandra Jameson, Parent of Matt '97 and Cal

Caroline's Vidalia Onion Pie

½ cup milk
1 teaspoon salt
3 tablespoons all-purpose
   flour
1½ cups sour cream
2 eggs, lightly beaten

3 cups sliced Vidalia onions
4 strips bacon, fried and
   crumbled
1 (9-inch) pastry shell,
   unbaked

Mix milk, salt, flour, sour cream, and eggs. Arrange onions and bacon in pie shell. Pour egg mixture over onions. Bake in preheated 350° oven for 45 minutes to 1 hour or until center is set.

Caroline Withers, Parent of Katherine '97 and Jonathan

Golden Potato Casserole

6 medium potatoes
¼ cup butter
2 cups shredded cheddar
   cheese
2 cups sour cream

⅓ cup chopped green onions
1 teaspoon salt
¼ teaspoon white pepper
2 tablespoons butter
Paprika (optional)

Cook potatoes in skins; chill. Peel and grate into mixing bowl. Combine butter and cheese in saucepan over low heat, stirring often until almost melted. Remove from heat; blend in sour cream, onions, salt, and pepper. Pour over potatoes; stir lightly and turn into 2-quart casserole dish. Dot with 2 table-spoons butter. Sprinkle with paprika. Bake in preheated 350° oven for 45 minutes. Serves 6 to 8.

Judy Brustad, Parent of Andrew, Jennifer and Theresa

New Potato Casserole

12 medium-size new potatoes
¼ cup chopped pimento
¼ cup chopped onion

1 pound processed cheese
loaf, cubed
1 cup bread crumbs
¼ cup butter, melted

Boil potatoes about 10 minutes – potatoes should not be completely cooked. Cut into bite-size pieces. Arrange potatoes in baking dish. Sprinkle with chopped pimento and onion; add cheese cubes. Sprinkle with bread crumbs and pour butter over the top. Bake in preheated 350° oven for 20 minutes. Serves 6.

Liza Latella '94

Cheesy Potato-Carrot Foil Bake

3 large potatoes, thinly sliced
3 medium carrots, peeled and
shredded
¼ cup sliced green onions
Salt and pepper to taste

¼ cup butter or margarine
4 slices bacon, fried and
crumbled
1 cup shredded Monterey Jack
cheese

Fold a 36x18-inch piece of heavy duty foil in ½ to make an 18-inch square. Fold up sides, using your fist to form a pouch. Place potatoes into pouch; add carrots and green onions. Sprinkle with salt and pepper; dot with butter. Fold edges of foil to seal pouch securely, leaving space for expansion of steam.

Grill over slow coals 55 to 60 minutes or until done; turn several times. Open package; stir in crumbled bacon and cheese. Close pouch; return to grill for 2 minutes or until cheese melts. Serves 6.

Blair Broadfoot Knowlton '84

Two-Cheese Potatoes

6 medium-size potatoes
2 cups small-curd cottage
  cheese
1 cup sour cream
1 small onion, finely chopped

2 tablespoons finely chopped
  parsley
1 teaspoon dried dill weed
1½ teaspoons salt
½ cup shredded cheddar
  cheese

Cook potatoes with small amount of water until tender; cool slightly. Peel and thinly slice potatoes into large bowl. Combine cottage cheese, sour cream, onion, parsley, dill, and salt; add to potatoes, stirring gently. Spoon potato mixture into a lightly buttered 1½-quart casserole; sprinkle with shredded cheese. Bake in preheated 350° oven for 30 to 40 minutes. Serves 8.

Frances Bowyer, Parent of Robert '90 and Wendell '88

Rotel Potatoes

5 or 6 large potatoes, peeled
  and cut in chunks
1 green pepper, diced
1 onion, diced

½ cup butter or margarine
1 pound processed cheese
  loaf
1 can diced Rotel tomatoes

In large pan, boil potatoes until tender. Drain. Place in casserole. Sauté green pepper and onion in butter. Add cheese; stir until melted. Add tomatoes; pour over potatoes in casserole. Bake in preheated 350° oven until hot and bubbly. Serves 8.

Bernice Oswalt, Grandparent of Allison and Jennifer

Potato Casserole

1 (2-pound) package frozen
  hashbrown potatoes
1 (16-ounce) container sour
  cream
½ cup margarine
1 can cream of chicken soup

1 can cream of mushroom
  soup
1 cup grated cheddar cheese
2 to 3 cups crushed
  cornflakes

Mix all ingredients except cornflakes together. Pour into 9x13x2-inch baking dish and bake in preheated 375° oven for 45 minutes. Remove from oven and add crushed cornflakes on top. Dot with more margarine and bake an additional 30 minutes. Serves 10 to 12.

Note: This may be prepared the night before. You may also substitute cream of potato soup for the chicken and mushroom soups.

Elizabeth Nunalee Hood '77
Mary Anne Dawkins, Parent of Johnny '77 and Dawn '81
Beckie Bishop, F.A. Faculty, Parent of Jenna and Megan

Spinach–Artichoke Casserole

½ cup chopped onion
4 tablespoons butter
1 (6-ounce) jar artichoke
  hearts, drained and
  chopped
2 (10-ounce) packages frozen
  chopped spinach, cooked
  and drained well

2 eggs, beaten
½ cup sour cream
¼ teaspoon garlic salt
2 tablespoons lemon juice
¾ cup Parmesan cheese,
  divided

Sauté onions in butter. Remove from heat; stir in spinach and artichoke hearts. In large bowl, combine eggs, sour cream, garlic salt, lemon juice, and all but 2 tablespoons cheese. Add vegetable mixture to sour cream mixture. Pour into greased 2-quart casserole. Sprinkle remaining cheese on top. Bake in preheated 350° oven for 25 to 30 minutes. Serves 6.

Irma Smith, Parent of CoCo

Texan Spinach

4 (10-ounce) packages frozen chopped spinach	1 teaspoon salt
½ cup butter or margarine, divided	½ teaspoon celery salt
	½ teaspoon garlic salt
1 small onion, chopped	2 teaspoons Worcestershire sauce
4 tablespoons all-purpose flour	12 ounces Monterey Jack cheese with jalapeños, cubed
1 cup evaporated milk	
1 teaspoon black pepper	1 cup bread crumbs

Cook spinach according to package directions. Drain well, reserving liquid for later use. In large saucepan, melt 4 table-spoons butter. Add onion and flour. Cook on medium-low 5 minutes. Do not brown. Stir in evaporated milk and 1 cup reserved liquid from spinach. Cook until thick. Add pepper, salt, celery salt, garlic salt, and Worcestershire sauce. Add cheese and stir until melted. Combine with drained spinach. Pour into greased casserole dish. Top with bread crumbs mixed with 4 tablespoons melted butter. Bake in preheated 350° oven for 30 minutes. Serves 10 to 12.

Meg Leyte-Vidal, Parent of Eddy and Tricia

Spinach Au Gratin

2 (10-ounce) packages frozen chopped spinach	Dash of nutmeg
	1 teaspoon onion powder
3 cups cooked rice	½ teaspoon salt
4 eggs, beaten	¼ teaspoon pepper
1 can cream of mushroom soup	¼ cup grated Parmesan cheese

Thaw, drain and separate spinach. Toss with rice. Combine eggs, soup, and seasonings; stir into spinach mixture. Turn into greased shallow 2½-quart casserole. Sprinkle with cheese. Bake in preheated 350° oven 30 minutes or until firm. Serves 6 to 8.

Virginia McQuillan, Grandparent of Brooke,
Garrett, Megan and Seth Ebel

Squash Casserole

2 medium onions, finely
 chopped
2 stalks celery, finely chopped
2 tablespoons butter
½ small package herb-
 seasoned stuffing mix,
 divided
1 (8-ounce) carton sour cream

2 pounds yellow squash,
 cooked whole and coarsely
 chopped
1 (8-ounce) can water chestnuts, finely chopped
1 can cream of chicken soup
1 (2-ounce) jar diced pimento

Cook onions and celery in butter until tender. Cover bottom of 2-quart casserole dish with part of stuffing mix. Mix all remaining ingredients. Pour over crumbs; cover with remaining stuffing mix. Bake in preheated 350° oven for 30 minutes or until bubbly. Serves 8 to 10.

Joyce Williams, Grandparent of Andrew, Jennifer and Theresa Brustad

South of the Border Squash

2 pounds yellow squash,
 sliced (about 6 medium)
2 cups crushed tortilla chips
1 (4½-ounce) can diced green
 chiles
¼ cup chopped onion
1 can cheddar cheese soup
1 can cream of mushroom
 soup

2 eggs, lightly beaten
2 tablespoons taco seasoning
 mix
1 cup shredded sharp cheddar
 cheese
4 slices bacon, cooked and
 crumbled

In saucepan, cover and cook squash in small amount of boiling water for 8 minutes or until tender; drain very well. Combine squash with tortilla chips, green chiles, onion, soups, eggs, and taco seasoning mix, stirring gently. Spoon into lightly greased 9x13x2-inch baking dish. Sprinkle evenly with cheese and bacon. Bake in preheated 450° oven for 30 minutes. Serves 8.

Marcia Kinlaw, Parent of Grey '98 and Zach

Butternut Squash

4 cups mashed squash or 2
(16-ounce) packages frozen
squash
2 eggs, beaten
⅓ cup butter, melted and
divided

¼ cup sugar
1½ cups cranberries, halved
½ teaspoon salt
⅛ teaspoon pepper
Dash nutmeg

Mix squash, eggs, and 3 tablespoons butter. Stir in sugar, cranberries, salt, and pepper. Spoon into buttered 2-quart casserole. Drizzle with remaining butter. Sprinkle with nutmeg. Bake in preheated 400° oven for 30 minutes. Serves 4 to 6.

Bea Elmen, Grandparent of Matt Benshoff

Sweet Potato Casserole

3 cups cooked, mashed sweet
potatoes
½ cup sugar
¼ cup milk
⅓ cup margarine, melted
1 teaspoon vanilla
2 eggs, beaten

Topping:
1 cup flaked coconut
1 cup firmly packed brown
sugar
⅓ cup all-purpose flour
⅓ cup margarine, melted
1 cup chopped pecans

Combine sweet potatoes, sugar, milk, margarine, vanilla, and eggs in large bowl; mix well. Spoon into greased 8x8-inch glass casserole. Combine topping ingredients and sprinkle over top. Bake in preheated 375° oven for 25 minutes or until golden brown. Serves 6.

Beth Bradford Davis '84, Parent of Brawley and Dottie
Gail Bolton, Parent of Meredith '97 and Trey '98

Tomato Pie

1 (9-inch) pie crust, unbaked
2 medium tomatoes, sliced and
    drained on paper towels
1 small onion, chopped
Basil

6 ounces cheddar cheese,
    grated
2 tablespoons mayonnaise
    (maybe slightly more)

Slightly bake pie crust. Do not brown. Layer tomato slices and onion. Sprinkle basil on top to taste. Mix cheese and mayonnaise so it is spreadable; spread on top. Bake in preheated 350° oven for 25 to 30 minutes. Serves 6 to 8.

Sharlene Riddle Williams '80

Turnips in Horseradish Cream

1¼ cups whipping cream
1¼ cups half and half
3 to 3¼ pounds turnips,
    peeled, halved, and thinly
    sliced

¼ cup cream-style horseradish
1 teaspoon minced fresh
    rosemary
Salt and pepper to taste

Lightly butter 8x8x2-inch glass baking dish. In large heavy saucepan, bring cream and half and half to boil over medium-high heat. Add turnips. Simmer until turnips just begin to soften, stirring occasionally, about 5 minutes. Using slotted spoon, transfer turnips to prepared dish. Mix horseradish and rosemary into liquids in pot. Season generously with salt and pepper. Pour liquids over turnips. Press firmly to compact. Cover dish with foil; bake in preheated 400° oven for 40 minutes. Uncover. Bake 30 minutes longer or until turnips are tender and top is browned. Let stand 10 minutes. Serves 6 to 8.

Janice McDaniel, Parent of Greg '76,
Grandparent of Jack

Susanne's Vegetable Casserole

1 (10-ounce) package frozen
  cauliflower, thawed
1 (16-ounce) jar carrots
1 (16-ounce) jar whole onions
1 (15½-ounce) can peas
1 (6-ounce) can sliced water
  chestnuts

½ pound sharp cheddar
  cheese, grated
2 cans cream of mushroom
  soup
1 cup fresh bread crumbs
1 tablespoon melted butter

Drain all vegetables. Arrange in greased casserole dish. In saucepan or microwave, melt sharp cheese with mushroom soup; pour over vegetables. Mix bread crumbs with melted butter and sprinkle on top of casserole. Bake in preheated 350° oven for 30 minutes.

Susanne Hux Long '77, Parent of Caroline and Claire

Vegetable Trio with Zippy Sauce

Vegetable Trio:
1 (10-ounce) box frozen lima
  beans, cooked and drained
1 (10-ounce) box frozen peas,
  cooked and drained
1 (10-ounce) box frozen
  French-style green beans,
  cooked and drained

Zippy Sauce:
1 cup mayonnaise
2 hard-boiled eggs, chopped
3 tablespoons lemon juice
2 tablespoons minced onions
1 teaspoon Worcestershire
  sauce
1 teaspoon prepared mustard
¼ teaspoon garlic salt

Mix hot vegetables and pour into serving dish. In small saucepan, mix sauce ingredients. Heat to warm and pour over hot vegetables. Serves 6 to 8.

Herma Delgado, Grandparent of Jennifer Godman '99

Marinated Chinese Vegetables

I am named for my mother's sister, Elizabeth. She is a fine lady of southern heritage. As is so often the case in churches in the south, certain persons are "expected" to bring certain things to the covered dish suppers. This is the dish Aunt Libba is always expected to bring. She shared the recipe with me when I was visiting one summer about 10 years ago and I always think of her when I fix it. I consider it a blessing to be named for her because she is so special. An interesting aspect to our personalities and careers is that she was the Director of Volunteer Services for the University of Mississippi Medical School Hospital, and I am the Volunteer Coordinator at Cape Fear Valley Health System.

1 (16-ounce) can French style
   green beans
1 (12-ounce) can small
   English peas
1 (14-ounce) can fancy
   Chinese vegetables
1 (6-ounce) can water chestnuts, sliced thin
1½ cups chopped celery
3 medium onions, chopped
1 (2-ounce) jar diced pimento
1 (6-ounce) jar marinated
   artichoke hearts, chopped

Marinade:
½ cup sugar or appropriate
   amount of Equal
1 teaspoon salt
Pepper to taste
¾ cup apple cider vinegar

Drain all canned vegetables. In large bowl, combine all vegetables. Set aside. In small bowl, mix marinade ingredients. Pour over vegetables. Refrigerate overnight.

Libbie Crabtree, Wife of Headmaster Ben Crabtree

Roasted Vegetables with Dip

Dip:
½ cup mayonnaise
¼ cup sour cream
2 tablespoons salsa
1 teaspoon minced garlic

Vegetables:
12 fresh mushrooms
1 medium red pepper, cut into
   strips
1 yellow squash, sliced
5 red potatoes, sliced and
   boiled until tender
3 tablespoons vegetable oil

Combine dip ingredients in small bowl and refrigerate for at least 2 hours. (Dip can be made ahead and refrigerated overnight.) Coat vegetables with oil. Place on baking sheet in single layer. Bake in preheated 450° oven for 10 minutes. Serves 4 to 6.

Martha DeGaetano, Parent of Robert

Summer Vegetables

Vegetable cooking spray
4 cloves garlic, minced
2 cups sliced zucchini
2 cups sliced yellow squash
1 cup chopped tomato

½ cup julienned green pepper
½ cup chicken broth
1 tablespoon chopped fresh
   basil or 1 teaspoon dried
   basil

Coat skillet with cooking spray. Heat over medium-high heat until hot. Sauté garlic 1 minute. Add zucchini, yellow squash, tomato, green pepper, and chicken broth. Cook 3 minutes or until vegetables are crisp tender, stirring constantly. Stir in basil. Serves 6.

Betty Dumas, Grandparent of Harry and Lacy Godwin

Barb's Veggie Casserole

2 (15-ounce) cans mixed
  vegetables, drained
1 cup chopped celery
1 cup chopped onions
1 (8-ounce) can sliced water
  chestnuts

1 cup grated sharp cheddar
  cheese
1 cup mayonnaise
½ cup round buttery cracker
  crumbs
½ cup margarine, melted

Combine mixed vegetables, celery, onions, water chestnuts, cheese, and mayonnaise; mix thoroughly. Spread mixture into non-greased 9x12-inch casserole dish. Sprinkle top with cracker crumbs. Drizzle margarine over top. Bake in preheated 350° oven for 30 minutes. Serves 8.

Barbara E. Lambert '76, F.A. Staff

Beth's Vegetable Casserole

2 (16-ounce) cans
  French-style green beans,
  drained
1 (16-ounce) can shoepeg
  corn, drained
1 can cream of celery soup
½ cup sour cream
½ cup chopped celery
½ cup chopped onion

Topping:
1 cup shredded cheddar
  cheese
1 cup cheese-flavored cracker
  crumbs
¼ cup butter

Mix vegetables, soup, sour cream, celery and onions. Pour into greased 9x13x2-inch casserole dish. Mix topping ingredients and sprinkle over casserole. Bake in preheated 350° oven for 45 minutes to 1 hour. Serves 8.

Beth Ray, F.A. Faculty

Fruit

Hot Fruit Compote

12 almond macaroons, crumbled

4 cups canned mixed fruit, drained

½ cup slivered almonds, toasted

¼ cup brown sugar

½ cup sherry

¼ cup butter, melted

Cover bottom of buttered 2½-quart casserole dish with ¼ of macaroons. Alternate fruit and macaroons in layers, ending with macaroons. Sprinkle with almonds, sugar, and sherry. Bake in preheated 350° oven for 30 minutes. Pour melted butter on top and serve. Serves 8.

Nan Goldwasser, Grandparent of Ashley and Justin Rosen

Scalloped Pineapple

3 eggs

1½ cups sugar

1 (20-ounce) can crushed pineapple with juice

4 cups white bread, crust removed and cubed

¼ cup margarine, cut in small pieces

Beat eggs; add sugar, pineapple, bread cubes, and margarine. Mix well. Pour into buttered casserole. Bake in preheated 350° oven for I hour. Serves 4 to 6.

Christopher White '97
Marion Bryan, Parent of Jessica and Kate
Tottee Clark, Parent of Cyndee '89 and Ashleigh

Pineapple Casserole

1 (20-ounce) can pineapple chunks	1 cup grated sharp cheddar cheese
½ cup sugar	14 round buttery crackers, crumbled
3 tablespoons all-purpose flour	¼ cup butter or margarine, melted

Drain pineapple; reserve 3 tablespoons juice. Mix sugar and flour; add juice. Stir in pineapple and cheese. Mix well. Pour into greased casserole dish. Mix cracker crumbs with butter; sprinkle on top of casserole. Bake in preheated 350° oven for 20 to 30 minutes. Serves 8 to 10.

Sharlene Riddle Williams '80
Bettye Grady, F.A. Faculty

Apples and Cheese

1 cup sugar	1 (8-ounce) processed cheese loaf, room temperature
¾ cup all-purpose flour	
½ cup margarine, room temperature	1 (21-ounce) can apple slices (not pie filling)

Mix sugar and flour by hand; set aside. Mix margarine and cheese by hand; set aside. Layer apples in 9x9-inch baking dish. Mix sugar mixture with cheese mixture. Drop cheese mixture by spoonful over apples; mixture will spread while cooking. Bake in preheated 350° oven for 45 minutes. Serves 8 to 10.

Teri Mascia Williams '80, Wife of Stuart '80, Parent of Jared and Justin

Cakes, Cookies and Candy

Cakes, Cookies, Candy

Cakes
Apricot Bundt Cake

Cake:
4 eggs
1 cup apricot nectar
¾ cup sugar
½ cup vegetable oil
1 yellow cake mix
3 teaspoons lemon extract
  (optional)

Glaze:
Juice of 2 lemons
1¼ cups powdered sugar

In large bowl, mix eggs, apricot nectar, sugar, and oil. Stir in cake mix and lemon extract; beat by hand about 130 strokes or until no lumps remain. Grease and flour Bundt or 10-inch tube pan. Bake in preheated 350° oven for 1 hour. Cool in pan while preparing glaze.

Mix glaze ingredients, stirring to dissolve powdered sugar. Poke holes in top of cake with toothpick to allow icing to run through cake. Pour glaze over warm cake.

Sue Belvet, Parent of Benita
Paula Keeton, F.A. Faculty, Parent of Caitlin, Rachel and Will

Dawa's Hot Milk Cake

This is an old recipe from my husband's family. It makes a quick, no nonsense, small sponge cake and can be whipped up while dinner is cooking.

2 eggs, well beaten
1 cup sugar
1 cup flour
1 teaspoon baking powder

1 teaspoon vanilla
½ cup milk
2 tablespoons butter

Add sugar to eggs and beat well. Stir in flour, baking powder, and vanilla. Heat milk and butter nearly to a boil. When scalding hot, pour into batter and mix. Pour into 8x8-inch pan. Bake in preheated 350° oven until done.

Joan Ingalls, F.A. Faculty

Chocolate Praline Cake

Cake:
½ cup butter
¼ cup whipping cream
1 cup firmly packed brown
    sugar
¾ cup chopped pecans
1 devil's food cake mix with
    pudding added
1¼ cups water
⅓ cup oil
3 eggs

Topping:
1¾ cups whipping cream
¼ cup powdered sugar
¼ teaspoon vanilla

In saucepan, combine butter, whipping cream, and brown sugar. Cook just until butter is melted. Pour into two 9-inch cake pans. Sprinkle evenly with pecans.

Combine cake mix, water, oil, and eggs at low speed until moistened. Beat at high speed for 2 minutes. Carefully spoon over praline mixture. Bake in preheated 325° oven for 35 to 45 minutes. Cool 5 minutes before removing from pans. Cool completely.

For topping, beat whipping cream until soft peaks form. Blend in powdered sugar and vanilla. Beat until stiff peaks form.

To assemble, place one layer on serving plate, praline side up. Spread with half of topping. Top with second layer, praline side up. Top with remaining whipped cream, leaving sides of cake plain. Garnish with chocolate curls or pecan halves. Keep refrigerated.

Linda Bradford, Grandparent of Brawley and Dottie Davis

Carrot Cake

Cake:
2 cups sugar
1½ cups oil
4 eggs
1 teaspoon vanilla
2½ cups all-purpose flour
1 teaspoon baking soda
2 teaspoons cinnamon
3 cups grated carrot

Icing:
½ cup butter or margarine,
    softened
1 (8-ounce) package cream
    cheese, softened
1 teaspoon vanilla
4 cups powdered sugar
    (1 16-ounce box)
1 cup chopped nuts

In large mixing bowl, beat sugar, oil, eggs, and vanilla until well blended. Sift dry ingredients together; add to first mixture. Stir in grated carrots. Pour batter into 2 greased 9-inch cake pans. Bake in preheated 350° oven for 30 to 40 minutes. Let cool completely.

To make icing, cream butter and cream cheese until well blended. Add vanilla and powdered sugar; mix well. Slice each cake into 2 layers and spread each layer with icing. Ice top and sides of cake and sprinkle with nuts. Store in refrigerator.

Jeanne Schmidt, Grandparent of Jason

Succulent Carrot Cake

2 cups sugar
1½ cups vegetable oil
4 eggs
3 cups all-purpose flour
2 teaspoons baking powder
2 teaspoons baking soda

2 teaspoons cinnamon
½ teaspoon salt
1 teaspoon vanilla
4 cups grated carrots
1 cup chopped nuts (optional)
¾ cup raisins

Cream together sugar, oil, and eggs. In separate bowl, sift together flour, baking powder, baking soda, cinnamon, and salt. Beat dry into wet ingredients. Stir in remaining ingredients. Pour into greased springform or 9x13x2-inch baking pan. Bake in preheated 300° oven for 1 hour. Frost with cream cheese icing, if desired.

Joan Bitterman, Parent of Johanna and Jeffrey

New York Cheesecake

5 (8-ounce) packages cream
cheese, softened
1¾ cups sugar
2 tablespoons all-purpose
flour

2 teaspoons vanilla
5 eggs
2 egg yolks
½ cup whipping cream

Have all ingredients at room temperature. In large bowl, beat cream cheese until creamy (30 seconds). Scrape bowl and beaters well; gradually add sugar and flour until smooth (1 to 2 minutes). Beat in vanilla. Beat eggs and egg yolks in 1 at a time. Scrape bowl and beaters after each addition. On low speed, beat in heavy cream. Pour batter into greased 9-inch springform pan; smooth the top. Bake in preheated 325° oven for 50 minutes.

Check for doneness by tapping pan gently; when it barely jiggles, turn oven off and leave in 10 more minutes. After 10 minutes, open door slightly, and let cool in oven for 1 hour. Remove to rack and let cool completely before unmolding. Cover and refrigerate for at least 6 hours, preferably 24 hours before serving.

Elizabeth Coats, Grandparent of James Morgan

Low-Fat Chocolate Chip Cheesecake

2 cups crushed reduced-fat
creme-filled chocolate
sandwich cookies
(24 cookies)
¼ cup shortening, melted
3 (8-ounce) packages fat-free
cream cheese, softened

1 (14-ounce) can fat-free
sweetened condensed milk
3 eggs
2 teaspoons vanilla
1 cup mini chocolate chips,
divided
1 teaspoon all-purpose flour

Combine crumbs and shortening; press firmly on bottom of 9-inch springform pan. In large bowl, beat cream cheese until fluffy. Gradually beat in sweetened condensed milk until smooth. Beat in eggs and vanilla. Toss ½ cup chocolate chips with flour to coat; stir into cheese mixture. Pour over crust. Sprinkle with remaining chips. Bake in preheated 350° oven for 55 minutes or until center is set. Cool. Chill several hours or overnight.

Matthew Franzeen, Student

Classic Cheesecake

Crust:
1 (8-ounce) bag Pepperidge Farm Bordeaux cookies, finely crushed
¼ cup butter, melted

Filling:
2 cups sugar
4 (8-ounce) packages cream cheese, softened
6 eggs, individually beaten
2 teaspoons vanilla
1 (16-ounce) container sour cream

Mix cookie crumbs with butter; spread on bottom only of greased springform pan. Set aside.

In large mixing bowl, beat cream cheese on low speed. Gradually add sugar, beating until light and fluffy. Add beaten eggs 1 at a time, mixing thoroughly after each addition. Add vanilla. Beat sour cream briefly to smooth texture, then fold into cheese mixture. Pour into prepared springform pan. Bake in preheated 375° oven for 45 minutes. Turn oven off, leaving cheesecake in for 1 hour. Remove cheesecake after the hour and cool to room temperature, approximately three hours. Remove the pan's outer ring. Refrigerate for 8 hours before serving.

Optional topping is fresh fruit (strawberries, blueberries, pineapple) on top of a thin layer of sweetened whipped cream.

Cake may not look done after 45 minutes, but will continue to bake after oven is turned off. Cake must be at room temperature before placing it in refrigerator.

Sylvia Schmidt, Parent of Jason

Tad's Poppy Seed Cake

1 yellow cake mix
1 (3-ounce) package instant
   vanilla pudding mix
1 (8-ounce) container sour
   cream

4 eggs
1 (2-ounce) jar poppy seeds
½ cup dry sherry
¾ cup oil

Mix all ingredients and beat well. Pour into greased Bundt pan and bake in preheated 350° oven for 1 hour.

Jean Schaefer Moore '80, F.A. Faculty,
Parent of Hampton and Kirkland

Love Cake

1 yellow cake mix
½ cup water
4 eggs
½ cup oil
1 cup sour cream

1 (3-ounce) package instant
   vanilla pudding
1 (4-ounce) bar sweet German
   chocolate, melted
1 cup chocolate chips
   (1 6-ounce bag)

In large mixing bowl, beat together all ingredients except chocolate chips; mix well. Stir in chips and pour into greased Bundt or 10-inch tube pan. Bake in preheated 350° oven for 55 to 60 minutes.

Catherine Allison, Grandparent of Janene '99, Cara and Jacqueline

Chocolate Chip Cake

1 chocolate cake mix
1 (3-ounce) package chocolate
   pudding mix
1 cup sour cream

3 eggs
1 cup chocolate chips
   (1 6-ounce bag)
½ cup water

In large mixing bowl, mix all ingredients until well blended. Pour batter into greased 9x13x2-inch pan. Bake in preheated 350° oven for 40 minutes.

Sue Hockman, Aunt of Cassandra

Strawberry Cake

Cake:
1 white cake mix
1 (3-ounce) package strawberry
  flavored gelatin
3 tablespoons all-purpose
  flour
¾ cup oil
½ cup water
4 eggs
1 (10-ounce) package frozen
  strawberries, thawed,
  reserve ¼ cup for frosting

Frosting:
¼ cup reserved strawberries
4½ cups powdered sugar
½ cup margarine, softened

In large mixing bowl, blend cake mix, gelatin, flour, oil and water. Add eggs 1 at a time, beating well after each addition. Mix in ¾ cup strawberries. Pour into 3 greased and floured (8-inch or 9-inch) cake pans. Bake in preheated 350° oven for 30 to 35 minutes or until done. Let cool.

Combine remaining ¼ cup strawberries, powdered sugar, and margarine in small bowl. Beat until smooth. Frost layers, top, and sides. Serves 12.

Lee Holmes Zettel '75

Pumpkin Chocolate Chip Cake

4 eggs
2 cups sugar
1 cup oil
2 cups all-purpose flour
2 teaspoons baking soda

2 teaspoons cinnamon
½ teaspoon salt
2 cups canned pumpkin
2 cups chocolate chips
  (1 12-ounce bag)

Beat eggs with sugar until light and well mixed. Add oil; mix well. Mix dry ingredients separately in small bowl. Gradually stir dry ingredients into egg mixture. Add pumpkin; continue to stir. Add chocolate chips; stir thoroughly. Pour batter into greased and floured Bundt or 10-inch tube pan. Bake in preheated 350° oven for 1 hour and 10 minutes, or until toothpick inserted in center comes out clean. Let cool before slicing. Serves 8.

Lisabeth Wasson Peterson '86

Pig Pickin' Cake

1 golden butter or yellow cake
  mix
½ cup oil
4 eggs
1 (11-ounce) can mandarin
  oranges, drained and juice
  reserved

Icing:
1 (3-ounce) package instant
  vanilla pudding mix
1 (8-ounce) container frozen
  nondairy whipped topping
Flavor icing with:
1 (10-ounce) package frozen
  strawberries, drained,
  chopped, and juice reserved
  with ½ cup milk
OR
1 (15-ounce) can crushed
  pineapple and juice

Beat cake mix, oil, eggs, and reserved juice from oranges; fold in oranges. Pour evenly into 3 greased 8-inch cake pans. Bake in preheated 350° oven for 20 to 25 minutes. Frost with icing flavor of your choice.

For strawberry icing: Mix pudding mix with reserved strawberry juice and milk. Fold in nondairy whipped topping and strawberries. Let stand 5 minutes in refrigerator. Ice top and sides of all layers. Refrigerate.

For pineapple icing: Add pudding mix to nondairy whipped topping and pineapple. Spread over cake layers. Refrigerate.

Gail Bolton, Parent of Meredith '97 and Trey '98
Debbie Steadman, Parent of Adam, Cameron, Caroline, and Grant

Vegetarian Cake

1 (16-ounce) container sour
  cream
2 cups sugar

2 cups cream of wheat
½ teaspoon baking powder
2 teaspoons vanilla
Chopped pecans (optional)

Mix sour cream, sugar, and cream of wheat; let set for 1 hour. Add baking powder, vanilla, and pecans. Pour into greased 10x10-inch baking pan. Bake in preheated 350° about 1 hour. Cool. Serves 8.

S. D. Devasthali, Grandparent of Manisha and Rakhee

Hummingbird Cake

Cake:
3 cups all-purpose flour
2 cups sugar
1 teaspoon baking soda
1 teaspoon salt
1 teaspoon ground cinnamon
3 eggs, beaten
1 cup vegetable oil
1½ teaspoons vanilla
1 (8-ounce) can crushed
  pineapple

1 cup chopped pecans
1 cup chopped bananas

Frosting:
1 (8-ounce) package cream
  cheese, softened
½ cup butter, softened
4 cups powdered sugar
  (16 ounces)
1 teaspoon vanilla

Combine flour, sugar, baking soda, salt, and cinnamon in large mixing bowl. Add eggs and oil; stir only until dry ingredients are moistened. Do not beat. Add vanilla, pineapple, pecans, and bananas. Divide batter evenly into 3 greased and floured 9-inch baking pans. Bake in preheated 350° oven for 25 to 30 minutes. Cool in pans.

Combine cream cheese and butter; beat until fluffy. Gradually add sugar; add vanilla. Beat until fluffy and light. Frost sides and top of cooled cake. (Freezes well)

Doris Conaway, Grandparent of Robert White

Applesauce Cake

½ cup shortening
1 cup sugar
1 egg
1¾ cups all-purpose flour
1 teaspoon baking soda

¼ teaspoon salt
1 teaspoon cinnamon
1 teaspoon cloves
1 cup applesauce
1 cup raisins (optional)
½ cup nuts (optional)

Cream together shortening, sugar, and egg. Stir in flour, baking soda, salt, cinnamon, and cloves. In saucepan, heat applesauce to boiling point. Stir into batter. Add raisins and nuts, if desired. Mix; pour into greased 9x13x2-inch pan. Bake in preheated 350° oven for 35 minutes. Frost as desired or serve with whipped cream.

Eileen Haefele, Grandparent of Trey Bright

Red Velvet Cake

Cake:
1 cup butter
2 cups sugar
2 eggs
1 tablespoon white vinegar
1 tablespoon cocoa
½ teaspoon salt
1½ teaspoons baking soda
2½ cups cake flour
1 cup buttermilk
1 teaspoon vanilla
2 ounces red food coloring

Frosting:
10 tablespoons flour
1¼ cups milk
1¼ cups shortening
1¼ cups sugar
2 teaspoons vanilla
1 cup chopped nuts

Cream butter and sugar. Add eggs and beat until fluffy. Make a paste of vinegar and cocoa; add to creamed mixture. Sift salt, baking soda, and flour. Add to creamed mixture alternating with buttermilk. Add vanilla and food coloring blending well. Pour into greased 9x13x2-inch cake pan. Bake in preheated 350° oven for 30 minutes. Cool.

In saucepan, blend flour with milk. Cook over low heat until thick. Let cool. Cream together shortening and sugar. Add cooled flour mixture and vanilla; beat at high speed for 6 minutes. Fold in nuts. Spread on cake.

Sue Holden, F.A. Staff, Parent of Candace

Self-filled Cupcakes

1 devil's food cake mix
1 (8-ounce) package cream
  cheese, softened
½ cup sugar
1 egg
Dash salt
1 cup chocolate chips
(1 6-ounce bag)

Mix cake as directed on package; fill baking cups ½ full. Beat cream cheese and sugar until fluffy; add egg, salt, and chocolate chips. Drop teaspoonful of cream cheese filling on top of cupcake batter. (Batter will rise during baking and enclose filling.) Bake in preheated 350° oven for 18 to 20 minutes. Makes 3 dozen.

Betty Campbell, Grandparent of Janene '99,
Cara, and Jacqueline Allison

Dead Teacher's Cake
(Chocolate Coconut Cake)

1 devil's food cake mix	Frosting:
	1½ cups sugar
Glaze:	½ cup evaporated milk
1 cup evaporated milk	½ cup butter
½ cup sugar	1 cup chocolate chips
24 large marshmallows	(1 6-ounce bag)
1 (14-ounce) bag coconut	

Prepare cake mix as directed on package in greased 9x13x2-inch cake pan.

While cake is baking, combine evaporated milk, sugar, and marshmallows in saucepan over low heat; stir until marshmallows are melted. Add coconut. When cake is done, poke 15 holes in top with handle of wooden spoon. Pour marshmallow mixture on top; spread. Set aside to cool.

In small saucepan, bring sugar, evaporated milk, and butter to boil; stir constantly for 1 minute. Remove from heat; add chocolate chips. Stir until melted. Pour frosting over coconut mixture.

Cornelia Hilburn, Parent of Ben and Amanda

"On Time" Brownie Frosting

My husband, Rick, says this frosting makes brownies "On Time;" hence, the name!

3 tablespoons butter	2 tablespoons milk
2 tablespoons cocoa	1 teaspoon vanilla
1½ cups powdered sugar	

In medium saucepan, melt butter over low heat. Stir in cocoa until dissolved. Add powdered sugar, milk, and vanilla. Stir until smooth. Add milk, if necessary to soften consistency. Frost brownies; let set until firm. Recipe will frost 1 9x13-inch pan of brownies.

Elizabeth Frederick Carter '78, F.A. Staff, Parent of Richard

Streusel Kuchen

Batter:
1½ cups biscuit/baking mix
½ cup sugar
1 egg
¼ cup milk
2 tablespoons butter, softened
1 teaspoon vanilla
3 apples, peeled and cored

Topping:
1 cup sugar
2 cups all-purpose flour
1 cup cold butter

Beat all batter ingredients except apples in mixing bowl for 3 to 4 minutes until very smooth. (It will be thick). Spread in greased 9x13x2-inch pan. Grate apples and distribute evenly over batter. Mix sugar and flour in large bowl. Cut in butter using a fork or your fingertips. Make crumbs of varying sizes; sprinkle over apple layer. Bake in preheated 350° oven for 30 to 40 minutes or until light golden brown.

Maria Castellot, Grandparent of Elaine Erteschik

Red Velvet Pound Cake

1½ cups solid vegetable
   shortening
3 cups sugar
7 eggs
1 teaspoon vanilla
2 ounces red food coloring
3 cups self-rising flour
2 tablespoons cocoa
1 cup buttermilk

Icing:
½ cup margarine, softened
1 (8-ounce) package cream
   cheese, softened
4 cups powdered sugar
   (1 16-ounce box)
3 tablespoons milk or lemon
   juice

Cream together shortening and sugar. Add eggs 1 at a time, beating after each addition. Add vanilla and food coloring. Combine flour and cocoa. Add dry ingredients alternating with buttermilk beginning and ending with flour. Pour into greased and floured 10-inch tube pan. Bake in preheated 325° oven for 1½ hours. Cool. Mix all icing ingredients well and spread on cake. (Cake can also be made in 3 greased and floured 9-inch layer pans. Reduce baking time accordingly.)

Mary Warren, Parent of Patrick

Pound Cake

1 cup butter, softened	3 cups all-purpose flour
¼ cup solid vegetable	½ teaspoon baking powder
shortening	½ teaspoon salt
2¾ cups sugar	1 teaspoon vanilla
6 eggs	1 cup milk

Cream butter, shortening, and sugar. Add eggs 1 at a time mixing well after each egg. Mix flour, baking powder, and salt. Mix vanilla with milk. Alternately add liquid and dry ingredients to butter mixture, beginning and ending with dry. (One third at a time). Pour into pound cake pan (round or oblong). Bake in preheated 350° oven for 1 to 1¼ hours. Cool. Frost with your favorite frosting, if desired. Serves 10 to 12.

Addie Williford, Grandparent of Lindsay '98 and Carlin

Addie's Chocolate Frosting

½ cup butter	4 cups powdered sugar
2 to 3 ounces unsweetened	(16 ounces)
chocolate	
¼ cup milk (additional 1 to 2	
tablespoons, if needed to	
achieve spreading	
consistency)	

In saucepan, melt butter and chocolate over low heat, stirring frequently. Add milk. Gradually beat in powdered sugar; mix well. Spread on top and sides of pound cake.

Addie Williford, Grandparent of Lindsay '98 and Carlin

Mrs. Lincoln's Pound Cake

This was handed down through a friend who had an ancestor in Indiana who married Patricia Hanks, a relative of Nancy Lincoln. Mrs. Lincoln made the cake and liked it very much, as did the President!

1 cup butter, softened	2 cups all-purpose flour
1⅔ cups sugar	½ teaspoon nutmeg
5 eggs	

Cream butter and sugar thoroughly. Add eggs 1 at a time; beat well after each addition. Sift flour with nutmeg. Add gradually to creamed mixture; mixing well. Pour into greased and floured or paper-lined tube pan. Bake in preheated 325° oven for 1½ to 1¾ hours.

Ursula M. LeFevre, Grandparent of Jordan Ethington

Mini Pound Cakes

Cake:	Glaze:
1 cup butter, softened	2 cups powdered sugar, sifted
1¼ cups sugar	2½ tablespoons milk
4 eggs	1 teaspoon vanilla
2 cups cake flour	
1 teaspoon baking powder	Garnish:
¼ teaspoon salt	Pecan halves
⅓ cup milk	
1 tablespoon brandy	
1 teaspoon vanilla extract	

Cream butter. Gradually add sugar, beating at medium speed until light and fluffy. Add eggs 1 at a time; beat after each addition. In separate bowl, sift together cake flour, baking powder, and salt. Add to creamed mixture alternating with milk; begin with milk and end with flour. Mix just until blended after each addition. Stir in brandy and vanilla. Pour batter into 3 small greased and floured loaf pans. Bake in preheated 325° oven for 35 to 40 minutes or until toothpick comes out clean. Cool 10 to 15 minutes in pans. Remove from pans; cool on wire racks. Mix glaze ingredients until smooth. Spoon glaze over cakes. Garnish with pecans.

Dee Dee Kells, F.A. Faculty, Parent of Rich '98 and John

Deluxe Pound Cake

1 cup butter, softened
½ cup solid vegetable
  shortening
3 cups sugar
5 eggs

3 cups all-purpose flour
½ teaspoon baking powder
1 cup milk
1 teaspoon rum extract
1 teaspoon lemon or coconut
  extract

Cream together butter, shortening, and sugar. Add eggs 1 at a time, mixing well after each egg. Sift flour with baking powder. Add to batter alternating with milk. Add extracts. Pour batter into greased Bundt pan. Bake in preheated 325° oven for approximately 1 hour or until toothpick inserted in center comes out clean.

Mary Martinez, Parent of Mario

Dick's Pound Cake

1 cup butter, softened
2 cups sugar
6 eggs

2 cups all-purpose flour
Pinch of salt
1 teaspoon vanilla

Cream together butter and sugar until smooth. Add eggs one at a time. Blend in flour gradually; then add salt and vanilla until thoroughly combined. Place in cold oven; set heat to 325° and bake for 1 hour.

Dick Wiess, Grandparent of Caswell Prewitt

Board of Trustees' Bribe

Chocolate Cream Cheese Pound Cake

Warning! *This is not a cake your friendly cardiologist would recommend for his/her patients! (But a piece or two shouldn't do you in.) In spite of this, I do enjoy making it for the Board of Trustees on nights when the Headmaster has warned me there will be a long meeting. After several years of imbibing on this artery clogging dessert, our dedicated D.A. has discovered that it may have been the cause of some rather sleepless nights. I am sorry, Ed!*

2 ounces unsweetened baking chocolate	3 cups sugar
1½ cups butter (not margarine), room temperature	5 eggs, room temperature
	3 cups all-purpose flour
1 (8-ounce) package cream cheese (not low-fat), room temperature	1 tablespoon vanilla

In top of double boiler, melt baking chocolate being careful not to burn it. In large mixing bowl, beat butter and cream cheese together; add melted chocolate. Continue to mix until well blended. Gradually add sugar, 1 cup at a time; beat until most granules are dissolved. Add eggs, 1 at a time, beating well after each addition until mixture is fluffy. On low speed, gradually add flour. Beat until all flour has been well blended; add vanilla. Pour into greased and floured 10-inch tube pan. Bake in preheated 350° oven for 1 hour. Do not overcook. Cool 5 minutes; invert onto baking rack and release from pan.

Libbie Crabtree, Wife of Headmaster Ben Crabtree

Pumpkin Roll

Cake:
3 eggs
1 cup sugar
⅔ cup pumpkin
1 teaspoon lemon juice
¾ cup all-purpose flour
1 teaspoon baking powder
1 teaspoon baking soda
2 teaspoons cinnamon
1 teaspoon ginger
½ teaspoon nutmeg
½ teaspoon salt
1 cup chopped pecans
½ cup powdered sugar

Filling:
1 (8-ounce) package cream
  cheese, softened
4 tablespoons butter, softened
1 cup powdered sugar
1 teaspoon vanilla

In large mixing bowl, beat eggs on high for 5 minutes. Add sugar; beat until mixed. Stir in pumpkin and lemon juice. Stir together flour, baking powder, baking soda, cinnamon, ginger, nutmeg, and salt; add to batter. Stir in nuts. Spray 10x15x1-inch jellyroll pan with cooking spray and line with wax paper. Pour batter into prepared pan. Bake in preheated 375° oven for 15 minutes. Allow to cool in pan for 5 minutes. Sprinkle powdered sugar on clean dish towel or 2 paper towels. Invert cake onto towel and roll up starting with long side. Let cool. Mix together ingredients for filling; beat until smooth. Unroll cake and spread filling. Reroll and chill. Cake freezes well.

Kathy Taylor, Parent of Phillip

Quick Caramel Frosting

½ cup butter (not margarine)   ¼ cup milk (or half and half)
1 cup brown sugar   1½ to 2 cups powdered sugar

Melt butter over low heat. Add brown sugar. Boil slowly, stirring constantly for 2 minutes. Add milk. Stir until mixture comes to a boil. Remove from heat. Cool. Gradually add powdered sugar, beating with hand held mixer until thick enough to spread. Recipe will frost 9-inch 2 layer cake.

Mary Frederick, Parent of Elizabeth '78 and Susan '78
Grandparent of Richard Carter

Chocolate Decadence

Cake:
13 ounces semisweet
chocolate, chopped
1 cup plus 3 tablespoons
unsalted butter
1 cup plus 3 tablespoons
sugar
⅓ cup water
6 large eggs, at room
temperature
¼ cup sugar

Ganache:
18 ounces semisweet
chocolate, chopped
1½ pints whipping cream

Mousse:
1 pound imported white
chocolate
½ teaspoon unflavored gelatin
7 tablespoons whipping
cream

Topping:
1⅓ cups cold whipping cream

For cake: Melt chocolate and butter over low heat in double boiler or microwave; stir until smooth.

Cook sugar and water in small pan over low heat, stirring until sugar dissolves. Increase heat and bring to a boil. Whisk into chocolate mixture. Cool for 15 minutes.

Beat eggs and sugar in mixer for 10 to 15 minutes until the mixture is pale yellow and very fluffy. Add chocolate mixture and beat until mixed.

Spray 9-inch springform pan with cooking spray. Line bottom of pan with parchment paper. Wrap outside of pan, bottom and sides, with foil. Pour batter into prepared pan. Place in large roasting pan and pour hot water in pan to reach the level half way up cake pan. Bake in preheated 350° oven for about 45 minutes until cake looks dry on top and feels firm in the center. Remove from water bath and let cool completely. Cake will fall slightly. Peel off foil. Let cool.

continued on next page

Chocolate Decadence *continued*

For ganache: Melt chocolate and cream in microwave or double boiler. Stir until smooth. Cool for 20 minutes. Pour ½ over cake in pan. Refrigerate. Reserve other ½ for cake sides.

For mousse: Melt chocolate in double boiler or microwave. Stir until smooth. Sprinkle gelatin over 7 tablespoons cream in small saucepan. Let soften for 10 minutes. Cook over low heat until gelatin dissolves, stirring constantly. Whisk cream mixture into melted chocolate. Cool for 5 minutes.

Topping: Beat cream until soft peaks form. Fold ½ into white chocolate mixture to lighten it. Gently fold in remaining cream. Spoon mousse over top of ganache covered cake. Shake to even it.

Pipe concentric circles on top of mousse with chocolate ganache, spacing circles ½-inch apart. Starting at center, draw tip of a knife through spirals to edge of pan. Move knife 1½-inches around pan sides, then draw tip of knife through spiral from edge of pan to center. Repeat moving around pan to form a spiderweb design, spacing evenly and alternating direction of strokes. Chill until mousse sets - at least 2 hours.

Run knife around edge of pan between pan and cake to loosen. Remove pan sides. Spread remaining ganache over sides of cake, icing completely. Garnish with berries and mint. Serves 12.

DeLafayette Restaurant

Cookies

Noel Cookie Gems

½ cup shortening
¾ cup sugar
1 egg
1 teaspoon vanilla
2⅔ cups all-purpose flour
½ teaspoon salt
¼ teaspoon baking powder

¼ teaspoon baking soda
½ cup sour cream or plain
yogurt
1¼ cups finely chopped nuts,
approximately
Jam or jelly of your choice

In large bowl, combine shortening, sugar, egg and vanilla; mix well. Sift together flour, salt, baking powder, and baking soda. Add to shortening mixture alternating with sour cream; mix well. Shape into 1¼-inch balls; roll in nuts. Place 1-inch apart on greased baking sheets. Press thumb in center of each ball. Fill imprint with jam. Bake in preheated 400° oven for 10 to 12 minutes or until lightly brown. Makes about 4 dozen cookies.

Carolyn Campbell, F.A. Faculty,
Parent of Kathryn '89, Kristen '93 and John '95

Forgotten Cookies

2 egg whites, at room
temperature
¼ teaspoon salt
¾ cup sugar

1 teaspoon vanilla
1 cup chocolate chips
(1 6-ounce bag)

Preheat oven to 375° before starting cookies. Beat egg whites and salt until stiff peaks form. Add sugar very slowly, beating until mixture is stiff and glossy. Beat in vanilla. Using large spatula, stir chips into mixture. Drop by teaspoonful onto greased cookie sheets. Place in preheated oven and immediately TURN OFF HEAT. Leave in oven, without opening, for at least 8 hours. Cookies can be made at night and left in the oven until morning.

Marion Bryan, Parent of Kate and Jessie

Grandma Anderson's Chocolate Chip Cookies

These were the cookies everyone raved over at all my high school events! They are the best I've ever had.

1½ cups all-purpose flour	1 teaspoon hot water
1 teaspoon baking soda	1 teaspoon vanilla
1 teaspoon salt	2 cups chocolate chips
1 cup shortening	(1 12-ounce bag)
¾ cup brown sugar	2 cups quick-cooking oatmeal
¾ cup sugar	1 cup nuts (optional)
2 eggs	

Sift together flour, baking soda, and salt; set aside. In mixing bowl, cream shortening; gradually add sugars. Add eggs, beating well. Add hot water, then flour mixture and vanilla. Fold in chocolate chips, oatmeal, and nuts. Mix thoroughly. Drop on greased cookie sheet. Bake in preheated 375° oven for 8 minutes. Makes 4 dozen.

Morgan Anderson '94

Biscotti

1 cup margarine	5 cups all-purpose flour
1½ cups sugar	3 teaspoons baking powder
6 eggs	1 cup sliced almonds, sliced
1 teaspoon vanilla or anise extract	

Beat margarine and sugar together until fluffy; add eggs, beating well. Add extract, flour, and baking powder; mix well. Add nuts by hand. On a large cookie sheet, spoon dough to form a 14x5-inch loaf. Bake in preheated 375° oven for 20 to 25 minutes or until brown. Remove from oven for 15 minutes to cool. Reduce heat to 300°. Cut loaf crosswise into ½-inch slices. Place cut side up and toast each side about 10 minutes. Makes 5 loaves.

Marie A. Gagliano, Grandparent of Amanda and Lauren

Anise Biscotti

4½ cups all-purpose flour
1 teaspoon baking powder
1 teaspoon baking soda
½ teaspoon salt
2 eggs
1¾ cups sugar
¾ cup of vegetable oil
½ cup sour cream
1 teaspoon vanilla

½ teaspoon anise extract
½ teaspoon anise seeds
½ cup chopped walnuts
½ cup raisins

Egg wash:
1 egg
1 teaspoon water

Whisk together flour, baking powder, baking soda, and salt; set aside. In mixing bowl, beat eggs, sugar, and oil until well combined. Beat in sour cream, vanilla, anise extract, and seeds. Add flour mixture gradually, beating until mixture forms a dough. Stir in walnuts and raisins. Turn dough out onto lightly floured surface and divide into 3 pieces. Form each piece into a log about 14-inches long and 2-inches wide; arrange a few inches apart on lightly greased baking sheet. Mix together egg wash; brush over logs. Bake in middle of preheated 350° oven for 30 minutes or until pale golden. Cool logs on baking sheet 10 minutes and carefully transfer to cutting board. Cut each log diagonally into 1-inch thick slices and cool on racks. Sliced biscotti can be reheated in preheated 325° oven for 10 to 15 minutes for extra crispness. Watch carefully!

Janice McDaniel, Parent of Greg '76,
Grandparent of Jack McDaniel

Chocolate Chip Oatmeal Pecan Cookies

2 cups dark brown sugar	2 teaspoons baking powder
2 cups sugar	2 teaspoons baking soda
2 cups solid vegetable	2 teaspoons salt
shortening	4 cups chocolate chips
4 eggs	(1 24-ounce bag)
4 teaspoons vanilla	4 cups old-fashioned oatmeal
4 tablespoons milk	1 cup chopped pecans
4 cups all-purpose flour	

In large mixing bowl, cream together sugars, shortening, eggs, vanilla, and milk until fluffy. Sift together flour, baking powder, baking soda, and salt; add gradually to creamed mixture. Mix well with spoon. <u>Do not beat</u>. Stir in chocolate chips, oatmeal, and pecans. Drop by teaspoons on lightly greased cooking sheet. Bake in preheated 350° oven for 12 to 15 minutes or until light brown. Do not overbake. Makes 6 dozen.

Diane Riel, Parent of Andrew

"Special K" Cookies

½ cup vegetable oil	½ teaspoon baking soda
⅔ cup sugar (light brown or	½ teaspoon salt
white)	½ to 1 cup raisins or chopped
1 egg	dates (optional)
1 teaspoon vanilla	3 cups Special K cereal
1 cup all-purpose flour	

Mix oil, sugar, egg, and vanilla together. Sift together flour, baking soda, and salt. Mix together egg mixture and flour mixture. Stir in raisins and cereal mixing well. Drop by teaspoonful onto ungreased cookie sheet. Bake in preheated 375° oven for 7 to 10 minutes. Remove from cookie sheets and cool on rack. Makes 5 to 6 dozen.

Mary Flagg Haugh, Parent of Jamie

Almond Macaroons

2 egg whites, at room
   temperature
⅔ cup sugar
¼ teaspoon cinnamon

½ teaspoon almond extract
½ cup ground almonds
½ cup finely chopped
   almonds

In medium bowl, beat egg whites until soft peaks form. Gradually beat in sugar and cinnamon; beat until stiff, glossy peaks form. Beat in extract. Combine ground almonds and chopped almonds; fold into egg white mixture. Drop by rounded teaspoons, 1½-inches apart, on foil-lined baking sheets. Bake in preheated 250° oven for 30 to 35 minutes or until golden. Cool on baking sheets. Store in airtight container. Makes 15 cookies.

Steffi Schnabel, Parent of Jason

Flo's Fruit Cake Cookies

1 (15-ounce) box golden
   raisins
1 pound candied mixed fruit
1 pound candied pineapple,
   chopped
3 pounds pecans, chopped
1 pound red candied cherries,
   chopped

1 pound dates, chopped
4 cups self-rising flour,
   divided
2 cups butter, softened
2¼ cups sugar
10 eggs
¼ cup vanilla

In large bowl, mix fruit and nuts with 1 cup flour; set aside. In mixing bowl, cream butter and sugar. Add eggs; mix well. Add vanilla and remaining flour; mix until thoroughly combined. Pour dough over fruit and nut mixture; mix well. Proceed with baking or store dough in refrigerator until needed, up to 7 days. When ready to bake, drop by teaspoonful on cookie sheet. Bake in preheated 250° oven for 30 minutes. Cool and store in airtight container.

Florence Wellons, Grandparent of Kristin

Molasses Cookies

1 cup sugar	1 cup oil
⅔ cup molasses	2 eggs
2 teaspoons baking soda	4 cups all-purpose flour
2 teaspoons vanilla	Raisins (optional)

Mix all ingredients in large bowl. Drop by teaspoonful onto greased baking sheet. Bake in preheated 350° oven for 10 to 15 minutes. Makes 2 dozen.

Elizabeth Croll '87

Wedding Ring Cookies

2 cups butter, softened	10 cups all-purpose flour
1½ cups margarine, softened	6 cups chopped pecans
2 cups powdered sugar	½ cup powdered sugar, sifted
2 tablespoons vanilla	

In extra large mixing bowl, cream together butter, margarine, and powdered sugar. Add vanilla, flour, and nuts; mix well. Roll into thin fingers and then shape into rings. Bake in preheated 300° oven for 25 minutes. Cool, then roll in sifted powdered sugar. Makes 220 cookies.

Mary Frances Monroe, Grandparent of Maggie Ruth

Lemon Crisp Cookies

1 lemon cake mix	1 egg, beaten
1 cup crisp rice cereal	1 teaspoon grated lemon peel
½ cup butter or margarine, melted	

In large bowl, combine all ingredients until well mixed (dough will be crumbly). Shape into 1-inch balls. Place 2-inches apart on ungreased baking sheets. Bake in preheated 350° oven for 10 to 12 minutes or until set. Cool for 1 minute; remove from pan to wire rack to cool completely. Makes 4 dozen.

Connie Koonce, F.A. Faculty

Turtle Cookies

These were a favorite of mine as a child. My mom always made chocolate chip cookies, but her friend, Pearl, made these and I loved them!

Cookie dough:
4 ounces unsweetened
  chocolate
1 cup butter
4 eggs, beaten
1½ cups sugar
2 cups all-purpose flour
2 teaspoons vanilla

Frosting:
1 ounce unsweetened
  chocolate
1 cup brown sugar
½ cup water
5 teaspoons butter
1 teaspoon vanilla
Powdered sugar

In saucepan over very low heat, melt chocolate with butter. Add eggs, sugar, flour, and vanilla. Drop by teaspoonful onto hot waffle iron. Bake 1 to 2 minutes. Remove and let cool.

For frosting, melt chocolate, brown sugar, water, and butter. Boil for 3 minutes; add vanilla. Cool. Beat in powdered sugar as needed to make spreadable.

Maggie Franzeen, F.A. Staff, Parent of Matthew

"Smith College" Cinnamon Cookies

1 cup + 2 tablespoons butter
  or margarine, softened
1½ cups sugar
1½ cups brown sugar
3 eggs, well beaten
1½ teaspoons vanilla
1 teaspoon salt
4½ cups all-purpose flour
1½ tablespoons cinnamon
1½ cups chopped nuts

Cream butter and sugars until light and fluffy. Add eggs and vanilla; beat well. Add salt, flour, and cinnamon; mix well. Stir in nuts. Pack dough into well greased loaf pans and refrigerate overnight. When ready to use, cut dough into narrow strips. Bake in preheated 325° oven for 10 to 15 minutes. Makes 7½ dozen.

Mary Werner, Grandparent of Gordon McCambridge

Prize Nut Cookies

1 cup brown sugar
1 cup sugar
1 cup oil
3 eggs, well beaten
4½ cups all-purpose flour

1 teaspoon salt
2 teaspoons baking soda
1 teaspoon cinnamon
½ teaspoon nutmeg
1 cup chopped black walnuts

In mixing bowl, combine sugars and oil. Add eggs; beat well. Add dry ingredients; mix in nuts. Divide dough in half. Place each half onto waxed paper and shape into long rolls, about 2-inches in diameter. Refrigerate overnight or in freezer for 2 hours. When ready to bake, thinly slice dough (about ¼-inch thick). Place on ungreased cookie sheet and bake in preheated 425° oven for 8 minutes.

Robena Keatley, Grandparent of Caitlin, Rachel and Will Keeton

Peanut Butter Cookies

1 cup peanut butter
1 cup sugar

1 egg
1 teaspoon baking soda

Mix all ingredients. Drop by teaspoonful onto baking sheet. Bake in preheated 350° oven for 10 minutes.

Note: These cookies contain no flour.

Lloyd Hamlet, Grandparent of Hunter and Sarah-Ann Howell

Praline Crackers

1 cup butter
1 cup brown sugar
1 cup chopped pecans

1 teaspoon vanilla
Buttery crackers

Bring butter, brown sugar, pecans, and vanilla to boil; boil hard for 3 minutes. Layer crackers on baking sheet with sides. Pour mixture over crackers. It will spread as it bakes. Bake in preheated 350° oven for 10 minutes. Before crackers cool, remove and place on waxed paper.

Lisa Thompson '79

Auntie Em's Creme de Menthe Bars

Crust:
½ cup butter
4 tablespoons cocoa
½ cup powdered sugar
1 egg
1 teaspoon vanilla
2 cups graham cracker
  crumbs

Middle Layer:
½ cup butter, softened
4 to 5 tablespoons crème de
  menthe
2 cups powdered sugar
2 tablespoons instant vanilla
  pudding mix

Frosting:
½ cup butter
2 cups chocolate chips
  (1 12-ounce bag)

Melt butter and cocoa together; cool. Add powdered sugar, egg, and vanilla; mix well. Add crumbs; mix. Press into lightly greased 9x13x2-inch pan. Refrigerate for 1 to 2 hours.

Beat ingredients for middle layer until smooth. Spread over crust and refrigerate for ½ hour.

Melt frosting ingredients together; mix well. Spread on top. Refrigerate.

Matthew Franzeen, Student

Love Bars

1 yellow cake mix
1 egg
½ cup margarine, softened
1 (8-ounce) package cream
  cheese, softened

2 eggs
4 cups powdered sugar
  (1 16-ounce box)

Mix cake mix, egg, and margarine. Spread in greased 9x13x2-inch pan. In mixing bowl, beat cream cheese, eggs, and sugar until well blended. Spread on top of first layer. Bake in preheated 350° oven for 45 to 50 minutes. Remove from oven; sprinkle with powdered sugar.

Diane Harrell, Parent of Greg and Steven

Seven Layer Bars

½ cup butter
1 cup graham cracker crumbs
1 cup shredded coconut
2 cups chocolate chips
(1 12-ounce bag)

2 cups butterscotch chips
(1 12-ounce bag)
1 cup walnuts
1 cup sweetened condensed
milk

Melt butter in 9x13x2-inch metal pan. In layers, evenly spread graham cracker crumbs, coconut, chocolate chips, butterscotch chips, and walnuts. Pour condensed milk evenly over top. Bake in preheated 350° oven for 30 minutes. Makes 20 to 25 bars.

Linda Rosen, Parent of Ashley and Justin

Pumpkin Bars

4 eggs
1½ cups sugar
1 cup oil
16 ounces fresh or canned
pumpkin
2 cups all-purpose flour
2 teaspoons baking powder
2 teaspoons cinnamon
1 teaspoon salt
1 teaspoon baking soda

Icing:
1 (3-ounce) package cream
cheese, softened
½ cup butter
2 cups powdered sugar
1 teaspoon vanilla

Cream eggs, sugar, oil, and pumpkin until light and fluffy. Add flour, baking powder, cinnamon, salt, and baking soda; beat until smooth. Pour into ungreased 10x15x1-inch pan. Bake in preheated 350° oven for 25 to 30 minutes. After baking, let cool completely. Combine ingredients for icing; beat until creamy. Spread over top and cut into bars.

Norma Ginn, Parent of Gregg '87 and Doug '88

Gooey Butter Squares

1 yellow cake mix
½ cup butter, melted
3 eggs, divided
(not separated)

4 cups 4x powdered sugar
(1 16-ounce box)
1 (8-ounce) package cream
cheese, softened

Combine cake mix, butter, and 1 egg. Pat into well-greased and floured 9x13x2-inch pan. Mix powdered sugar, 2 eggs, and cream cheese; beat 3 minutes. Pour over cake mixture. Bake in preheated 350° oven for 30 to 35 minutes. When cool, cut into squares. Makes 24 small squares.

Karen Bullard, Parent of John

Cookie Dough Brownies

1 (22½-ounce) package fudge
brownie mix
½ cup chocolate chips
½ cup margarine or butter
½ cup firmly packed brown
sugar
¼ cup sugar
2 tablespoons milk
1 teaspoon vanilla
1 cup all-purpose flour

Glaze:
1 cup chocolate chips
(1 6-ounce bag)
1 tablespoon oil
¾ cup chopped pecans

Grease bottom of 9x13x2-inch pan. Make brownies following directions on box, adding ½ cup chocolate chips. Bake in preheated 350° oven for 30 to 35 minutes. Cool completely.

In large bowl, beat margarine and sugars until light and fluffy. Add milk and vanilla, blending well. Add flour. Spread over cooled brownies.

In small microwave-safe bowl, make glaze by melting chocolate chips and oil on medium, about 1 to 2 minutes. Stir until smooth. Carefully spoon glaze over filling. Sprinkle with nuts, pressing down lightly. Cut into bars and store in refrigerator.

Tricia Brooks, Parent of Tracey '99

Crunchie Fudge Squares

1 cup butterscotch chips
  (1 6-ounce bag)
½ cup peanut butter
4 cups crisp rice cereal

1 cup chocolate chips
  (1 6-ounce bag)
½ cup powdered sugar
2 tablespoons margarine
1 tablespoon water

Melt butterscotch chips and peanut butter over very low heat. Mix with cereal. Put half mixture in greased 8x8-inch pan and chill. Combine remaining ingredients; stir over low heat until smooth. Spread over cereal. Top with remaining cereal. Chill and cut into bars.

Meredith McCambridge, Parent of Gordon

Creme de Menthe Brownies

1 cup butter, softened and
  divided
1 cup sugar
4 eggs
1 cup all-purpose flour
½ teaspoon salt
1 (16-ounce) can chocolate
  syrup

2 cups powdered sugar, sifted
1 teaspoon vanilla
2 tablespoons crème de
  menthe
1 cup chocolate chips
  (1 6-ounce bag)

Cream ½ cup butter. Gradually add sugar, beating until light and fluffy. Add eggs, 1 at a time, beating well after each addition. Combine flour and salt. Add to creamed mixture alternating with chocolate syrup; begin and end with flour mixture. Stir in vanilla. Pour batter into greased and floured 9x13x2-inch baking pan. Bake in preheated 350° oven for 25 to 28 minutes. Cool completely.

Cream ¼ cup butter; gradually add powdered sugar and crème de menthe, mixing well. Spread evenly over brownies. Chill 1 hour.

Combine chocolate chips and remaining ¼ cup butter in top of double boiler over gently simmering water. Cook until chocolate melts. Spread over brownies. Chill for at least 1 hour. Cut into squares.

Paula Keeton, F.A. Faculty, Parent of Caitlin, Rachel, and Will

Candy
Tootsy's "Never Fail Fudge"
(If you follow the recipe exactly)

½ cup butter or margarine
¼ cup cocoa
2 cups sugar, divided
1 (5-ounce) can Pet brand
  evaporated milk

1 teaspoon vanilla
1 cup chopped nuts (pecans
  or English walnuts)

Melt butter; remove from heat and add cocoa. Add 1 cup sugar and stir. Add milk and stir. Add other cup of sugar and cook (medium to medium-high) until mixture forms soft or medium-soft ball when dropped into cool water. Remove from heat. Add vanilla and beat until mixture begins to thicken. Quickly add nuts; stir and pour into buttered dish. Cut into squares before fudge is completely cool.

Mrs. Barbara B. Lambert, F.A. Faculty, Parent of Barbara '76

Filtch (potato candy)

1 potato (about egg-sized)
4 cups 4x powdered sugar
  (1 16-ounce box)

½ teaspoon vanilla extract
  (optional)
Peanut butter

Peel and boil potato. Mash potato with fork until smooth. Gradually add powdered sugar; mix until dough forms. Add vanilla.

Lightly coat surface of cutting board with powdered sugar; roll mixture to ¼-inch thickness. Spread thin layer peanut butter on rolled mixture. Roll up sheet, loosening it from board with knife as you roll. Cut into slices and serve.

Emily Wetzel, Grandparent of Deanna and Duncan

Mozhee (molasses hard candy)

1 cup barrel molasses (the loose, old-fashioned type, not blackstrap molasses)
1 cup sugar
1 cup water

1 teaspoon vanilla
¼ cup butter
Walnuts, peanuts, coconut (optional)

Combine molasses, sugar, and water in large cast iron frying pan, stirring over medium heat until dissolved and then occasionally until mixture forms a hard crack stage (about 290° on candy thermometer). Reduce heat; add vanilla and butter. Mix thoroughly. If desired, add walnuts, peanuts, or coconut. Pour onto buttered baking sheet. Let cool and harden.

Emily Wetzel, Grandparent of Deanna and Duncan

Date Nut Balls

1 cup chopped dates
½ cup butter
1 cup sugar
1 egg, beaten

1 teaspoon vanilla
2 cups crisp rice cereal
½ cup nuts
Powdered sugar

In saucepan, combine dates, butter, sugar, egg, and vanilla; cook over medium heat for 10 minutes, stirring constantly. Add cereal and nuts. Let cool. Form into balls; roll in powdered sugar. These freeze very well.

Sue Holden, F.A. Staff, Parent of Candace

Covered Pecans

1 large egg white
¾ cup light brown sugar

1 teaspoon vanilla
2 cups pecan halves

Beat egg white until stiff; add sugar and vanilla. Coat pecans with mixture. Separate each pecan half and place on greased baking sheet. Bake in preheated 250° oven for 30 minutes.

Shirley Jenkins, Grandparent of Daniel and Tyler Britt

Candied Pecans

1 egg white	1 cup sugar
1 teaspoon vanilla	½ teaspoon salt
1 tablespoon water	1 teaspoon cinnamon
4½ cups pecan halves	

With fork, beat egg white, vanilla, and water until blended. Add pecans and coat well. Mix sugar, salt, and cinnamon; pour over pecan mixture. Stir well; spread on baking sheet. Bake in preheated 300° oven for 20 minutes. Remove from oven; stir. Reduce oven temperature to 250°; bake pecans for 30 more minutes.

Susan Sansverie, Parent of Kimberly

Wood Pile Candy

2 cups chocolate chips (1 12-ounce bag)	2 (7-ounce) cans shoestring potatoes
2 heaping tablespoons creamy peanut butter	1 cup chopped nuts

Melt chocolate over very low heat. Add peanut butter; stir until melted. Stir in potatoes and nuts. Mix well. Cover cookie sheets with waxed paper. Drop by teaspoonful onto baking sheets. Refrigerate for several hours.

Nan Goldwasser, Grandparent of Ashley and Justin Rosen

Chocolate Caramels

2 cups sugar	2½ ounces unsweetened chocolate
½ cup light corn syrup	4 tablespoons butter
1 cup half and half or evaporated milk	1 teaspoon vanilla

Butter heavy saucepan; cook sugar, syrup, milk, chocolate, and butter to 238°. Remove from heat. Add vanilla and pour into buttered 8x8-inch square glass dish. When cool, cut into squares.

Paulette Banks, Parent of James

Puppy Kibbles

It's fun to serve this from a ceramic dog food dish. It really looks like puppy food but tastes so much better!

2 cups chocolate chips
  (1 12-ounce bag)
1 cup creamy peanut butter
½ cup margarine or butter

9 cups Crispix cereal
3 cups powdered sugar,
  divided

Melt chocolate chips, peanut butter, and margarine together. Pour over cereal, stirring to coat. Put 2 cups powdered sugar into plastic bowl or large brown paper bag. Add cereal mix and put remaining powdered sugar on top. Cover (or close the bag) and shake vigorously to coat.

Doris Johnson, Grandparent of Matthew Franzeen

Mounds

1 (14-ounce) can sweetened
  condensed milk
½ cup butter, melted
8 cups powdered sugar
  (1 32-ounce bag)
2 (3½-ounce) cans flaked
  coconut

2 cups chocolate chips
  (1 12-ounce bag)
1 square paraffin wax,
  chopped or grated

Combine milk and butter. Add sugar and coconut; mix well. Chill for two hours. Roll into balls, flatten, and place on waxed paper. Chill for two hours.

In double boiler, melt chocolate chips and wax. Dip balls and dry on wax paper. After dry, keep candy chilled.

Catherine Allison, Grandparent of Janene '99, Cara and Jacqueline

Cream Cheese Horns

1 (8-ounce) package cream
cheese, softened
1 cup butter or margarine,
softened
2 cups all-purpose flour

Filling:
1 cup finely chopped nuts
½ cup sugar
Milk
Powdered sugar

Blend cream cheese, butter, and flour to form soft dough. Shape into round disk; wrap in plastic and store in refrigerator overnight. Roll dough to ¼-inch thickness and cut into 2-inch squares. Combine nuts, sugar, and milk to form soft paste. Fill dough with nut filling and roll up as you would a jellyroll. Bake on ungreased cookie sheet for 15 minutes or until slightly brown. Sprinkle with powdered sugar.

Jean Wychock, Grandparent of Jack McDaniel

Peanut Butter Delights

2 cups sugar
½ cup milk
½ cup margarine
4 tablespoons cocoa

2 teaspoons vanilla
2½ cups oatmeal (regular or
quick-cooking)
½ cup peanut butter

Mix sugar, milk, margarine, and cocoa. Bring to boil for 1½ minutes. Remove from heat. Add vanilla, oatmeal, and peanut butter. Mix well; drop by teaspoonfuls onto waxed paper. Allow to harden. Makes 1 dozen large (size of 1 cup) or 2 dozen small (size of 2 tablespoons).

Hannah Mendelsohn, Parent of Edie and Caroline

Pies and Desserts

Pies and Desserts

Pies
Japanese Fruit Pie

½ cup butter, softened
1 cup sugar
2 eggs
1 tablespoon vinegar
1 teaspoon vanilla
½ cup frozen coconut (flaked
  or shredded coconut may
  be used, but it is sweeter, so
  adjust sugar accordingly)

2 cups chopped pecans
½ cup golden raisins
Pinch of salt
1 (9-inch) pie shell, unbaked

Mix butter and sugar. Add eggs; beat well. Add vinegar, vanilla, coconut, pecans, raisins, and salt; mix well. Pour into pie shell. Bake in preheated 350° oven for 30 to 35 minutes.

Ronald Hodul '76
Mrs. Martin L. Davis, Grandparent of Brawley and Dottie

Sour Cream Apple Pie

2 cups peeled, cored, and
  chopped Granny Smith
  apples
¾ cup sugar
1 egg, beaten
Pinch salt
2 tablespoons all-purpose
  flour
1 cup sour cream
1 (9-inch) pie shell, unbaked

Topping:
⅓ cup sugar
⅓ cup butter, softened
1 teaspoon cinnamon

Mix apples, sugar, egg, salt, flour, and sour cream. Pour into pie shell; bake in preheated 375° oven for 30 minutes or until custard sets.

While pie is baking, combine topping ingredients. Remove pie from oven and reduce oven temperature to 350°; punch holes in custard with fork; mix topping and smooth onto custard and into holes. Return to oven for additional 30 to 40 minutes.

Ethel Bonifant, Grandparent of Courtney and Hillary Robinson

Sweet Potato Pecan Pie

1 pound sweet potatoes,
   cooked and peeled
¼ cup butter or margarine
1 (14-ounce) can sweetened
   condensed milk
1 teaspoon cinnamon
1 teaspoon grated orange rind
1 teaspoon vanilla
½ teaspoon nutmeg
¼ teaspoon salt
1 egg
1 (9-inch) graham cracker pie
   crust

Pecan Topping:
1 egg
2 tablespoons dark corn syrup
2 tablespoons firmly packed
   brown sugar
1 tablespoon butter, melted
½ teaspoon maple flavoring
1 cup chopped pecans

With mixer, beat hot sweet potatoes and butter until smooth. Add condensed milk, cinnamon, orange rind, vanilla, nutmeg, salt, and egg; mix well. Pour into crust. Bake in preheated 425° oven for 20 minutes. While pie is baking, prepare pecan topping: mix together egg, syrup, sugar, butter, and maple flavoring. Stir in pecans. Remove pie from oven; reduce temperature to 350°. Spoon pecan topping on pie. Bake 25 minutes longer or until set.

Patsy Markham, Parent of George '86 and Chris '94

"Grape" Pie

1 (14-ounce) can sweetened
   condensed milk
1 (12-ounce) container frozen
   nondairy whipped topping,
   thawed

2 (.14-ounce) packages unsweetened grape drink mix
   powder
1 (9-inch) graham cracker pie
   crust

Mix condensed milk and nondairy whipped topping by hand. Gradually add grape powder with large spoon; the mixture will turn a darker purple as you mix it. Spoon into crust; refrigerate at least 1 hour before serving. This keeps for 2 weeks in the refrigerator.

Note: Other flavors may be used, but grape makes a surprising lavender dessert. This is easy for children to make.

Celine Shoup, Parent of Mary

Lemon Meringue Pie

Crust:
1¼ cups crushed vanilla
  flavored cookies
⅓ cup melted butter

Filling:
3 eggs
1 (14-ounce) can sweetened
  condensed milk
½ cup lemon juice
1 teaspoon grated lemon rind
¼ teaspoon cream of tartar
¼ cup sugar

Mix together cookie crumbs and butter. Press firmly into 9-inch pie plate. Refrigerate crust until set.

Separate egg yolks from whites; set whites aside. Combine condensed milk, lemon juice, and rind. Mix in egg yolks. Pour into cooled crust. Beat egg whites with cream of tartar until soft peaks form. Slowly add sugar until stiff peaks form. Spread meringue over pie, carefully sealing to edge of filling.

Bake in preheated 325° oven for 12 to 15 minutes or until lightly browned. Cool to room temperature to serve.

Rhonda Dees, Board of Trustees Chair, Parent of Sarah

Aunt Kitty's Chocolate Pie

8 ounces German sweet
  chocolate
½ cup margarine
3 eggs

1 tablespoon all-purpose flour
1 cup sugar
1 teaspoon vanilla
1 (9-inch) pie shell, unbaked

Melt chocolate and margarine over very low heat. Beat eggs lightly. Sift flour and sugar; add to eggs. Stir into chocolate and margarine mixture. Add vanilla. Pour into pie shell. Bake in preheated 350° oven for 45 to 60 minutes. Serve with whipped cream or vanilla ice cream.

Tottee Clark, Parent of Cyndee '89 and Ashleigh

Mary Anne's Lemon Chess Pie

1½ cups sugar
1 tablespoon white cornmeal
1 tablespoon all-purpose flour
¼ teaspoon salt
4 large eggs
½ cup buttermilk

⅓ cup unsalted butter, melted
   and cooled
1 tablespoon finely shredded
   lemon peel
⅓ cup lemon juice
1 teaspoon vanilla
1 (9-inch) pie shell, unbaked

Combine sugar, cornmeal, flour, and salt. Beat eggs well. Add sugar mixture; mix well. Add buttermilk, butter, lemon peel, lemon juice, and vanilla; beat until well combined. Pour into shell. Bake in preheated 350° oven for 40 minutes or until golden brown and custard is set. Cool completely and serve with whipped cream.

Note: There will be some unabsorbed butter when pie is removed from oven, but it will be absorbed as pie cools.

Mary Anne Dawkins, Parent of Johnny '77 and Dawn '81

Cracker Pie

24 round butter flavored
   crackers, crumbled
¾ cup + 3 tablespoons sugar,
   divided
1 teaspoon vanilla
1 cup pecans

3 egg whites
1 (8-ounce) container frozen
   nondairy whipped topping,
   thawed
½ package frozen coconut,
   thawed

Grease 9-inch ovenproof glass baking dish with butter. Combine crackers, ¾ cup sugar, vanilla, and pecans. Beat egg whites with 3 tablespoons of sugar. Fold into cracker mixture. Spoon into pie plate. Bake in preheated 350° oven for 20 to 25 minutes. Cool pie. Spread top with whipped topping and sprinkle with coconut.

Barbara E. Lambert '76, F.A. Staff

Key Lime Pie

Crust:
2½ cups graham cracker
    crumbs
½ cup firmly packed light
    brown sugar
⅔ cup salted butter, melted

Topping:
2 teaspoons vanilla
2 cups whipping cream
⅓ cup powdered sugar

Filling:
8 eggs, lightly beaten
2 cups sugar
⅔ cup key lime juice
¼ cup grated lime rind
Dash salt
1 cup unsalted butter

Mix crust ingredients; divide evenly and press into 2 9-inch pie pans. Bake in preheated 375° oven for 6 to 8 minutes.

Combine eggs, sugar, lime juice, lime rind, and salt in top of double boiler over gently simmering water. Whisk constantly until mixture thickens. Add butter; continue to whisk until butter melts and mixture thickens. While hot, pour into crusts. Bake in preheated 300° oven for 20 minutes or until set. Cover and chill 8 hours.

Whip topping ingredients until stiff. Spread on immediately before serving.

Dena Lingle, Trustee, Parent of John and Margaret

Caramel Pies

4 (14-ounce) cans sweetened
  condensed milk
2 graham cracker pie crusts
1 (12-ounce) container frozen
  nondairy whipped topping,
  thawed
1 chocolate-covered toffee
  candy bar, coarsely
  chopped

Pour condensed milk into crockpot. Cook, covered 6 to 7 hours, stirring every half hour with wire whisk. When it is peanut butter colored, pour into pie crusts. Cool. Spread whipped topping on top, and sprinkle candy around edges. Cover and chill.

Edward House, Student

Fresh Strawberrry Pie

1½ cups water
1 cup sugar
2 tablespoons corn starch
1 (3-ounce) package
  strawberry flavored gelatin
1 deep-dish pie shell, baked
1 pint fresh strawberries,
  hulled and sliced

Bring water, sugar, and corn starch to boil. Boil 5 minutes. Add gelatin; cool completely. Put strawberries in pie shell. Pour gelatin mixture on top. Put in refrigerator until firm. Serve with whipped cream.

Billie Hankins, F.A. Staff

Judye's Lemon Chess Pie

1 lemon, quartered with seeds
  removed
4 eggs
½ cup butter, softened
2 cups sugar
1 teaspoon cornmeal
2 (9-inch) pie shells, unbaked

Place lemon in blender and grate. Add eggs, butter, sugar, and cornmeal; blend. Pour into pie shells. Bake in preheated 350° oven for 30 to 35 minutes. Refrigerate after baking. Serve with whipped topping.

Judye Bleecker, Parent of Happy '96 and Leigh

No Fool's Fruit Pie

6 tablespoons margarine,
 melted
¾ cup sugar
¾ cup self-rising flour

¾ cup milk
1 quart fruit (apples, peaches,
 or strawberries)

Spread melted margarine in bottom of 9x13x2-inch baking dish. Stir together sugar, flour, and milk. Pour over margarine. Put fruit on top. Bake in preheated 350° oven for 30 minutes.

Catherine Allison, Grandparent of Janene '99, Cara, and Jacqueline

Praline Pies

1 (14-ounce) can sweetened
 condensed milk
1 (8-ounce) package cream
 cheese, softened
1 (16-ounce) container frozen
 nondairy whipped topping,
 thawed
3 graham cracker pie crusts

Topping:
½ cup butter or margarine
1 (7-ounce) can shredded
 coconut
1 cup chopped nuts
1 (6-ounce) jar caramel ice
 cream topping

Mix together condensed milk, cream cheese, and whipped topping. Divide equally into pie crusts. Melt butter; mix with coconut and nuts. Pour onto cookie sheet; broil in preheated oven until golden brown. Sprinkle over pies and drizzle caramel on top. Freeze until ready to serve.

Beckie Bishop, F.A. Faculty, Parent of Jenna and Megan

Coconut Pie

2 eggs, beaten
1 cup sugar
1 tablespoon all-purpose flour

1 cup coconut
1 cup milk
1 (9-inch) pie shell, unbaked

Mix eggs, sugar, flour, coconut, and milk; pour into pie shell. Bake in preheated 350° oven 25 to 30 minutes or until done.

Mary Jane Ingram, Parent of Charlotte '81

The Best Blueberry Pie

1 (9-inch) pie shell, unbaked
4½ cups blueberries (frozen or fresh)
4 tablespoons all-purpose flour
1½ tablespoons fresh lemon juice
¾ cup sugar
2 tablespoons butter

Topping:
1 cup all-purpose flour
¾ cup rolled oats
⅔ cup butter
½ cup packed brown sugar

Mix blueberries, flour, lemon juice, and sugar. Pour into pie shell; dot with butter. Crumble together all topping ingredients to form crumbs. Spread over pie. Bake in preheated 425° oven for 35 to 40 minutes.

Caroline Withers, Parent of Katherine '97 and Jonathan

Apple–Pecan Pie

6 Granny Smith apples, peeled, cored, and sliced
1 (9-inch) pie shell, unbaked
2 tablespoons sugar
2 tablespoons lemon juice
1 teaspoon cinnamon

½ cup firmly packed brown sugar
½ cup all-purpose flour
¼ cup butter
½ cup chopped pecans

Place apples into pie shell. Cover with sugar, lemon juice, and cinnamon. Mix brown sugar, flour, and butter until corn meal consistency. Add nuts; sprinkle evenly over apples. Bake in preheated 400° oven for 1 hour. Serve with whipped cream or vanilla ice cream.

Sadie Floyd, Great-Grandparent of Daniel and Tyler Britt

Desserts
Lemon or Chocolate Delight

1 (3-ounce) package instant lemon OR chocolate pudding mix	½ angel food cake, cut into 1-inch cubes
2 (8-ounce) containers lemon OR vanilla yogurt	1 (8-ounce) container frozen light nondairy whipped topping, thawed

Mix pudding according to package directions. Mix in yogurt. Layer in the following order: cake, pudding/yogurt mixture, and nondairy topping; repeat. Refrigerate. If using chocolate version, drizzle chocolate syrup over dessert. Serves 8.

Mrs. Robert Bryan, Grandparent of Bobby and Bucky Brown

Almond Torte

¼ teaspoon baking powder	Topping:
½ cup flour	2 cups whipping cream
6 eggs, separated	(1 pint)
2 cups sugar	4 tablespoons powdered
2 cups ground almonds with skins	sugar
1 teaspoon vanilla	1 teaspoon almond extract
	1 teaspoon vanilla

Stir baking powder into flour. Beat egg whites until foamy. In separate bowl, beat egg yolks; add sugar, almonds, flour, and vanilla. When flour mixture gets very stiff, add a tablespoon of beaten egg white. Fold in remaining egg whites. Put in 2 9-inch pans (round or square) that have been lined with greased waxed paper. Bake in preheated 325° oven about 40 minutes or until light tan and crusty on top. Turn out immediately and cool completely.

Whip cream with powdered sugar, almond extract, and vanilla. Spread on cake and refrigerate. Best if made one or two days ahead of serving. Serves 16.

Libba Pate, Former F.A. Faculty

Deb's Homemade Ice Cream

Basic Vanilla Ice Cream:
5 cups evaporated milk
3 (14-ounce) cans sweetened
  condensed milk
3 cups cold milk
3 tablespoons vanilla

Fruit Ice Cream:
4 cups evaporated milk
2 (14-ounce) cans sweetened
  condensed milk
2 cups cold milk
2 tablespoons vanilla
3 cups fruit, drained and
  sweetened

Choose which flavor ice cream you are making. Mix ingredients well; pour into 4-quart electric ice cream freezer. Add ice and salt to freezer as needed until freezer stops and ice cream is ready.

Wanda Williford, Parent of Lindsay '98 and Carlin

Fruit Pizza

1 roll refrigerated sugar
  cookie dough
1 (8-ounce) package low-fat
  cream cheese, softened
½ cup sugar
2 bananas, sliced

Strawberries, sliced
1 (8-ounce) can pineapple
  tidbits
1 (14-ounce) can mandarin
  oranges
½ cup apricot preserves

Line a pizza pan with aluminum foil (this makes it easier to remove the fruit pizza to a pretty serving tray or platter). Press out dough to cover pan. Bake according to directions on cookie dough package. Let crust cool completely. Mix softened cream cheese with sugar. Spread over cookie crust. Drain all juice off canned fruit. Soak sliced bananas in juice for 2 minutes to keep them from turning dark. Arrange fruit in a pretty design over cream cheese. Warm apricot preserves in microwave until liquid. Drizzle over fruit to coat. Serves 8 to 10.

Note: Use any combination of fresh and canned fruit.

Susan Frederick Flanagan'78

Apple Squares

4 cups peeled, cored, and
  diced apples
½ cup oil
2 cups sugar
2 eggs
1 cup chopped walnuts

1 teaspoon vanilla
2 cups all-purpose flour
2 teaspoons cinnamon
2 teaspoons baking soda
¾ teaspoon salt

In large mixing bowl, mix apples, oil, sugar, eggs, walnuts, and vanilla. Combine flour, cinnamon, baking soda, and salt; blend until just moistened. Pour into greased 9x13x2-inch pan. Bake in preheated 350° oven for 45 to 55 minutes. Serve with whipped cream. Serves 8.

Kappy Prosch, F.A. Faculty, Parent of Bo

Pears with Yogurt

3 medium pears, peeled, cored,
  and cubed
¼ teaspoon cinnamon
1 tablespoon sugar

1 (8-ounce) container vanilla
  yogurt
1 teaspoon almond extract

In 2-quart saucepan over high heat, combine pears, cinnamon, sugar, and ¼ cup water; heat to boiling. Reduce heat to low; cover and simmer 15 minutes or until pears are tender. Refrigerate covered at least 1½ hours. In small bowl, combine vanilla yogurt and almond extract. Spoon pear mixture onto dessert dish; top with yogurt crème. Serves 4.

Bea Elmen, Grandparent of Matt Benshoff

Strawberry Trifle

1 angel food cake, cubed
2 (2-ounce) boxes sugar free
  vanilla pudding, prepared
  according to box

1 quart strawberries
1 (12-ounce) container frozen
  light nondairy whipped
  topping, thawed

In a 10x12-inch pan or dish, place cake pieces. Pour pudding on top. Add strawberries; cover with whipped topping. Refrigerate 4 to 6 hours. Serves 10.

Barbara Hinkle, Grandparent of Eve Greene

Cold Banana Pudding

3 (3-ounce) boxes vanilla
instant pudding
5 cups milk
1 (8-ounce) container sour
cream

1 (12-ounce) container frozen
nondairy whipped topping,
thawed
1 (16-ounce) box vanilla wafers
5 to 6 bananas

Mix pudding with milk; add sour cream and half of whipped topping. Line 3-quart dish or 9x12x2-inch pan with vanilla wafers. Top with layer of sliced bananas. Cover with ⅓ of pudding mixture. Repeat for 3 layers. Dot remaining whipped topping on top; spread out. Refrigerate for several hours before serving.

Cheryl Atkinson Haigh '84
Sharon Bullard, Parent of Christopher

Apple Crisp

5 cups peeled, cored, and
sliced apples
1 cup butter, softened
2 cups sugar

1½ cups all-purpose flour
2 teaspoons cinnamon
Dash salt
Dash nutmeg

Place enough apples to fill 9x13x2-inch glass baking dish a little more than ¾ full. Combine butter with remaining ingredients until mixture resembles streusel. Spoon over apples and pat down lightly. Bake in preheated 375° oven for 50 minutes. Serve with whipped cream or vanilla ice cream.

Virginia McQuillan, Grandparent of Brooke, Garrett, Megan and Seth Ebel

Warm Peach Crinkle

1 (29-ounce) can sliced
peaches, drained
1 teaspoon grated lemon rind
1 (9-ounce) package pie crust
mix

⅔ cup firmly packed light
brown sugar
¼ cup butter
Vanilla ice cream

Place peaches in lightly greased 8x12x2-inch baking dish. Sprinkle with lemon rind. Combine pie crust mix and brown sugar; sprinkle over rind. Dot with butter. Bake in preheated 425° oven for 15 to 20 minutes. Serve with ice cream.

Michelle Caviness, F.A. Faculty

Pretzel Salad

Crust:
2 cups coarsely crushed
  pretzels
¾ cup butter or margarine,
  melted
4 tablespoons sugar

Filling:
1 (8-ounce) package cream
  cheese, softened
1 cup sugar
1 (8-ounce) carton nondairy
  whipped topping, thawed

Topping:
1 (6-ounce) package
  strawberry or raspberry
  gelatin
2 cups boiling water
2 (10-ounce) packages frozen,
  sweetened strawberries or
  raspberries

Mix crust ingredients. Press into 9x13x2-inch pan. Bake in preheated 400° oven for 6 minutes; cool completely. Cream together cream cheese and sugar. Fold in nondairy whipped topping; spread over cooled pretzels.

Dissolve gelatin in boiling water; stir in both packages of frozen strawberries. Stir until berries separate. Place in refrigerator until gelatin is partially set, then pour over cheese filling. Refrigerate until serving time.

Judy Brustad, Parent of Andrew, Jennifer and Theresa
Kelley Ebel, F.A. Staff, Parent of Brooke, Garrett, Megan and Seth

Blueberry Surprise

2 cups blueberries, fresh or
  frozen
1 cup Grape Nuts cereal
1 packet artificial sweetener

1 tablespoon margarine, cut
  into pieces
¼ cup water
1 teaspoon vanilla

Mix all ingredients in microwave safe dish. Cook in microwave on high for 5 minutes. Serve hot. Delicious if served with nondairy whipped topping. Serves 2.

Peggy Beverly, F.A. Staff

Crepes

1⅛ cups all-purpose flour	1½ cups milk
4½ tablespoons sugar	1 tablespoon melted butter
1 pinch salt	1½ tablespoons brandy
3 eggs, beaten	(optional)

In deep bowl, sift flour, sugar, and salt. Combine beaten eggs and milk; add to flour mixture stirring until smooth. Add melted butter and brandy. Let stand for two hours.

In 6-inch sauté pan, heat 1 tablespoon butter. When butter is hot, pour in 1 tablespoon of batter. Rotate pan quickly to spread batter. Cook for 1 minute; flip and cook for 1 minute on the other side. Place crepes flat, using waxed paper to separate them. Store in refrigerator or freeze tightly wrapped for later use. Serve with fresh fruit and whipped cream, jam, chocolate sauce, or Grand Marnier.

Kelli Koba, F.A. Faculty

Mammaw's
Chocolate Eclair Dessert

3 cups milk	Icing:
2 (3½-ounce) packages instant French vanilla pudding	¼ cup butter, melted
1 (8-ounce) container nondairy whipped topping	3 cups powdered sugar, sifted
Graham crackers	3 tablespoons cocoa
1 (16-ounce) can chocolate icing OR homemade icing	¼ cup milk
	1 teaspoon vanilla

Mix milk and pudding. As it begins to set, mix in whipped topping. Line 6x10-inch baking dish with graham crackers. Pour ½ pudding mixture on top. Make layer of graham crackers. Pour remaining pudding mixture on top. Make top layer of graham crackers. Microwave chocolate icing for 30 seconds and pour over top layer of graham crackers. (If using frosting recipe, mix all ingredients. If too thick, add more milk. Pour over graham crackers.) Refrigerate overnight. Serves 10.

Winnie Grannis, Parent of Whitaker '99 and McBryde
Susan Frederick Flanagan '78

Chocolate Eclair Dessert

Good for diabetics or people watching their weight.
Pyramid Exchange is equal to 1 bread, 3 milk, 2 fat.

24 low-fat graham crackers
2 (1-ounce) boxes sugar free
  instant vanilla pudding
3 cups skim milk, divided

1 (12-ounce) container frozen
  light nondairy whipped
  topping, thawed
1 (1-ounce) box sugar-free
  instant chocolate pudding

Place 8 graham crackers in bottom of 9x13x2-inch pan. Mix vanilla pudding and 1½ cups milk. Allow to set for 2 minutes. Gently fold in nondairy whipped topping. Pour half on graham crackers. Top with 8 graham crackers. Pour remaining pudding over graham crackers. Top with last 8 graham crackers.

Mix chocolate pudding with remaining milk. Allow to set 2 minutes and spread over graham crackers. Chill 6 hours in refrigerator to soften crackers. Strawberries may be served on top for garnish. Serves 18.

Eva Kleckley, Grandparent of Matt '97 and Cal Jameson

Blender Chocolate Bavarian

2 envelopes unflavored gelatin
½ cup cold milk
2 cups chocolate chips
  (1 12-ounce bag)
1 cup hot milk
2 eggs

1 cup heavy cream
⅓ cup sugar (or less to taste)
2 tablespoons light rum
  (optional)
1 cup cubed or crushed ice

Sprinkle gelatin over cold milk in 5 cup blender. Let stand until granules are moist. Add chocolate chips (reserve some for garnish) and hot milk. Cover; blend at low speed until chocolate melts. Stop blender; add eggs, cream, sugar, and rum. Cover; blend at high speed until well mixed. With blender running, remove center cap of lid; add ice cubes one at a time. Blend until ice melts. Pour at once into individual dessert dishes; chill until set, about 30 minutes. Garnish with whipped cream and reserved chocolate pieces.

Mary Joan Fredette, Parent of Chris '94 and Jon

Bubert ja Kissell

(Estonian Egg Custard with Cranberry Sauce)

Custard:
4 eggs
1½ cups sugar
1 pinch salt
3 cups + 3 tablespoons milk,
  divided
1 tablespoon corn starch
3 tablespoons all-purpose
  flour
1 teaspoon vanilla

Cranberry Sauce:
1 bag of cranberries
⅓ cup sugar
3 tablespoons corn starch

Separate egg yolks from whites. Beat egg yolks with sugar and salt. Bring 3 cups milk to boil. Mix corn starch, flour, and 3 tablespoons milk until paste forms. Slowly add flour paste to milk. Reduce heat; simmer gently. Add vanilla. Add egg yolk mixture, stirring constantly. Remove from heat. Beat 2 egg whites until stiff; fold in. Chill.

Cook cranberries in water until they pop; strain. Add water to make 3 cups liquid. Sweeten with sugar and reheat, stirring in corn starch to thicken. Cool.

Spoon custard into individual dishes. Slowly pour cranberry sauce around it. Eat a spoonful of sweet and sour together.

Ann Hamlet, Grandparent of Hunter and Sarah-Ann Howell

Pineapple–Orange Sherbet

2 cans sweetened condensed
  milk
1 (64-ounce) bottle orange
  soda

2 cups crushed pineapple with
  juice

Pour all ingredients into one gallon ice cream freezer; freeze according to manufacturer's directions.

Kim Howell, Parent of Hunter and Sarah-Ann

Viennese Ice Cream Torte

This recipe sounds difficult, but according to Mrs. Frederick, it is not. It's a delicious dessert which may be wrapped well and kept for several weeks.

Crust:
18 large cinnamon graham crackers
4 ounces toasted almonds
⅓ cup butter

Topping:
¾ cup amaretto
¾ cup honey
¼ teaspoon cinnamon
2½ ounces toasted almonds

Filling:
½ gallon vanilla ice cream
1 quart chocolate ice cream
½ gallon coffee ice cream
2½ teaspoons cinnamon

Crust: Using steel blade on food processor, crush cinnamon graham crackers and chop almonds. Add butter and blend. Pat mixture into buttered 9-inch springform pan. Bake in preheated 375° oven for 10 minutes. Remove from oven and cool.

Filling: Soften ice creams in refrigerator for 15 minutes. Spread softened chocolate ice cream on sides and lightly in bottom of crust. Return to freezer to harden. Spread coffee ice cream in thick layer on top of chocolate layer. Return to freezer to harden. Place vanilla ice cream and cinnamon in mixer; blend on low speed. Spread cinnamon ice cream on top of coffee layer and freeze for 24 hours.

Topping: Combine amaretto, honey, and cinnamon. Remove sides of springform pan. Slice into serving pieces. To garnish, sprinkle with toasted almonds and spoonful of honey mixture.

Mary Frederick, Parent of Elizabeth '78 and Susan '78,
Grandparent of Richard Carter

Pumpkin Pie Crisp

3 eggs
1½ cups sugar
1 (13-ounce) can evaporated
   milk
1 (16-ounce) can pumpkin

1 teaspoon cinnamon
1 yellow cake mix
1 cup chopped pecans
½ to ¾ cup butter, melted

Mix eggs, sugar, milk, pumpkin, and cinnamon together; pour into ungreased 9x13x2-inch pan. Mix dry cake mix with pecans; sprinkle over pumpkin mixture in pan. Drizzle melted butter over cake mixture. Bake in preheated 350° oven for 1 hour or until knife comes out clean. To serve, cut in squares and top with whipped cream. Sprinkle with cinnamon sugar. Refrigerate leftovers.

Sally Swanson, F.A. Faculty

Leslie's Chocolate Mousse

3 (4-ounce) bars German
   chocolate
4 tablespoons water

6 eggs, separated
1 package lady fingers
1 cup whipping cream

Break chocolate into top of double boiler; add water and melt slowly. Line loaf pan with waxed paper. Split lady fingers and place half in pan bottom. Arrange the remainder along the sides. Beat the egg yolks 1 at a time into the chocolate. Beat reserved egg whites until stiff; fold into chocolate mixture. Pour chocolate into loaf pan. Refrigerate 24 hours. Invert onto serving plate and cover with whipped cream. Garnish with shaved chocolate or crushed peppermint candy.

Cheryl Bacon, Parent of Elizabeth and Rebecca

Index

Index

Index

Celebrations ... Food, Family, and Fun!
The Fayetteville Academy
Attn: Cookbook Request
3200 Cliffdale Road
Fayetteville, NC 28303
(910) 868-5131

Please send _____ copies of Celebrations ... Food, Family, and Fun!

at $19.95 each (includes sales tax) _____

Plus shipping and handling at $5.00 each _____

Total _____

Name: _____

Address: _____

City: _____ State: _____ ZIP: _____

Phone: _____

Make checks payable to: **The Fayetteville Academy**
Prices are subject to change. Call for verification.

— —

Celebrations ... Food, Family, and Fun!
The Fayetteville Academy
Attn: Cookbook Request
3200 Cliffdale Road
Fayetteville, NC 28303
(910) 868-5131

Please send _____ copies of Celebrations ... Food, Family, and Fun!

at $19.95 each (includes sales tax) _____

Plus shipping and handling at $5.00 each _____

Total _____

Name: _____

Address: _____

City: _____ State: _____ ZIP: _____

Phone: _____

Make checks payable to: **The Fayetteville Academy**
Prices are subject to change. Call for verification.